FAMILY
POLITICS

FAMILY POLITICS

Love and Power
on an Intimate Frontier

LETTY COTTIN POGREBIN

McGraw-Hill Book Company

New York   St. Louis   San Francisco
Toronto   Hamburg   Mexico

1 2 3 4 5 6 7 8 9 D O C D O C 8 7 6 5 4 3

ISBN 0-07-050386-9

Library of Congress Cataloging in Publication Data

Pogrebin, Letty Cottin.
Family politics.
Includes index.
1. Family—United States. 2. Family policy—United
States. 3. Power (Social sciences) I. Title.
HQ536.P63 1983 306.8'5'0973 83–9818
ISBN 0–07–050386–9

Book design by Roberta Rezk

To the memory of my parents,
Cyral Halpern Cottin (1901–1955)
Jacob Cottin (1900–1982)

Contents

Author's Introduction

WHEN IT COMES to family life, I feel I've seen it all. In fact, it takes me twenty minutes to give an accurate answer to the simple question "Have you any sisters or brothers?" I began my life in a traditional two-parent family but thanks to divorce, adoption, death, and remarriage, I've also had a single parent, a stepparent, a full sister, a half sister, a stepbrother and a stepsister. For the past twenty years, I've been married to my first and only husband and together we are raising three children. My life has been enriched by these dense family connections plus an even more convoluted extended family that has taught me first hand, the legitimate dignity of the diverse marital, sexual, racial, and economic family configurations flourishing in America today. Nevertheless, I leave it to others to survey the particular pleasures and problems of "alternative" families, stepfamilies, and single-parent families. Here I limit myself to a discussion of belief systems that underlie family interaction, regardless of who is in the cast of characters.

The title of this book, *Family Politics,* suggests my two-fold analytical objective: to explore the use and misuse of family issues in American politics, and to examine the politics operating within conventional families—that is, the power relations that exist among women, men, and children who live together.

For the most part, this book is addressed to people who tend to include children in their family life. This is because I think of the reader as someone like myself, a modern parent reared by old-style parents—a member of a unique, transitional generation that is critical of many aspects of traditional family life but also recognizes its virtues, especially for the rearing of children. Our generation is looking for ways to preserve those virtues while changing what is unsatisfying about the family of the past. I believe there are millions of us who want to live in families that distribute happiness more equally; families fueled by reciprocity, not domination; families that strike a balance between intimacy and autonomy, between adventure and security, between individual freedom and group harmony.

In one sense, then, *Family Politics* is about the *meaning and feeling of family*. But it is also an inquiry into *the place of family* in today's society and *the political uses of families* in the public sphere. I hope to help readers clarify their families' strengths and weaknesses, reconsider the power relations in their households, and understand how social policy and political institutions affect every part of their family lives.

Books written in praise of traditional family structures, such as Rita Kramer's *In Defense of the Family,* Burton Pines' *Back to Basics,* Jeanne Westin's *The Coming Parent Revolution, The War over the Family,* by Brigitte and Peter L. Berger and Christopher Lasch's *Haven in a Heartless World,* keep beating the same dead horses. Ignoring real life and real people's situations, they campaign for Dick-and-Jane nuclear households in which fathers earn the money and exercise authority, mothers take care of the house and children, girls and boys respect their elders, and families solve their own problems.

Although these authors come at their theses from various angles, to some degree they each blame professional experts, social service agencies, government "interference," the women's movement, "decadence" schools, child-care centers, and television for disturbing traditional household hierarchies and eroding the good old–fashioned virtues of initiative, hard work and individualism. Somehow, when you finish these books, you sense it is all your fault if your family is not up to snuff. You shouldn't have lost your job, your husband, your health, control of your kids. You shouldn't need any help. Pull yourself together. The traditional all-American family was an independent, self-sufficient, rugged little unit; what's the matter with yours?

In this book, I demonstrate that reality supports a totally different analysis, one that reveals how families have been exploited and then manipulated to blame themselves for their hardships. I try to interpret the larger forces pressing upon families and to locate the original source of our troubles both inside and outside our own walls. *Family Politics* is not a superficial how-to book; it is a book that I hope will influence legislators, sociologists, politicians, journalists, family counselors, and teachers. I would also like it to help women, men, and children reevaluate their treatment of each other and reorganize the ways their families function so that the home becomes a happier place for everyone in it.

Very simply, I hope to preserve family life by saving what is best about it and changing what isn't.

1

Whose Family Is It, Anyway?

THE FAMILY IS A HOT ISSUE. Judging by the proliferation of magazine cover stories, television features, talk show discussions, academic research, and public policy discourse being devoted to the state of the American family, it seems safe to say that what civil rights and Vietnam were to the Sixties, and women's rights and the environment were to the Seventies, family issues have become to the Eighties. People care about their own families, of course, but of late they also seem terribly concerned about the *idea* of family and the future of family life in this country.

I share that concern, but I have also begun to worry about the way the family debate has been skewed. I am afraid we won't be able to make reasonable decisions about family needs and problems if we are misled by distorted notions of what families are and want to be. I'm afraid of a phenomenon I think of as "the asparagus syndrome."

As a child, I hated asparagus. I hated the smell of it cooking and my disgust was confirmed by one taste of the soggy, gray stalks my mother boiled to mush. Much later in life, I discovered that asparagus offers other choices: it is delicious raw, crisp as a carrot, dunked into a dip, steamed and glossed with melted butter or lemony hollandaise sauce, or served cold under a fresh vinaigrette, to mention just a few possibilities.

So it wasn't true that I hated asparagus, only that I had been given *a false choice:* overcooked asparagus or none at all. No one told me there were other options.

2

The same sort of false choice is now being offered in the family debate. Some people would have us believe that there are only two alternatives: the old-fashioned, confining, authoritarian family or no family at all.

Paul Weyrich, founder of the Committee for the Survival of a Free Congress, calls the ultra-right's fight for the traditional family "the most significant battle of the age-old conflict between good and evil, between the forces of God and the forces against God that we've ever seen in this country."[1]

Other political conservatives and religious fundamentalists warn that "secular humanism" is destroying the family; or feminism is, or public education is, or the Equal Rights Amendment would, or reproductive freedom will. Any social change that might promote pluralism or empower individuals, the ultra-right labels "a threat to the family." Some conservatives have established what they call the "pro-family" movement. Legislation to "protect the family" is at the top of their national agenda. Their magazines and direct mail solicitations hammer away at the need to "strengthen," "defend," or "save" the family. Their books carry such combative titles as, *The Battle for the Family*, *In Defense of the Family*, and *The War over the Family*.[2]

Estimates of the number of people who count themselves part of the political or religious right range from five million to fifty million.[3] Whatever their number, their voices are loud, their leaders well-connected and politically powerful, and their movement slickly publicized and well-financed. The top ten TV ministries raise up to $90 million *each* per year, and the Moral Majority alone had revenues of $5.7 million in 1981.[3a] More alarmingly, their message has permeated the public consciousness to a point where even people who are unaffiliated with the ultra-right have unwittingly begun to adopt its apocalyptic vision and to doubt the validity of their own family lives.

But what is this entity we are supposed to defend? When you and I hear "family," do we understand it to mean what someone like Paul Weyrich means? Judging by current varieties of usage, the answer is no.

"Family" is not a precise, universally understood label

for a particular living unit; it has different meanings and produces different results in different contexts. The word is both symbolic and functional. Used prescriptively, it seems able to coerce people into roles, to transform nostalgia into votes, and to create a national ethos out of a myth of domestic bliss. Used descriptively, it is more powerful as an Idea to be distorted and manipulated than as a Reality to be examined for the common good.

Who Is the Family?

In childhood, we say "my family" and mean our parents and siblings. After marriage, few people call a spouse "my family"; we tend to continue using the term "my family" to mean our family of origin until we have children of our own. But if children make a family, then what do we call two adult brothers who live together, or a married couple who cannot or choose not to have children or, for that matter, the 24 million households in which married couples live without children at home? (The 1980 census found that today's women plan to have fewer children than ever before—2.048 births each—and a national poll found that more than eight in ten Americans now believe it is acceptable to be married and not have children.[4])

Familiar lines, such as "the author lives with his wife and family," "in a family way," and "when are you two going to settle down and raise a family?" suggest that "family" is just another word for *children.* Yet we call orphans "children without a family," and when abused children are removed from the custody of their father and mother, officials say the children were "taken from the family." So maybe "family" is just another word for *parents.*

The definition is further muddled by the fact that families are often identified by the marital status of the parents: in the phrase "single-parent family," we know "parent" usually means *mother.* When a question of authority is involved (asking permission from a "parent," having a "parent" sign a loan, going into the "family" business), "parent" or "family" most often means *father,* but when it's a question of care—as in "parenting courses," "class parent," Parent-Teacher Association or *Parents* magazine (80 percent of whose readers are women)—"parent" means *mother*.

When traditionalists talk about The Family, they mean an employed father, a mother at home, and two school-aged children, a profile that fits only 5 percent of American households.[5] One out of six youngsters now lives in a one-parent, usually female-headed family (16 percent of all families). Are these mothers and children to be excluded from America's family of families? People such as Jo-Ann Gasper, a self-described pro-family leader, would answer yes: "In the 'good ole days,' " she writes, sanctimoniously, "there were only two 'family forms'—a family and a broken family."[6]

"Broken family" and "single-parent family" describe what the U.S. Census Bureau used to call a "female-headed household." (There was no category for a "male-headed household" because a qualifier is not necessary for what is considered normal.) Regardless of how prevalent it has been across time and cultures, or how solid it may feel to the woman and children in it, the female-headed household has been considered broken, inferior, and abnormal.

What Is the Family?

If *who* is family is a complicated question, *what* is family is a contradictory mess:

When a fellow slays his wife and children, the bewildered neighbors often express shock because he was a "real family man." What do they mean by "family"? Are family men on a continuum with family murderers? Is a family man somehow distinct from other husbands and fathers? Would neighbors call the average wife and mother a "real family woman"?

When policy-makers question "the effect of a working mother on the family," they put a woman in opposition to a hallowed entity. What policies would result if instead we probed "the effect of sex discrimination on a working mother and her family" or "the effect of an uncooperative, demanding husband on the energies of a working mother"? Rather than make mother seem the cause of "family problems," why not address the legitimate problems and conflicting interests of family members?

When researchers ask "How does domestic violence affect the family?" do they mean to imply that some disembodied object gets beaten up every night, or that domestic violence is experienced in the same way by both the batterer and the victim?

When right-wing spokeswoman Phyllis Schlafly says she doesn't want "unmarried parents and lesbians to have the same social status as a family,"[7] what family does she mean: Godfather Corleone's? The feuding Hatfields and McCoys? The imbecilic inbred Jukes and Kallikaks? Shall we disregard a family's character and award it social status simply because it is legal ("heterosexual marriage or relation by birth, blood or adoption"[8]), while simultaneously denying social status to self-proclaimed families that are far better practitioners of the art of family love?

When Chief Justice Warren Burger rules that "important considerations of family integrity"[9] require a doctor to notify the parents of a girl seeking an abortion, does he mean that the courts can force families to be confidantes and invade a daughter's privacy as no one else's privacy is invaded in our society? Can there be "family integrity" if there is no primary integrity for each person in the family?

When Ronald Reagan says "we have witnessed an extremely disturbing decline in the strength of families,"[10] and at the same time the Russian government subsidizes the purchase of wedding rings because "they are a wonderful tradition that helps strengthen the family,"[11] can we assume strong communist families are the same as strong capitalist families?

When Pope John Paul II tells the Nigerians that contraception and abortion are "the modern enemies of the family,"[12] does he mean that the alternatives of underdevelopment, overcrowding, starvation, disease, and poverty are *friends* of the family? Nigeria's alarming population growth is among the world's highest. What *is* "the family" if to save it we are willing to destroy the quality of life within it?

Why this defensiveness, this talk of enemies and attacks? And why is the campaign for the traditional family picking up so much steam?

Family as Fetish

> fe•tish (fĕ′tĭsh), *n.* 1. an inanimate
> object, regarded with awe as being the
> embodiment or habitation of a potent spirit.
> 2. any object of blind reverence.

Like a sexual fetish (commonly a shoe or undergarment), an ideological fetish is dehumanized and dehumanizing, the object of compulsive rather than volitional devotion. A fetish triggers a response based on obsession or conditioning, not sense or sentience. The Family has become that kind of fetish for people who prefer inanimate concepts to organic human institutions. They want The Family to be concrete and to deliver fixed pleasures as predictable as those the shoe or silk panties deliver to the sexual fetishist.

After the social upheavals of the Sixties and Seventies, the Eighties brought a kind of national passivity borne of an unstable economy and shifting values. What is embodied in The Family—that is, the *traditional* family promoted by conservatives—is something concrete, secure and orderly: the structure and spirit of patriarchy.

The relationship of a family to its patriarch creates a paradigm for every other power hierarchy in western culture: The team coach controls the captain, the starting lineup, and down to the last guy on the bench. The generals head the chain of command in the military. American corporations and the country itself have their own pyramids of authority, each topped by a president.

Dominance depends on hierarchy and hierarchy begins at home with Big Daddy. Sophocles put these sentiments in the mouth of King Creon centuries ago:

> . . . Nothing
> Should come before your loyalty to your father.
> . . . If I allow
> My own relations to get out of control,
> That gives the cue to everybody else.
> People who are loyal members of their families
> Will be good citizens too. . . .
> Once a man has authority, he must be obeyed—

In big things and in small, in every act,
Whether just or not so just.

—*Antigone*[13]

In the 1980s, would-be kings like Paul Weyrich use Scripture to buttress the same politics: "The Bible ordains the family with the father as head of household and the mother subject to his ultimate authority. The father's word has to prevail."[14] After all, *somebody* has to be in charge; for the sake of efficiency, discipline, division of labor, basic order, natural law, and of course, God's will. Whatever the rationalizations, at root the traditional family is defended because it is the core model for all authoritarian patriarchal structures. (Try substituting "male supremacy" for "family" in those previously quoted pronouncements of the Pope, Justice Burger, Reagan, or Schlafly, and watch the hidden meaning be revealed).

The strategists of the right are scared. If there is an erosion of the elemental Big Daddy model of dominance, what would happen to every other hierarchy? Would people cease to obey their "superiors"? Would capitalist organizations founder? Would soldiers stop following orders? Would the nation "weaken," lose its "supremacy," be conquered and forced to take a lower place in *somebody else's hierarchy?*

With this construct, father dominance is the prerequisite for world dominance. Think of it this way: When "God is Dead" became the slogan of a generation that dared to question all authority, only the Born Again could be counted on to submit. When open education and affirmative action blurred class distinctions, the preserves of the privileged were democratized. When blacks stopped genuflecting to whites and racial mixing and racial pride went public, the satisfactions of white supremacy were eliminated. Now male supremacy is in peril. The women's movement has challenged man's hegemony in business, politics, law, medicine, sports, the media, finance, education, and virtually every other field. Laws have been passed that support women's advancement in the public sphere. Now traditionalists, defenders of the old order, are determined to hold the line at the door to a man's castle. In other words, save the family. They contend that the measure of a nation depends on the health of its families, and they go on to define a healthy family—not in terms of its physiological and economic well-being—but in terms of a norm that puts men in power and keeps women in the home.

> *Item:* Howard Baker, Jr., the Senate majority leader, was apprehensive when his twenty-six-year-old daughter Cynthia made an appointment with him.
>
> "For two days I worried, as any father can worry about a daughter. Thought of the most terrible things she could say. I finally decided she was getting married to someone I didn't like."
>
> What Cynthia came to say was, she was running for Congress. "I still haven't decided if I should be relieved or not," said Baker.[15]
>
> *Item:* Explaining his vote in favor of tax breaks for families in which the husband works while the wife keeps house, Alabama Senator Jeremiah Denton said: "The guy likes to come home and get supper and a couple of martinis from a woman who is reasonably rested."[16]

What do these legislators' comments tell us about life in their families, their sex-stereotyped view of women and men, and how it affects their representation of American families' interests? If his twenty-six-year-old *son* wanted to see him, would Baker have worried about a bad marriage? And had the son declared for Congress, would the father be ambivalent? Does Senator Baker not believe a woman's place is in the House? Does he think marriage is the be-all and end-all for daughters?

As for Senator Denton, would he favor the same tax break for *men* who stay home? Who is going to subsidize someone to get supper and martinis for the millions of single working women? Should masculine comfort be supported by the American taxpayer? Does Denton think keeping house is a *restful* occupation?

Decoding the Strategies on the Right

In essence, family fetishism and its political strategies are a reaction to, and attack on, the two major barriers to male dominance: uppity women and uppity children.

According to the ultra-right creed, The Family has been eroded by federal "intrusion," by which is meant government empowerment of those who are "supposed to be" subordinate. Thus, traditionalists oppose legislation and federal agencies that *protect women against sex discrimination,* and *protect both children and women against exploitation and abuse.* Although in an everyday sense, most troubled people look for help to relatives, neighbors, or religious organizations, the guarantee that those who need it must have direct access to government assistance and legal redress has strengthened women and children who are under severe duress. The possibility of a federal ally has reduced their powerlessness. That's what bothers traditionalists; they want father to be the only public person, the only family member with direct access to law and government. They complain about government violations of the right to privacy but they mean *man's* right to privacy, the privacy to do as he wishes in his own home. Government must not protect women because that's men's job; government must not regulate women's rights because those rights contradict her higher obligation to serve men. Says one TV evangelist:

> Women have great strength, but they are strengths to help the man. A woman's primary purpose in life and marriage is to help her husband succeed, to help him be all God wants him to be.[17]

I'm reminded of a political cartoon in which President Reagan is saying, "A gun in every holster. A pregnant woman in every kitchen. Make America a *man* again!"[18] Nothing less than national virility depends on confining women to the family. Surely female submissiveness is not too much to ask when the stakes are so high.

This ideological maneuver has a long history.[19] Whenever and wherever patriarchal exclusivity has been threatened, inevitably someone proclaims a greater good, or a mortal threat. "The historic family has depended for its existence and character on woman's subordination," writes Carl N. Degler. "The equality of women and the institution of the family have long been at odds with each other."[20] In nineteenth-century America, they said educating women's brains would atrophy their wombs; giving women the vote would divide husbands and wives and lure women from children's bedsides into public life. Hitler insisted strong families were the key to a strong Reich; feminists' early-twentieth-century gains in German politics, law, and art were destroyed in the name of Aryan reproduction, and women were instructed to mother the Master Race. In the United States after World War II, hundreds of thousands of Rosie the Riveters were forced out of jobs for which women had been actively recruited; by 1945, government propaganda characterized a "real" woman as one who retreated to her family and gave up her job so that a man could work.

Today, any move for women's political or sexual freedom—from the defeated Equal Rights Amendment to contraceptive education—is labeled "anti-family." Reactionary priests and ministers and Orthodox rabbis proselytize for full-time motherhood and service to the family. Even the respectable Howard Phillips, National Director of the Conservative Caucus, has said the first step in the downfall of The Family was giving women the vote. Phillips sees women's suffrage as "a conscious policy of government to liberate the wife from the leadership of the husband. It used to be that in recognition of the family as the basic unit of society, we have one family, one vote."[21] The husband's vote. Howard Phillips and the other Good Ole Boys miss The Good Old Days. But in the 1980s, most people with reactionary intentions don't come right out and say it quite so flagrantly. If you favor male supremacy, fear the loss of patriarchal power, and hate the idea that women and children might control their own destinies, you can mask your indelicate views behind a clever all-American slogan: Call yourself "pro-family" and all you have left to worry about is defining the *kind* of family "family" is, so that you can comfortably be for it. Then anyone who's against it is "anti-family."

Pro-family strategists call any change in women's or children's dependency on the father "anti-family." They dismiss women's career goals as "selfish" and children's striving for autonomy as "rebellion" born of family "permissiveness." They disdain children's *rights* in preference for children's *training*, a sacred responsibility that cannot be left to any influence but the family—meaning the influence and control of the father transmitted through the care of the mother. The only right they guarantee to children is the right to be raised by their mother, which also happens to coincide with the father's right to have *his* woman raising *his* children.

"Ninety percent of our problems with children," explains a pro-family booklet, "are probably the result of a mother who has 1) failed to learn how to really love her man and submit to him, 2) tried to escape staying at home, or 3) hindered her husband in the discipline of the children."[22]

Other than in the disciplinary role, many men fear having to deal directly with children. They require the neutralizing agent of the mother. They see that infants and small children, however adorable, are inadequate twenty-four hour companions for a grown person, that childrearing is hard work at no pay, that it is far from an honored profession in this culture, and that people who care for children are isolated from the rest of human discourse. Many a man is consciously or unconsciously afraid that if his woman refuses to be the old-style, buck-stops-here, primary parent, then *he* will have to take responsibility for the isolated, exhausting world of child care. Men do not want to have to take care of children. Rule them, yes. Play with them, yes. Take credit for their achievements, certainly. But not care for their bottles, diapers, mess, spills, tears, tantrums, laundry, lunches, nightmares, and the million daily details of childhood.

Even with the Pro-Family line and the romance-of-the-family rhetoric, strategists on the right are still confounded by laws and public agencies that shield women and kids from discrimination, exploitation, and abuse. To pierce that shield, and to keep Mother's child care role primary, the ultra-right must sever the connection between the powerless and their government. They must dismantle the civil rights laws of the Sixties and Seventies and pass new laws to protect an interest that they can make seem larger and more important than women and children: The Family, of course.

The Family Protection Act

Written by Robert Billings, executive director of The Moral Majority, and first introduced in the U.S. Senate in 1979 by Senator Paul Laxalt, the Family Protection Act is an omnibus bill whose expressed purpose is "to strengthen the American Family and promote the virtues of family life through education, tax assistance, and related measures."[23] The Act begins with this warning: "A reversal of Government policies which undermine the American family is essential if the United States is to enter the twenty-first century as a strong and viable nation."

The sleight of hand is dazzling: To enter the twenty-first century as a virile nation, we need a nineteenth-century family with eighteenth-century status for women and children. Whether or not the Act is ever passed in its omnibus form, I view it as the handwriting on the wall. Since it has the enthusiastic support of the President, and since it spells out the social program of the Conservative agenda without mincing words, it tells us what our future would be if we do not resist the interest groups and politicians who are pledged to:

• *protect the right of parents and other authorized individuals to use corporal punishment against children.* The Reverend James Roy, a Baptist minister in Syracuse, New York, is an example of a father who would be "protected." He forbade his fourteen-year-old daughter to wear slacks. She refused to obey, so he paddled her with a shingle. He was convicted of child abuse and his daughter is now living with guardians. The Rev. Roy remains incensed that the state could step into his family affairs.[24]

• *repeal federal laws relating to child abuse and wife beating and discontinue intervention programs that treat or shelter their victims.* Jo-Ann Gasper, former publisher of *The Right Woman* and now assistant secretary for social services policy at the Department of Health and Human Services, ridicules domestic violence by characterizing it as "belittling," "yelling," "teasing," or "failure to provide warmth—I guess if you don't set the electric blanket high enough." I rather doubt that yelling or teasing qualified for the police blotter and yet there are millions of family violence charges filed each year.

• *repeal all federal laws that grant educational equity to both sexes (and all races).* This means that schools would once again teach only girls to sew and cook, and only boys to run track and fix cars—as was the case before passage of Title IX of the Education Amendments Act of 1972.

• *require that marriage and motherhood be taught as the proper career for girls, and deny federal funds to schools whose textbooks show women in nontraditional roles.* On the trash heap would go biographies of Margaret Mead, Rachel Carson, Amelia Earhart, Golda Meir, and such. If you want to see which textbooks would be acceptable to the pro-family folks, get yourself on the mailing list of the leading right-wing censors: Parents' Alliance to Protect Our Children (44 East Tacoma Avenue, Latrobe, PA 15650) or The Mel Gablers Newsletter (P.O. Box 7518, Longview, TX 75607).

• *prohibit the "intermingling of sexes in any sports or other school-related activities."* Besides the fact that separate has never been equal, sex segregation does not inspire the friendship and understanding that males and females will need when and if they work together or join forces to make a family. Sex segregation in school may protect prudish parents from uncomfortable fantasies about their children's sexual "intermingling," especially across racial lines. It does not protect The Family.

• *provide for parents' unlimited classroom visits, review of courses, and censorship of textbooks.* This could cause intellectual freedom to disappear with the stroke of a pen.

• *impose prayer in the schools.* Add to the usual concerns for church-state separation the specter of the fundamentalist

Biblical view of sex roles becoming part of your child's morning prayer . . .

• *provide tax incentives that discourage women's employment and promote wives' economic dependence on husbands.* For instance, the child-care deduction could only be taken by married women doing volunteer charitable or religious work, not by wage-earning women.

• *give a $1,000 tax exemption for the birth or adoption of a child, but only to a married couple.* Obviously, this is not intended to alleviate the cost of having a child, or to encourage adoption of hard-to-place kids, but to reward legal marriage.

• *offer tax breaks for home care of the aged and handicapped.* While this innovation would be a boon to some, it also would create a financial incentive to tie women to the home, caring for relatives long after their children have left; further, it would discourage the development of the kinds of group care "hotels" or "centers for independent living" that many disabled and old people prefer. Instead, why not provide a subsidy for care of the aged and handicapped and let each family decide how and where it should be spent?

• *require that parents be notified before their daughters can receive counseling on or medical help for venereal disease, contraception, or abortion.* (More on this in Chapter Eight.)

• *prohibit federally funded legal services for abortion, divorce, homosexual rights, or school desegregation complaints.* A government that refuses to *defend* its citizens' civil rights is a government that can *withdraw* those rights.

The Family Protection Act is careful to talk in terms of *parents'* rights. Nevertheless, since male supremacy is inherent in the traditional constructs of God and family, *parents'* rights may be understood to mean *father* power. As all the male pronouns in the Act imply, its goal is to reestablish man's authority over *his* children, *his* spouse, *his* older dependents, *his* taxes, and *his* children's teachers (usually women).

Just as racists' crusades for white preference laws march under the banner of "states' rights," the patriarchs' lust for chattel is made politically respectable with slogans—if not about the evils of "government meddling," certainly with some sentimental plea for the restoration of the mythic "good old-fashioned family."

The Myth of the Happy Family

Since sentimentality obfuscates and family feelings are as inflammable as spilled gasoline, I want to be very clear about what I mean by the myth of the happy family. I am not saying that there aren't millions of contented families; I am saying that The Family that the right is promoting and protecting, the traditional nuclear family, is not *necessarily* or *automatically* a happy place.

The myth of the happy family is disproven daily in newspaper accounts of family violence, in the daily docket of our family courts, and in the despair of our friends' confided secrets. For the wife and mother, it is not a happy place when she feels trapped in the role of cook, cleaning woman, and child-caregiver—and taken for granted besides. It is not a happy place if she has to ask her husband's permission to go out in the evening, to spend $10, go to a meeting, or visit her friends. (Hundreds of women at the National Women's Conference in Houston testified that this was the case in their marriages.) It is surely not a happy place if it is the place where she is assaulted or raped by a husband who views the marriage license as a license to abuse his wife in the sacrosanct privacy of his home (see Chapter Five). For men, the family may be a source of unhappiness for psychodynamic reasons, but in this book I am concentrating on power relations and here men's complaints are minimal (again, see Chapter Five).

For children, the family is not a happy place when parents who are supposed to nurture and protect them, neglect or batter them instead. (In 1982, according to the National Center on Child Abuse, more than a million cases were reported,[25] and we can only guess how many incidents go unreported.) It is not a happy place when the arguments of incompatible parents become children's nightly lullaby, or when the frictions and jealousies of stepfamily life embitter everyone involved. It is not a happy place when divorcing parents play tug o'war with child custody, tearing apart the object to be won, or kidnap their child from each other like pickpockets stealing a wallet back and forth. (In 1980, roughly a hundred thousand children were snatched by one parent from the custody of the other.[26]) It's not a happy place when irrational parents beat sense into children by beating them senseless; when fanatical parents exorcise the devil by torturing the child; when religious parents refuse a child lifesaving medical treatment because of their faith; or when perverted parents pollute the family trust with the crime of incest.

The Gallup Poll found that one in five Americans is *personally* aware of serious cases of family violence.[27] Undaunted by such facts, ultra-right men insist families must remain "intact," however miserable. Undaunted by such lived experiences, right-wing women defend the patriarchal family because, as Andrea Dworkin points out, in a world largely hostile or indifferent to women, it seems to offer them the best deal. In return for sexual submission, child-rearing services, obedience, and household services, they get shelter, safety, order, and material well-being.[28] The alternatives to this deal, conservative women fear, are hedonism, prostitution, homosexuality, pornography, abortion, drug addiction, and "Godless humanism." Like the asparagus syndrome, it's a false choice and a phony deal.

It is too easy to say that The Family is the strength of the nation. But only the most cynical and rigid person would insist that any particular family is worth saving if it is a hollow container for dispirited lives. In the words of Rebecca West, "There is one point when it is permissible to break up the institution of the family; that is the point when it is changing from an institution to a mausoleum."[29] Or, one might add, a prison.

When is the family as an institution worth "saving"? How do we know when a family is neither a mausoleum nor a prison? When everyone in a particular family loses nothing and gains something by being in the family unit; *when the gains of one family member are not achieved at the expense of another.* In other words, when a family is a democracy.

The politics of the family are the politics of a nation. Just as the authoritarian family is the authoritarian state in microcosm,[30] the democratic family is the best training ground for life in a democracy. Those who want to "strengthen" American families must be willing to strengthen and empower each American—not toward the goal of national supremacy but for reasons of human justice.

In his book *Family Matters,* Lawrence H. Fuchs, a respected political scientist, wrote: "With its emphasis on personal independence and equality, American ideology is at war with the very nature of family life."[31] Rather than wish families could rise to the democratic ideology, Fuchs faulted the American "sacred cows" of independence and equality for contravening male authority. He argued that "the common pattern of mutual resentment and recrimination between husbands and wives is linked to the decline of patriarchy and the ensuing struggle for independence and equality by each family member."[32]

I would argue just the reverse. The traditional patriarchal family is democracy's "original sin"; it is the elemental flaw in an otherwise perfectible political system. When the traditions of The Family are permitted to supercede the legally guaranteed rights of individuals, democracy goes sour at its core.

Alexis de Tocqueville understood this 150 years ago when he wrote in *Democracy in America:*

> There are certain great social principles that a people either introduces everywhere or tolerates nowhere. In countries which are aristocratically constituted with all the gradations of rank, the government never makes a direct appeal to the mass of the governed . . . social institutions recognize, in truth, no one in the family but the father; children are received by society at his hands; society governs him, he governs them. . . .
>
> In democracies, where the government picks out every individual singly from the mass to make him subser-

vient to the general laws of the community, no such inter-
mediate person is required.[33]

Would we be able to call ourselves a representative government if any Act of Congress were to interpose the husband-
father between other family members and their government?
How can a national ethic extol the virtues of individual expression if women and children in the families of that nation are
systematically muzzled, or if their prescribed roles contravene
the full exercise of their right to life, liberty, and the pursuit
of happiness? Do such phrases as "land of opportunity" and
"free enterprise" mean anything if the economics of patriarchal family life perpetuate selective feudalism? How can children learn to treat people equally if inequality is intrinsic to
family relations? And most crucially, if family violence teaches
children that might makes right at home, how will we hope
to cure the futile impulse to solve worldly conflicts with force?

I'm certainly no patriotic chauvinist, but it seems to me
that in the current political lexicon, to be in the Pro-Family
movement is to be *un*-American. Listen to Dan Fore, Moral
Majority ideologue: "If you teach people their rights, you
breed rebellion and anarchy, but if you teach people responsibility, you breed a submissive society."[34]

If there is "an American way of life," the ultra-right is
subverting it through its family politics. Very simply, it is impossible to achieve the exalted goals of the democratic dream
and the free and full development of every person so long
as the basic unit of our society, the family, is undemocratic
and unfree.

2

The Enduring Nest

BUT WHY BOTHER arguing about all this? Many people who are dedicated to egalitarian, democratic principles have concluded that the family is not worth saving. For women at least. If one man's haven is another woman's housework—that is, if the male of the family consistently gets the best of the domestic deal —surely, in Katha Pollitt's words, "a woman is entitled to ask herself if it is wise to commit her destiny— and her children's well-being—to an institution she is given the responsibility but not the power to maintain."[1]

Maybe the family is moving toward a deserved extinction. There has been good reason to question its future ever since Cain slew Abel. In 1903, in the full flush of social progress, Charlotte Perkins Gilman found the home "the least evolved of all our institutions."[2] Thinkers from Plato to Alvin Toffler have explored alternatives to the family, analyzed the family's functions, and perennially declared the family "in crisis."[3] Virtually every social condition has been called the cause of family decline. In the nineteenth century, sin, heredity, materialism, and urbanism were the culprits. Early-twentieth-century prophets proclaimed the family (and thus Western civilization) lethally threatened by communism, miscegenation, the automobile, women's suffrage, and the end of prohibition. And in the years since World War II, the family has supposedly been doomed by Dr. Spock's permissiveness, television, the pill, working mothers, the counter-culture, open marriage, the human potential movement, no-fault divorce, rock music, legal abortion, government meddling, and homosexual rights.

If not in crisis all these years, the family has been "in transition." Depending on which theorist you read[4] it has been moving from an institutional to a companionship form, from an economic to an affectional unit, from a child-centered to a couple-centered entity, from one lifelong bond to serial connections, from asymmetrical to quasi-egalitarian roles, from kinship groups to extended families to nuclear to "reconstituted" families.

Many schools of family theory have interpreted these trends, but only feminists have asked the essential question: *Is the family an inherently oppressive institution?*

In her critical survey of contemporary feminist thought,[5] Jane Flax distills the complex ideas of seven influential writers who have addressed that question. Thanks to Flax's coherent clarity, I can boil them down even further to help illuminate whether the family is "worth saving."

1. *Betty Friedan*[6] located the source of woman's oppression in the "feminine mystique," the stultifying roles of wife and mother, and the many barriers that keep women from equality with men in the world outside the home. Friedan's solution: better jobs and education so that women can "have it all."

2. *Kate Millett*[7] saw the family as the primal training ground for patriarchal "sexual politics," and the "citadel of property and traditional interests." She defined patriarchy as a system whereby "male shall dominate female, elder male shall dominate younger," and said that the family pattern can be extended to state hierarchies. Within the family, Millett argued, patriarchy is bulwarked by *romantic love,* which obscures *women's economic dependence.* That dependence reinforces *male power,* which is also policed by *force.* To break this cycle, Millett prescribed "cultural revolution": an altered social consciousness that would give rise to new structures and behaviors.

3. *Shulamith Firestone*[8] followed the branches of patriarchy inward and found the roots of women's oppression in biology. Her "dialectic of sex" begins with female childbearing, the origin and model for the family's sexual division of labor. She says pregnancy and birth tie mother and child together in interdependence, and make them rely on a man for their survival. This unequal distribution of power leads ultimately to oppressive class and caste systems. Firestone's solution is to circumvent female biology and dismantle the family; translation: produce children in test tubes and diffuse childrearing responsibility among many households.

4. *Juliet Mitchell*[9] saw women's oppression originating not in patriarchy (men dominating women) but in class conflict (bosses dominating workers). She argued that the family unit cannot help being influenced by these exploitative production relations outside the family. She said families suffer too from an economic system that focuses on individual advancement, not group solidarity. While accepting Freud's Oedipal analysis as a description of how we acquire "patriarchal law" within the family, she distinguished between *oppression* in the family and class *exploitation* in the workplace, and for her, the economic factors are more determinative. Although she, along with many other Marxist and socialist feminists, has struggled to explain why sexism survives in socialist countries and to do what socialist masterminds of the past have failed to do: that is, integrate into their analysis women's reproductive labor and the value of housework.[10] Mitchell's solution, of course, is socialist revolution.

5. *Gayle Rubin*[11] asserted that the family is the source of women's oppression because it is where human beings are "engendered," that is, where *biological* sex is transformed into *culturally acceptable* sex, or what social scientists call gender. "Engendering" means making a biological boy into a "real" boy, say, one who likes sports and learns to control his emotions. Through a family's sexual division of labor and childrearing measures, a child born male is socialized to be "masculine" and a child born female is socialized to be "feminine" as the culture wishes those terms to be acted out. This family-based sex/gender system, according to Rubin, culminates in the subordination and "domestication" of women, i.e. girls are engendered to become the second sex in general, and mothers in particular.

6. *Dorothy Dinnerstein*[12] argued that the conventional family's childrearing arrangements have monumental repercussions. Human malaise, she says, originates in women's sole responsibility for infant care. Because all of us associate our infantile powerlessness with our fear and dependence on the all-powerful mother, we displace onto women all our larger rage about being powerless to control our fate as a species. To tame the infantile experience, women become mothers like their mothers; men distance themselves from women and from nature in order to dominate both. Men exclude women from history-making, and require females to represent humanity and nature, which men then exploit in unconscious retaliation against the female giant of the nursery.

7. *Nancy Chodorow*[13] agreed with Rubin and Dinnerstein, but added the psychodynamics: girls grow up to "mother"—i.e., nurture small children—and boys grow up to "non-mother" (stunting those human needs and retreating to the world of work and patriarchal domination) because the family's sexual division of labor creates in children a "division of psychological capacities." This, in turn, becomes our internalized model for all the race, class, and sex-stratified differentiations in the social order. The solution both Dinnerstein and Chodorow propose is full involvement of fathers in child care.

I was deeply influenced by these thinkers, especially Millett and Dinnerstein. At the same time, I continued to feel privately gratified by romantic love, motherhood, and family life. To reconcile the personal and political, I spent eight years researching family psychology and child development and writing *Growing Up Free,* a book-length blueprint for nonsexist childrearing and parity parenthood.

Here's the point: I believe one can acknowledge that the traditional patriarchal family oppresses women and creates distorted gender relations, but still choose not to jettison family as a way of life. Furthermore, I'm aware that for many women the family has been "a source of power" as often as a "tool of oppression."[14] I think it insulting, not to mention irresponsible, to overlook the psychological satisfactions many women find in marriage, motherhood, homemaking and heterosexuality.[15] What's more, in many black, white ethnic and poor communities, there is great pride in families' "adaptive resiliency and strength"[16] and there is more confidence in the reliability of the family for support, succor and sheer survival than might be the case in more affluent, educated classes where the luxury of individualism can be indulged.

With all this in mind, I concluded it won't do to just trash the family; we must transform it. Thousands of my contemporaries have reached the same conclusion. Moreover, regardless of what we conclude, the plain fact is that family living, in one form or another, remains the condition or the goal of a vast majority of Americans.

What is it about the family that survives dissection, defamation, reports of its imminent demise, and the burdens of its own imperfection? Why do seven out of ten divorced people choose to remarry within five years despite bitter experience, and make new families despite the problems of stepparenthood?[17] Why do so many people form "chosen families" to take the place of legal ones? (The latest census revealed that more than three million U.S. households are composed of unrelated people living together. According to *The New York Times*, what these unmarried couples, same-sex roommates, and elderly companions are seeking is not just cost-sharing but "the semblance of family," tribal attachments, and the sense of "coming home."[18]) Can family be all bad if the urge to have a family and be a family is so strong?

I find the beginning of an answer in metaphor:

If the family were a container, it would be a nest, an enduring nest, loosely woven, expansive, and open.

If the family were a fruit, it would be an orange, a circle of sections, held together but separable—each segment distinct.

If the family were a boat, it would be a canoe that makes no progress unless everyone paddles.

If the family were a sport, it would be baseball: a long,

slow, nonviolent game that is never over until the last out.

If the family were a building, it would be an old, but solid structure that contains human history, and appeals to those who see the carved moldings under all the plaster, the wide plank floors under the linoleum, the possibilities . . .

The possibilities are there for the family as well, if we can figure out what is worth preserving and what to discard. To rethink the family's design, purpose, and meaning, we must begin with some "essence of family" that is pure and true. And for me the essence of family is:

> who it is,
> how it feels, and
> what it does.

That is not so flabby a thesis as it sounds. Stay with me.

FAMILY IS WHO IT IS

By this I mean that *families must be able to define themselves;* no one else can tell them what or who they are. In a sense, they always have. Generations ago, death caused as many "broken" families as divorce does today; in fact, there were *more* single-parent families in the United States in 1940 than in 1978.[19] Of course, widowhood was more socially acceptable than divorce, so the community rallied around the widow. She may have taken in boarders, an aunt or a grandfather, or sent a child to live with a cousin, but her household was not stripped of the title "family." Today, we may make other accommodations, but whether truncated by death or divorce or by the departure of grown children, we don't stop being a family. And a family doesn't need two parents to make it a family. Once we stop "engendering" children, there is no need for a big Daddy and a medium-sized Mommy to teach Baby Bear how to act out sex roles. Either sex can teach any child how to be a complete human being. Nor does a family need children to make it a family. While 54 percent of Americans think the ideal family has two children—14 percent think four or more kids is ideal—studies show that many childless people are perfectly content, and that in many families, childrearing is incidental to marriage.[20] Disenchanting though it may be, research suggests that many couples feel *happiest* when their children are grown up and gone, and the wife and husband have the leisure and wisdom to use their time well.[21]

The family is the most intimate expression of self beyond the primal I. "This is me," we say. "And this is my family." That recognition of "us," that need to sense a special "we" in this huge, homogenized, Neilsen-numbed country, is a longing many of us satisfy at home. When a family is free of abuse and oppression, it can be the place where we share our deepest secrets and stand the most exposed, a place where we learn to feel distinct without being "better," and sacrifice for others without losing ourselves.

A family is a unit that demands reduced selfhood and yet cultivates individuality; it cultivates the One while nourishing concern for the Many. Therefore, our society acts against its own interests by making it hard for people to live in families of their own choosing. Whether you are part of Ethel Kennedy's or Rosa Martinez' single-parent clan, or a group of lesbian mothers collectively caring for their children, or a priest and his adopted son, or a simple adult twosome, or some grownups with foster kids, when you become family you become an outpost against selfishness. When adults and children act for their common good while cherishing each other's individuality, their family becomes a precious affirmation of mutuality and connection, not *because* it is legal, but *if* it is lived.

Nevertheless, at any given time, says the Census Bureau, "a sizeable majority of the population lives in a family maintained by a married couple" (nearly 50 million out of 84 million U.S. households as of 1982).[22] The hunger to capture that special "us" in specific marital ritual seems timeless and universal: Witness how many Americans were distraught when the Reverend Sun Myung Moon took over Madison Square Garden for the mass wedding of four thousand of his cult followers— brides in identical gowns and grooms in blue suits. The event also aroused for the first time a unified reaction from the major faiths who joined to issue the statement that "marrying such large numbers of people at one time negates the dignity and sanctity of what has traditionally been a highly personal and solemn rite."[23]

Modern couples may "no longer regard the married state as significantly better than being single," but 90 percent of young Americans expect to marry; they may be marrying later, signing "prenuptial agreements" to clarify each partner's financial rights and radically altering the balance of power within their marriages, but most young people are still getting married—two and a half million of them each year between May and September alone[24]—(and they're doing it one couple at a time) because for many couples, marriage remains a meaningful way to proclaim that their union is extraordinary to them. But because most people *want* to marry does not mean all families *must* begin with a married couple. Whether state-sanctioned or ritualized by private commitments, whether heterosexual or homosexual behind the bedroom door, whether related by blood or consanguinity of spirit, all kinds of families who love and support their members should on that basis alone be welcomed into the family of families. Because in its first distilled essence, your *family is who it is,* whoever *you* say it is.

FAMILY IS HOW IT FEELS

Public opinion polls tell us Kenneth Keniston's upside-down aphorism was right: "the heart is where the home is."[25] Most people seem to overlook the downside of family life in favor of its rewards and pleasures. They enjoy "knowing I have someone who loves and cares for me."[26] Nine out of ten say they value "traditional family ties"—not the *structure,* but the emotional linkages.[27]

A majority of Americans have an abstract yearning for an "old-fashioned family" but an inaccurate notion of what families of the past were really like. They want the "warmth and closeness" they believe existed, but not if it means going back to traditional work roles, sex roles, or sexual relations.[28]

"Having a good family life" is the most important goal for people of every age—more important even than physical

health, self-respect, personal happiness, and "a lifetime of interesting experiences"; and far more important than a high
income, nice house, or expensive car.[29] Both women and men
say they feel "fulfilled" when they have satisfying intimate
family relations, rather than when they've succeeded in the
performance of traditional roles, because families are "clearly
more central to self-definition" than are work or leisure
activities.[30]

In short, despite decades of social and political upheaval,
and a disturbingly high incidence of domestic abuse, the family
is, according to comparative studies, "probably stronger and
certainly happier today than it was in the 1920s."[31]

Some feminists would attribute this rampant positivism
to "false consciousness" (people don't know enough to know
how bad off they are), but at a certain point theory must bow
to felt-experience. And whatever a particular family's inade-
quacies, millions of children as well as adults feel and experience their own families in a positive way.

When I asked my three teenagers to free-associate about
"how family feels," these are the words they blurted out:

team	home base
comrades	backbone
comfort	launching place
inspiration	forum
laboratory	rehearsal hall
testing ground	escape
haven	security
unity	warmth

How closely those words echo what Harriet Beecher
Stowe wrote in 1865: "Home is a place not only of strong
affections but of entire unreserve; it is life's undress rehearsal;
its backroom; its dressing room from which we go forth to
more careful and guarded intercourse."[32]

When I was in Sweden in 1981, children were polled
about what they wanted most. Believe it or not, the most
common answer was "cozy evenings, adults to be with and
talk to, someone to confide in"[33]—in other words, family life.

At a number of recent graduation ceremonies, seniors

rose spontaneously to applaud their parents in the audience as if to say "thank you."[34] Around the same time, a nationwide survey of thirteen- to eighteen-year-olds found family relations in dandy shape. Sixty percent of the youngsters said they get along "very well" with their parents, and 77 percent said if they needed help with a serious decision they would turn to their parents (only 18 percent would consult their best friends). In another study, 160,000 kids were asked their greatest fear. "It wasn't fear of atomic war or crime," reports Dr. Myron Harris. "It was the fear of losing their parents."[35]

Families feel important to the people in them. That feeling, wherever it comes from, cannot be dismissed. It's one of the things family *is*.

FAMILY IS WHAT IT DOES

Families used to provide for their members food, clothing, shelter, education, religion, succor, medical care, entertainment, *everything*. "To be everything may come close to being nothing," observes Carl Degler. The modern family, on the other hand, is free to concentrate on its primary functions— love, support, and affection—"without internal distraction. It is possible, in short, that not much of value has been lost at all."[36]

Different families do different things for their members at different times in the life cycle, but as I see it, all families have three enormous capacities: the capacity to humanize, to transmit history, and to resist.

The Capacity to Humanize. In the next chapter you will read about a father who hid his cross-eyed son from the world, and about Las Vegas parents who locked their four children in a dark room for six years. These parents did not "humanize" their children, they barely kept them alive. However, the word "kindness" and the word "kin" are not etymologically related by accident. Assuming one begins with kind, sane adults, the family is where each of us learns how to become a human being, an enterprise that takes great effort from all concerned. It is where we learn love, communication, trust, sharing, a sense of humor, a value system, and the control and expression of anger and of sexuality. It is where we experience the consequences of our actions, the limits of egoism, and the pleasures of pleasing others.

"To do all that learning," says psychologist Dorothy Dinnerstein, "you need to feel an intense trusting relationship with other people for whom your existence is important. . . . It's because you exist for them that you want to exist for yourself."[37] Dinnerstein extols the "essential humanizing functions of stable, longstanding, generation-spanning groups."[38] Couldn't a community of friends provide the same foundation? Dinnerstein thinks not: "If you can always withdraw from relationships, you never grow up, you're not stimulated to look into your own motives, to exert yourself to see another point of view." Since divorce and desertion statistics tell us that adults withdraw from blood relationships as well as chosen ones, though perhaps less easily, one might want to distinguish between *intense* chosen commitments and *emotionless* blood ties. But Dinnerstein insists, "To be able to live amicably, or in some sense cooperatively, with people you wouldn't choose . . . that is an irreplaceably humanizing experience."[39] On second thought, that involuntary quotient defines *children's* situations: they do not choose their parents, but they learn to live with us.

Historian Gerda Lerner says, for all its flaws, the family has an "emotional and sustaining meaning" matched by no substitute. It is "the last humanizing force left in society, and [most people] think, correctly, that it must be maintained."[40]

Perhaps that explains the national popularity of a video game in which the player's mission is to "save the last human family" by "hugging" them with an electronic blip. (Predictably, the family on the screen is a white, nuclear threesome: Mommy, Daddy, and little Mikey.) The game's inventor calls it "the answer to all those people who say that video games are destroying family life. Now you can put a quarter into the game to save the family. . . . It's humanity's last stand."[41] Is it cynicism or symbolism that society's ultimate humanizing institution, the family, is rescued by a "hug" from a machine?

The Capacity to Transmit History. When a family spans the generations, it advertises the facts of the human life span at close range: As you see a tiny infant grow into a vigorous adult or watch a lively relative turn gray and weak, you get, in Dinnerstein's words, "a sense of mortality that can't be gotten any other way."[42] Families of blood do transmit species history with special vividness because the family resemblance makes recognition of one's fate unavoidable. Right now, for instance, I am forty-three. My sister is fifty-seven, and just beginning to show age. Our mother died nearly thirty years ago; she was fifty-five when I saw her last. Now I see her again, suddenly, in the newly lined face of my sister.

With or without family resemblance, the physical evidence of continuity makes us want to transmit another kind of history through what some psychologists called "generational transfer" and business types refer to as "networking" or "mentoring." Although treated as a new discovery in the corporate world, families have always practiced this apprenticeship system, passing on values, passions, trade secrets, pieces of themselves; making their children the beneficiaries not just of wealth and property, but of the legacy of their families' *strengths.* Ideally, these strengths are transmitted without regard to blood or gender: My father, who had no sons, passed along to his daughters his lawyerlike rationality and argumentative rigor, passed them on with equal fervor to me, his natural child, and to my mother's daughter, whom he adopted. I hesitate to think what we would have gotten if he'd had a son as well.

Catharine Stimpson, child of a traditional church-going, picnicking, togetherness family, found herself at age forty in a *chosen* family helping another woman raise several children. "I have, then, both reconstituted and repudiated family history," she writes. "Being in a family means serving others, especially small dependent children." It also means Stimpson has taught one child to drive, another to play poker, introduced another to Nancy Drew mysteries, arranged their food with *her* mother's aesthetic, and equipped the children with her opinions of television and sex. "Though I will pass on little property and no name," Stimpson writes, "perhaps I wished to infiltrate another's memory."[43]

When we infiltrate another's memory, family history is a dialectic of love and learning. The adults teach the children, reaping as we sow, surprising ourselves with what we have to give and how much we relish their growing proficiencies and glory in their triumphs. In adolescence, for a brief moment in time, the two generations may be balanced on a horizontal seesaw, equalized by the same level of tennis playing or the same taste in movies. Inevitably, the seesaw tips and the children think differently, make their own mark, care about other issues. For some, this is a time of rancor and resentment. But if parents acknowledge that children have things to teach us, it can be the payback. Generational transfer comes full circle when we can enjoy our own multiple legacies to our children transmogrified by their world and sharpened by their perceptions.

The notion of children's necessarily rebelling against their parents, becoming "alienated" and rejecting their families, may have been a phenomenon of the age of immigration when parent and child embodied real clashes between the values of the old and new worlds. But today, all generations have the possibility of commonality and friendship, and the family's lifelong continuum of reciprocity could be the model for generational transfer, or generativity, on a wider scale from individual to family to community at large.

The Capacity to Resist. Both the capacity to humanize and the capacity to transmit history tend to be actualized in families without too much effort; each family does it differently but most families do it. However, the capacity to resist is a potential few families consciously develop or understand. For me, it is among the main reasons why families, however altered, must be supported and strengthened.

Classical philosophers charted how the family should school citizens in obedience and subordination to God and the state. As contemporary French sociologist Jacques Donzelot puts it, people without ties are hard to regulate.[44] Because family ties help maintain social order, society evolved from a government of families to a government *through* the family. In this view, family is seen as an agency of control.

More recent psychoanalytically inclined thinkers have diagrammed how the family reproduces the conformity the culture needs by repressing sexuality and channeling it into acceptable outlets. They argue that the family teaches us to experience our suffering as personal guilt, not societal injustice, and that *internalization* of suffering inhibits acts of rebellion. Again, the family is seen as an agency of repression.

Marxists have identified the family as the place where liberal ideals of justice and equality are undermined by class and sex inequality in property and family relations. And critical theorists have seen in the family the origin of the "authoritarian personality" and the seeds of fascism.

Although there is some truth in all these positions, there's another view, just as supportable and far more optimistic, that might explain why, in Donzelot's words, "fondness for family is associated with a feeling for liberty."[45] This view holds that the family can serve as *the* revolutionary cell in a repressive society, a place where nonconformity is validated and alternative values nourished. In short, an intimate agent of resistance.

With a few provisos, I find this position the one that offers the most enthusiastic hope for the families of the future, as it has for those of the past. The working-class family, for example, which has sheltered laborers from the full storm of capitalism, has also seeded class consciousness and facilitated trade union organizing. Exploring the ways that family solidarity both sustains workers in struggle and creates a model for class comradeship, Jane Humphries points out that "A radical tradition could be preserved within the family during times of oppression and perpetuated intergenerationally."[46]

The Nazis saw the family's subversive potential, too. "Although they exalted the family in ideology as indispensable to a society based on the 'blood' principle," explains Max Horkheimer, "in reality they suspected and attacked the family as a shelter against mass society. They looked at it as a virtual conspiracy against the totalitarian state."[47]

Christopher Lasch contends that political despotism rises

when family strength dissolves, because we are then vulnerable to new forms of domination; only the family gives us the ability to resist. Agreed. But this insight is spoiled by Lasch's sentimental notion of an utterly self-sufficient family that never was. His strong families are those who wrench free of the helping professions, go it alone, and contain dominant fathers. In my view, patriarchal authority may be a precondition for males to develop the capacity to resist other forms of domination, but for females it is *itself* a form of domination; what it preconditions is female inferiority and submission.

Of course, families have their limits. They cannot protect their members "from the brutalizing influence of the market and of bureaucratic organizations," notes Lasch, nor from "the brutalizing influence of the street."[48] The family's function as refuge and safe space is dependent on state or societal protection of that space. Thus, the capacity to resist can never be entirely privatized.

For instance, families can keep their Jewish identity alive under anti-Semitic torment, spawn universalism in a ghetto, inspire rebellion without armies or arms, sustain three people on one potato—but families are impotent if the Gestapo decides to kick down their doors and march them to the gas chambers.

Short of that, families are almost omni-powerful. As the first human society a child knows, the family occupies the cortical position as conscious and unconscious purveyor of ideology as well as behavior. It is within the family that the sex/gender system can be broken by women who resist oppression and men who relinquish male privilege. It is the place where children, reared on shared parenthood or raised by one parent who chooses to transcend sex-role behaviors, can be empowered to control their own lives, rather than become addicted to power over others.

It is within the family that industrial and corporate life can be neutralized and held at bay. Hegel argued that "family serves to moralize and communalize property, elevating it above mere selfishness and greed."[49] More concretely, the family is where children can learn to resist consumerism, commercialism, materialism, and status-seeking; where they can cultivate buying habits based on need and aesthetics, and an appreciation of old things, used things, and recycled goods. It is within the family that children can rise above the self-aggrandizing structures of the American system and nurture the impulse to give back, to share resources, and pay for justice through philanthopy (if that, for the time being, is the only way to get it). Furthermore, rearing children to reason, analyze, challenge, speak bitterness, and demand fair treatment is, it seems to me, a vaccination against the creeping passivity and powerlessness that end in the tolerance of slavery.

A national survey of American families[50] found that 43 percent of all parents are a "new breed" who have adopted nontraditional *attitudes* if not yet widespread nontraditional practices. They say they believe in the equal rights of parents and children, and in raising girls and boys with the same chances and choices. More than two out of three families worry about passing on their own prejudices to their children. Three families in four say they are not interested in the usual ethic of competition. Although these new beliefs may only slowly be translated into behavior, there is wonder in the fact that one family in four claims they do not teach children "my country right or wrong," and 40 percent no longer raise children to believe "people in authority know best."

What does it all add up to? Not as many ambiguities as you might expect. The essence of family is who it is, how it feels, and what it does: its capacity to humanize, to transmit history, and to teach resistance. The family endures because it has accommodated internal revolution with more resilience than any other institution; because, like a benevolent Hydra, it has remained "family" regardless of which of its functions or people are lopped off; and because, without the permission of Western culture, it has changed and thus managed to stay alive in new and diverse forms and has ultimately proven itself more useful, more responsive, and more humane than its critics may have dreamed possible.

The family endures because it offers the truth of mortality and immortality within the same group. The family endures because, better than the commune, kibbutz, or classroom, it seems able to both individualize and socialize its children, to make us feel at the same time unique and yet joined to all humanity, accepted as is and yet challenged to grow, loved unconditionally and yet propelled by greater expectations. Only in the family can so many extremes be reconciled and synthesized. Only in the family do we have a lifetime in which to do it.

3

Pedophobia: Ambivalence and Hostility toward Children

IN 1980, ANNA AND MICHAEL POLOVCHAK and their three children emigrated from the Ukraine to Chicago, Illinois, in search of a better life. After six months, the parents became disillusioned and decided the family should return to the Soviet Union. One son, Walter, twelve years old, and his older sister, Natalie, seventeen, preferred to remain in the United States. The parents insisted that Walter, who was underage, go back with them. He refused and took refuge with a cousin, declaring through lawyers that he had chosen freedom over repression and would be in danger if forced to return to the Soviet Union.

Suddenly, two sacrosanct principles were at loggerheads: the obligation of children to obey parents, and the obligation of the United States to protect a defector from communism. Whereas the imperative to honor thy father had always served to undergird the imperative to honor thy country, here the one was in direct contradiction with the other. Custody *vs.* asylum. Patriarchy *vs.* patriotism. How would the conflict be reconciled?

First, a Chicago judge made Walter a ward of the juvenile court, protecting him from his parents' reach.[1] Then the Illinois Appellate Court, reversing that ruling, ordered him returned to parental custody, and declared the state "had violated the Polovchaks' civil rights by intervening in the family's internal affairs."

In the meantime, however, the U.S. Immigration and Naturalization Service granted Walter asylum, and the boy stayed put, guarded twenty-four hours a day by two armed federal officers.

Next, the Appellate Court reaffirmed that Walter must go back to his parents. The Reagan administration countered by issuing an executive order preventing him from leaving the United States, and the Justice Department granted him "permanent residency status." The Soviet Union then accused the United States of "a crying violation of human rights" for not letting Walter return to the bosom of his family.

For each action the propaganda reasons are transparent, the ironies dense: the United States took a stand against the Soviet Union that put the Reagan administration in the "right" place in terms of cold war anti-communism but, at the same time, put Reagan in the politically embarrassing position of siding with a child against his parents. On the other hand, the state of Illinois, by siding with the parents, also stood with the Soviet Union.

As for the Polovchaks, Natalie said, the father was afraid of the Soviet government, which instructed him to return home with his entire family; the mother was afraid of the father, and did "what her husband told her to"; and the father insisted that Walter and Natalie had "a duty to return to their homeland." So it goes, from family duty to national duty in a single bound: The state commands the man, the man commands the woman and children. Patriotism imitates patriarchy, and patriarchy reciprocates.

But something begins to ring wrong. Why does a twelve-year-old choose to live in a strange land without his mother and father? Most children cleave to their parents so tightly that, even if there is family abuse or alcoholism, they opt to remain with their parents when given the choice; some profound need, some sense of loving and being loved despite parental inadequacy keeps them there. But when children *want* to leave their parents, that love-sense is missing, and no judge or dictator can create it.

In the Polovchak family, was there a Family worth "saving"? Mr. Polovchak said he loved his children "like a father"—a peculiar statement to come from their actual father. What's more, his children tell a different story.

"I never had love for my parents," said Natalie. "I was always a slave in their house." She also said her mother was "rarely present," and her father ignored the kids and spent all his time on work, night school, and his own friends. Just before the Soviets ordered the family home, her father had told relatives he planned "to give away Wally and Natalie."

For his part, Walter said, "I have never been close to my parents. I was raised by my grandmother until I was twelve years old. My father was coming home once a week and sometimes never." Reportedly, his parents never noticed that Walter badly needed dental care and eyeglasses. They never gave him lunch money. They never took him to a movie. They never came to school to watch him play soccer, his proudest effort. They left the United States without even trying to say goodbye.

When the myth of the happy family is dispelled, as it was in this case, one might expect reasonable people to look at the merits of the dispute and side with the aggrieved child. But one would have underestimated how deeply family fetishism is rooted in the political order, and how inextricably the defense of parental rights is linked to the defense of patriarchal power.

Interestingly, the major defenders of the parents against the child have been that great advocate of individual rights, the American Civil Liberties Union, and the "liberal" *New York Times*. An ACLU lawyer who represented the Polovchaks said the real issue was whether children should be allowed to live where they want just because "they feel like it." And the *Times* editorial, agreeing that Walter should be returned to the Ukraine, opined with Victorian pomposity: ". . . this case isn't about freedom from political oppression but the freedom of a boy to defy his parents."

So there it is. The Family isn't a place where parents must love children, but where children must obey parents. The pro-family impulse isn't a nostalgic longing for a caring circle of kin around the hearth, but a strategy against youthful insubordination and defiance. The awful truth is that this pro-family strategy touches a chord in millions of people who do not otherwise identify with ultra-right aims. It touches that chord because, contrary to the belief that we are collectively a child-loving people, *America is a nation fundamentally ambivalent about its children, often afraid of its children, and frequently punitive toward its children.*

As a society, we love children only when they are *under control.* We hate children who defy us, even when they defy us, like Walter Polovchak, to do something that we might otherwise applaud—such as choosing democracy. We fear children who want democracy for themselves, children who are independent, quirky, free-thinking, nonconformist, idiosyncratic, superior, or critical of adults.

Especially problematic are precocious children. Adult envy of youth—its innocence, physical freshness, carefree times—has always been tempered by the compensation of our greater adult wisdom. But precocious, gifted children rob us of that comparison, which may explain why few of them escape "the fear, indifference, hostility, envy, and sarcasm of society toward their giftedness." According to Bernard S. Miller, an expert on intellectually talented youngsters, such children are feared largely because "they are less willing to accept adult explanations that are based on force, age, or lack of logic, such as 'Do it because I say so!' "[2]

Although women have always used children as scapegoats of female frustration and powerlessness, in recent years many men have begun to focus on children as the finger in the dike of male dominion. Now that men have no animals to tame and no frontier to conquer; now that women are rebellious and machines are out-thinking and displacing men, children are the last remaining subjects of domination. Rulers need subjects. Therefore, children's equality cannot be permitted. No wonder conservatives were incensed when the United States Commission for International Children's Year recommended "that laws dealing with rights of parents be re-examined and changed where they infringe on the rights of children."[3] How the traditionalists hated that one—and still feel threatened by the concept of children's rights. The *Conservative Digest* even found it necessary to warn: "Under 'kiddie lib' children could sue their parents and could even choose to leave their parents and find a new set."[4]

The ultra-right rails against long hair, fashion fads, rock 'n roll, drugs, and teen pregnancy, not necessarily because of what these "evils" are in themselves or what they do to our children, but because they are measures of adults' failure to impose their authority on children. Despite their cries of too much government, and their attempt to eliminate the laws, sex education courses, and counseling services that circumvent the father and help mother and children *directly*,[5] they still want to legislate patriarchal family relations with whatever government interference is necessary.

Many of us fear our children's emancipation. Their self-sufficiency is proof of how dispensable we are. Already virtually helpless to affect economic conditions and world events, and feeling that we have lost control of our lives to technocracy, television, government, and experts, people cannot bear to lose control of their children, too.

Neil Postman, author of *The Disappearance of Childhood*, contends that children are growing up too fast; they are rushing into grown-up clothing styles, food tastes, and games, and are learning too soon the adult "secrets" of sexuality and aggression. I might agree with this analysis if I had not seen where it leads: The Women's Movement is "devastating to the power of the family," says Postman. Women should stay home and protect "the information environment of the young." It is women's job to see that childhood survives and being an adult remains a "distinction."[6]

Dressed up in fancy theory, or uttered plain, the fear is the same: If we who are so small in this vast and complex universe cannot feel more powerful, able, and knowing than children, then who and where are we in the hierarchy of the cosmos? To contemplate such existential dis-order is to fall into an abyss as desolate as an echo. We need to bounce our voices off children's silence. Men, especially, need children to anchor the bottom of the chain of command. When gender, race, and class comforts fail, children are the last order of necessary inferiors.

PEDOPHOBIA IN ACTION

In search of a shorthand term to describe this attitude, I've invented the word "pedophobia" from the Greek word elements *paed*, meaning "child," and *phobia*, meaning "fear, dread, aversion, or hatred." A doctor who specializes in treating children is a *pediatrician;* a teacher of children is a *pedagogue;* one who has a sexual love of children is a *pedophile,* so it seems reasonable that one who fears and hates children is a *pedophobe.* And I see a veritable epidemic of pedophobia in America today. Although most of us make exceptions for our own offspring, we do not seem particularly warmhearted toward other people's children. Collectively, we are heirs to a strong legacy of pedophobia from the past. The only thing new about it is giving it a name.

The Historical Anti-Child.[7] In ancient times, children were sacrificed to the gods, brutally beaten, neglected, and starved. Infanticide served the function of population control, especially to rid families of less-valued female babies. Poor families purposely mutilated their children to make them more pitiful or amusing beggars. Many were sold into slavery for a father's profit. Among the higher classes, children were used as political hostages, security for debts, and negotiable assets. Very young children were forced to marry to facilitate a father's acquisition of property. From the Greek and Roman era through Biblical times as recently as the rise of Calvinism, children were subject to the death penalty for offenses against their parents.

In the supposedly enlightened eighteenth and nineteenth centuries, parental indifference, child neglect, and raw cruelty appeared among Europeans of all classes. Children were considered "creatures apart." When they cried, they were given opium pacifiers. Violent cradle rocking was used to knock them into "the sleep of insensibility." Mothers allowed babies "to stew in their own excrement for hours on end." Often, they were left on the floor where they were attacked by farm animals or burned by sparks from the open hearth. Infants were "overlain" and suffocated by adult bodies, sometimes accidentally because of crowded sleeping conditions, sometimes purposely.

In mid-nineteenth-century France, families abandoned their children at the rate of thirty-three thousand a year. The foundling homes that absorbed them were disease-ridden and inadequate; in one, the mortality rate reached 80 percent. French and English babies of "good families" were routinely sent to mercenary wet nurses who operated "baby farms" out of their impoverished, filthy peasant hovels. In the care of wet nurses, infant death rates averaged 35 percent. When the cities suffered famines and plagues, it was not unusual to see in the streets the bodies of dead children ignored by passersby. Few parents showed signs of bereavement; fewer still attended a child's funeral.

Children who survived infancy were forced to work at hard, heavy labor. In England, for example, chimney sweeps as young as four years old were crammed into narrow chimney flues and made to clean them for hours at a time. Poor children were indentured in textile mills from age seven to twenty-one. It took sixty years after the criminalization of cruelty to animals for cruelty to children to be made punishable under English law.

In the young American republic, many of the same habits persisted. Parents fed babies rum to quiet them. A daily cold bath and a walk outdoors in thin-soled shoes were thought to toughen children's constitutions. Teachers "bestowed" the birch rod even for minor infractions, such as failure to memorize five thousand Bible verses. Penalties included humiliation by dunce cap. Girls were allowed neither education nor exercise until well into the nineteenth century.

To avoid spoiling them, Puritans "put out" their children to be servants in the homes of relatives or strangers. To avoid the "sin of idleness," children were expected to work almost from the time they could stand. In the slave South, children were sold away from their mothers. From age six onward, slave children worked in the fields or the great house. Near-naked boys waited on table. Older girls were taken at will to the master's bed. In every state a father could apprentice his son to a gambler or rum seller, bind his daughter to a brothel, or will his children away from their mother. Birch canings and Calvinism molded children's character. They were "broken" like horses: in 1833, a sixteen-month-old girl was whipped and shut in a closet for refusing to say "dear Momma"; in 1858, by similar means, a boy was taught never to cry in his father's presence. Later, Victorian standards of duty, deference, and delicacy made room for a view of the child as either Innocent or Savage, with nothing in-between. One of the worst of the little Savage's infractions was "self-abuse," an act punishable by binding and handcuffs and worse. "To prevent the transmission of moral insanity"—meaning mental or physical disability, poverty, "deliquency"—thousands of children of both sexes were sterilized, a "punishment" that is not unknown in some states to this day.

Industrialized America added brutalizing child labor to the oppressions of the young. For ten to fourteen hours a day, small children worked in fly-infested meat-packing plants or poorly lit factories, crawled in coal mines, tended dangerous machines, did mind-numbing feather or tobacco sorting, hauled loads heavier than themselves. Child labor was abolished in 1938, but children today are still doing stoop work in the fields and illegal "home" work in the garment industry, where a new wave of immigrant families, including children, is being exploited. At this writing, the Reagan administration has proposed a relaxation of child labor rules for all fourteen- and fifteen-year-olds.[8]

The Anti-Child of the 1980s. In our own era, pedophobia is more subtle. It is also more pernicious because it exists within the lie that Americans are a child-loving people. Today, we protest the cost of public education, child health programs, or food stamps. We object to children's shelters being located in our neighborhoods, where they might lower our property values. Public accommodations ignore the existence of children and their needs. Many transit systems, stores, and museums prohibit baby strollers. Some shops, restaurants, and movie houses prohibit children altogether. Curbstones, public benches, toilets, telephones, and door handles are too high for little ones. (Ironically, lowering these things for wheelchair access has made life easier for children in some localities.) The pornographic display of women's breasts is undeterred on newsstands and movie marquees, but official and unofficial prohibition of breastfeeding in public places forces nursing mothers and babies into unsanitary bathroom stalls. There are no child-care facilities for even the temporary amusement of children while parents shop.

More virulent pedophobia can be found in the great wave of books and movies in which children personify evil (*Children of Darkness, The Lucifer Child, The Firestarters, The Stepchild, The Moonchild,* and of course, *Rosemary's Baby* and *The Exorcist*). These stories suggest that, although they appear small and innocent, children cannot be trusted. Beneath their child disguises, they are monsters. Pedophobia also explains the sudden rash of books on the importance of spanking children (*Dare To Discipline; Spanking: Why, When, How?; Spank Me If You Love Me*).[9] And the growing phenomenon of "child-free" housing developments that bar sales or rentals to families with children. ("Don't get me wrong," said one resident. "I like kids. I just don't like them around."[10]) And the commonplace protests of adults who happen to get seated next to a child on a plane or near a family group in a restaurant.

Worse by far, there is little "pro-family" protest against the plague of child abuse—the physical and sexual violations committed in families, on the streets, and in child pornography. Ten percent of all American children are *reported* abused, and authorities say child abuse is grossly *under-*reported.[11] Where are the ultra-right crusaders on these family issues? Why is there no "pro-family" outcry about all the youngsters who disappear from home each year (in June 1982, fifty thousand kids were unaccounted for in this country; a thousand were among the unnamed, unclaimed dead); or for the one in six hundred babies affected by fetal alcohol syndrome, the seven million youngsters who currently live with an alcoholic parent, the more than one million teenagers who themselves have serious drinking problems, the quarter of a million who try to commit suicide each year, and the ten thousand who succeed?[12]

Individualized Pedophobia. I am sure every parent has done something that her or his child would consider cruel. But lately, I seem to be seeing the cruelty of many, many parents through the eyes of their children. I chafe at the sight of little kids' being hushed, cuffed, scowled at, or completely ignored during a meal or train trip. I cringe when adults talk to children in patronizing tones, smiling with mirthless cheer, or when they push, pull, smack, and scream at children who cannot fight back, talk back, or run away.

The other day at the supermarket, I watched a father give a child no older than six a heavy grocery sack to carry home. The father had two big sacks himself and he clearly needed another pair of hands, but instead of giving his child a bag full of light items, say bread and cereal boxes, he had given her the canned goods. Straining under the weight, she began to cry. He shouted that he couldn't carry another bag and threatened to leave her behind if she didn't keep up. I wanted to barge in, rearrange their loads, and scold the man for thinking too little and asking too much. But I just stood by, respecting the father's rights, and wondering whether parents would be kinder to children if they knew they were being watched.

Some public pedophobes certainly bear watching; in fact, a few are almost grotesquely fascinating:

• Greg Dixon, the Indiana Moral Majority leader who engineered a weakening of his state's child abuse laws because "the Bible instructs parents to whip their children with a rod." The Reverend Dixon believes "welts and bruises are a sign that a parent is doing a good job of discipline." He also persuaded Indiana Senator Richard Lugar to stop sending constituents a free government booklet entitled, "Your Child from One to Six." Why? Because the booklet implied that children might not be born with evil in them, and because it counseled parents not to spank children.[13]

• Phyllis and David York, founders of Toughlove, a self-help program for parents with "out-of-control teenage children." While absolving parents of all responsibility for their children's development (and blaming the kids and "today's culture"), Toughlove aims "to stop households from being controlled by unruly teenagers, rid parents of guilt feelings and enable parents and non-problem children to lead a normal family life." Toughlove's emphasis on *control* (which includes refusing to bail a child out of jail) suggests more commitment to the "tough" part than the "love" part.[14]

• Wisconsin Circuit Court Judge William Reinecke, who was re-elected after he had remarked from the bench that the victim of a sexual assault was "sexually promiscuous" and called her "the aggressor"—although she was only *five years old*. (And right behind him are the forty Wisconsin lawyers who signed a letter in support of the judge, contending that "a long and distinguished career should not be destroyed by a few ill-chosen words.")[15]

• Harry Zain, who lobbies Congress for his proposal to lower girls' marriage age to twelve in order to "end promiscuity." Zain seeks to forbid girls an education because school and careers for women have "made us a nation of boys instead of men and a nation of boys is a nation of slaves." Zain's views were not published in *Mad* magazine, but in six columns of *The New York Times*.[16]

• Michigan Probate Judge Donald Halstead, who refused to grant the abortion requested by an eleven-year-old girl who had been raped by her mother's boyfriend.[17]

• The Chicago "pro-life" group of anonymous moralists who mercilessly hounded a woman to prevent her from arranging an abortion for her pregnant eleven-year-old. They besieged the woman's house, harassed her by phone, and picketed the hospital. Then, rather like bombing a village to save it from communism, these fetus protectors hired a private detective to track down the little girl to tell her "abortion could have a terrible psychological as well as physical effect" on her.[18]

Individual pedophobia reaches its apotheosis in those unspeakable cases of child abuse in the form of torture and sexual terrorism. Every Halloween we read about poisoned trick-

or-treat candies and apples implanted with razor blades. Throughout the year, there are chilling stories of child prostitution rings and "boy love" sex clubs.[19] Some of these enterprises are flagrantly "sexploitation-for-profit"; others—such as the René Guyon Society, whose motto is "sex by eight, or it's too late—couch their activities in phony liberationist rhetoric, insisting that children's rights include the "right" to be sexually involved with adults. Notice that the disputed issue for two vastly different groups is children's freedom. Conservative authoritarians think kids are unruly or innocent untamed creatures who must be both protected and taught their place. "Boy-love" libertarians see children's free spirit as carnal and knowledgeable (in the sexual sense); they contend that kids are just like us and must not be deprived of intercourse with adults. Whether the thesis is that children are different or children are no different, these contrasting views of childhood have the same objective: *to control children for adult purposes.*

Each time a tabloid headlines another pedophobic atrocity story, one thinks the incidents cannot get any worse. But they do. There was the father who set fire to his 6-year-old's bed while the boy was asleep rather than give the mother custody of him, and the mother who shot her children rather than relinquish them to foster homes; the father who hid his son for fourteen years because the boy was born with crossed eyes, and the two men who kept a three-year-old girl and an eleven-year-old boy prisoners in a van for ten months while they raped and beat them. I would say the very worst was the "family" that locked its six children, aged eight months to six years, in one small dark room all of their lives.[20] Some would insist, logically, that murder is worse.

Nationwide, "homicide has become one of the top five causes of deaths in children, with *parents or stepparents responsible for a third of the slayings*" (emphasis mine). Since 1925, homicides of children under age four have increased sixfold; for children five to fourteen, they have more than doubled.[21]

Thus, the society that romanticizes the family and kneels before the commercial images of children like Strawberry

Shortcake, Peter Pan, Gary Coleman, Fat Albert, Holly Hobby, Charlie Brown, and Annie is the same society that murders its children, rapes them, starves them, whips them, shuns them, burns them, stunts them, poisons them, and hates them to death. And we who do not do it ourselves let it be done, not only in the families where most of our 64 million children live their lives, but in public policies and practices that testify to a kind of institutionalized pedophobia.

Institutionalized Pedophobia. America's collective disregard for its children is writ large in numerous areas:

EDUCATION. Although we think of ourselves as an educated and literate nation, a million school-aged kids are not enrolled in school. One disabled child in every five is not getting a basic education. Up to a third of city high school students are chronic truants. Thirteen percent of our seventeen-year-olds (47 percent of black youths) are functionally illiterate.[22] Yet the Reagan administration wants to divert Title I funds from public education programs that have proven effective with disadvantaged kids; "pro family" forces say children should not go to school until age eight or ten, by which time the parents' influence has armed them against liberal, humanist teachers and books; and the ultra-right calls Christian schools and "home schools" superior educators.[23]

POVERTY. Although we think of ourselves as a classless society, or at least one in which no single group is disproportionately deprived, the fact is that *the poorest people in America are children.* One in five children is poor; one in two black children. Poverty is the primary cause of prenatal and early childhood malnutrition, and malnutrition has been found to influence a person's behavior for the rest of his or her life. Poverty (not divorce or working mothers) is a major cause of children's academic and disciplinary problems. Each year, 11,000 children die of poverty-related causes, which adds up to more deaths in five years than the total of Americans killed in the Vietnam War.[24]

NUTRITION. Although we think of ourselves as a land of abundance—and indeed we have federal storehouses bulging with surplus cheese, dried milk, butter, and grain[25]—we cannot seem to scrape together enough food or money to provide food for hungry children. Three million schoolchildren have been cut from breakfast and lunch programs, hungry or not.[26] The Women, Infants and Children (WIC) food supplement program, which feeds pregnant women, nursing mothers, and infants, has measurably reduced infant mortality, anemia, and birth defects. It not only ensures as healthy a start for poor children as for privileged ones, it does so economically: a Harvard study found that each preventive dollar spent on WIC saves five to ten dollars that might be spent later to hospitalize malnourished babies. Nevertheless, the Reagan administration cut $1.46 billion from child nutrition programs. At the same time, it found $1.7 million for five private dining rooms in the Pentagon; $1.4 million for the pets of military personnel; and $5 million dollars for the military's "servant program."[27]

Bob Greenstein, former U.S. Administrator of Food and Nutrition, says, "The Reaganites want to give children prayers in school, but not breakfast." And to Reagan's argument that a great percentage of school lunch food is thrown out, Greenstein answers that the same percentage of wasted food exists in the military, but no one is suggesting that we starve our soldiers.

EMPLOYMENT. Although we think of ourselves as a people who put children's needs first, proportionately far more youngsters than adults are unemployed. Idle, unemployed teenagers do not acquire skills or good work habits; they tend to drop out of the job market entirely, forming a lifetime pattern. Yet the budget-cutters halved the appropriation for "Upward Bound," the federal job program for youths, and eliminated the CETA job training program altogether.[28]

HEALTH. Although we think of ourselves as a medically advanced nation, a greater percentage of American babies die at birth than infants of fifteen other countries (more than 11 deaths per 1000 live births and nearly twice as many deaths for black infants).[29] Once born, a child's health is virtually left to chance. "We spend more health care dollars per person in the last week of life than in the previous seventy-five years," says a leading pediatrician, "and with much less payoff."[30] Each family is assumed equally able to oversee and pay for its children's physical, mental, and dental health. But sharp disparities have been found in access to routine health care between "rich and poor, white and nonwhite, innercity dweller and suburbanite."[31] One child in six gets no health care at all. Eighteen million children have never seen a dentist.[32] And those numbers will get worse if the Reagan administration succeeds in eliminating Medicaid funding that covers health examinations for two million poor children.

INFANT FORMULA. Although we think of ourselves as the most humane nation of all, the United States was the *only* government that refused to sign a code controlling the sale of infant formula throughout the world. We know that babies acquire valuable immunities and nutrients from breast milk. We know that poor mothers who are given prepared formula tend to overdilute it to make it go further, or mix it with polluted water because they have no facilities for sterilization. Nevertheless, the United States chose to protect the manufacturers of infant formula and not the ten million babies whose diseases and malnutrition have been traced to improper bottle feeding.[33]

Here in the United States, 55 percent of all newborns are breastfed.[34] Although infant formula is a relatively safe option for American mothers and babies, Congress did pass a law requiring the Food and Drug Administration to test formulas before they reach the marketplace. Reagan delayed implementation of that law to allow time for the "cost benefit analysis" that business wanted. In the meantime, fifty thousand cans of formula lacking vitamin B-6 reached the stores. Without B-6 in their diets, babies are at high risk for mental retardation and cerebral palsy.[35]

MILITARISM. Although we think of ourselves as a people who draw the line at exploiting children for war (as opposed to the Vietnamese and the PLO, who have used children as walking grenades), we don't have clean hands either. United States Green Berets in Honduras are training children to be paratroopers. The children are so small that weights must be strapped to their bodies to reach the 110 pounds needed to force open their parachutes.[36]

LEAD POISONING. Although we think of ourselves as more "civilized" than the likes of Jim Jones, who poisoned his followers with spiked Kool-Aid, we poison our children almost as systematically with leaded gasoline emissions and lead-based paint. The Department of Housing and Urban Development found that up to two hundred thousand children are being poisoned by the paint still found in some 35 million homes built before current standards went into effect. And the Environmental Protection Agency says leaded gas fumes are a health hazard to small children.[37] Programs to solve these two problems are stalled in confusion and noncompliance.

IMMIGRATION. Although we have a law that allows any child of an American citizen to enter the country under a "first preference" status, until January 1983 our gates were virtually locked to eighty thousand Amerasian children who were fathered by American servicemen stationed in the Orient. A tiny trickle of these children has begun entering the United States, but for reasons of racism, personal embarrassment, or indifference, most of the children either have not been acknowledged by their fathers or have been rejected by the fathers who have claimed paternity.[38] Citing its worries about "fraud and abuse," the government had subjected each little immigrant to a blood test as though their facial features were not advertisement enough of their half-American parentage.

In terms of the children's rights issue, an Appellate Court decision in the case of Frank Serpico seems relevant here. Serpico was ordered to pay support for a baby he said he was tricked into fathering. The court said, even if a father is deceived, "how does it logically follow that the child should suffer?"[39] We can likewise ask: Whether an Asian woman was seduced by a G.I.'s promises or the soldier was deceived into the belief that he was having sex with no consequence—how does it logically follow that the child should suffer? Where citizenship is concerned, these children are born of American fathers, regardless of *which* man or what blood type.

CHILD ADVOCACY. Although we have more than enough child-oriented bureaucracies, child advocacy is about as popular a cause on official levels as, say, decriminalizing marijuana. The Children's Bureau in Washington is rarely heard from. The Department of Education is slated for phase-out. The White House Conference on Children, which has been convened by American presidents since 1909 to generate new programs to meet kids' needs, was downgraded by the "New Federalism" to a series of low-priority state meetings. Congressman George Miller's new Select Committee on Children, Youth, and Families sets priorities for children's programs but has no power to effect legislation. The United Nations Year of the Child, which was dedicated to alleviating world poverty and providing health and education to all children, was virtually ignored in the United States—except by "pro-family" forces, who attacked it. Pat Robertson, on the Christian Broadcasting Network, lumped The Year of the Child with such other evils as virulent Humanism, anti-God rebellion, blatant homosexuality, radical feminism, drug abuse, and the *youth revolt*[40] (emphasis mine). Americans Against Abortion called The Year of the Child "nothing but a communist front for attacking motherhood, the family and Christian values . . . an intense propaganda campaign to 'liberate' children from their parents."[41]

THE BALTIMORE CONNECTION

I've been collecting examples of pedophobia for years, but not until attending the 1980 White House Conference on Families did I understand the political uses of this resentment and fear of children. The conference I attended in Baltimore was one of three regional meetings covened by President Carter to assess the needs of America's families. Conference delegates were supposed to examine the impact of federal policy on families, and propose new programs that would help families become healthier, happier, and more financially secure. What could be bad?

To the Pro-Family Coalition—the group that for months discredited plans for the conferences, and then attended and tried to take over—the very idea of helping families is bad: Helping means interfering in the orderly relations between husband and wife, and parent and child. So the Pro-Family Coalition came to the conference not to solve families' problems, but to enforce traditional roles.

I watched them not only condemn progressivism and feminism as usual, but capitalize on something extra: the delegates' pedophobic desire to keep children under control. At the workshop sessions, in the hallways, lunchrooms, and caucuses, I understood for the first time that *anti-child feelings translate to "pro-family" votes for right-wing issues.* I heard a man accuse the government of "coddling" children with its summer jobs programs. I asked what he did for a living; he was unemployed. I heard a woman say that school sex education "usurps" the parents' role. When another delegate asked if she had taught the facts of life to her own children, she blushed and snapped, "They know *enough!*" I heard many people wave off the subject of child abuse; they were far more interested in defending parents' right to spank. Why is corporal punishment so important? I asked one man. "To teach them who's boss," he answered.

Throughout the conference, parents complained openly that their children talk back, care more about their friends, dress wildly, play loud music, watch TV, and don't mind their parents. I remember a well-dressed woman shaking with fury and shouting "Spare the rod and spoil the child" as if she had coined the phrase. My notes contain a litany of complaints: "Girls are getting pregnant to spite us." "I'm tired of hearing about children's rights! What about parents' rights?" "There are too many experts around; nobody trusts parents." "Kids have too much freedom!" "Will our children be responsible for us when we get old, like we took care of our parents?"

Parental frustration thickened the air. They've lost their

children and they don't understand why. They don't know how to win kids' respect except through the use of force and publicly sanctioned parent power. They've confused obedience with love. If only The Family meant something, they think, their own families would mean something. They're feeling impotent and mad and they want someone or something to give them control over their children.

The Pro-Family Coalition had all the answers in the form of authoritarian certainties and God-given rules. One pro-family advocate from Atlanta was firm about fathers having the sole responsibility for discipline and guidance of their children. A panelist countered, "I see many cases of abuse and sexual molestation of children. Don't you feel that the government, through law enforcement, has some role in this matter?"

"Absolutely not," answered the man. He believed the father should take care of such matters.

The panelist then asked, "But my experience indicates that the father himself is frequently the abuser and sexual molester. Does not the government have some role in that?"

"Absolutely not," the man declared again. "The father must answer to his maker and God will punish him when the time comes."

Thus was a national conference on families derailed to questions of *control*, not care. During the planning stages, Lawrence D. Pratt, a member of the Virginia House of Delegates put a fine point on the pro-family position: "The main issue is who owns the children, the parents or the government."[42]

THE FAMILY AS CHASTITY BELT

The most relentless campaign for ownership of children is, not surprisingly, directed at female children who do not seem to be following men's rules about women's sexual behavior. In response, three government actions are demanded by conservatives who otherwise demand hands-off policies:

1. *The Parental Notification Bill,* one of the items extracted from the Family Protection Act (see Chapter One),

demands that parents be notified when a daughter goes to a federally funded clinic for information or medical services related to venereal disease, contraception, or abortion. (Sixty-three percent of Americans believe minors shouldn't be allowed abortions without their parents' *consent*.[43] The Supreme Court has ruled the requirement of parental consent unconstitutional, but not parental *notification*.) The same forces that deplore government intrusion and insist on the right to privacy for men and corporations want the government to interfere in the private life of a teenage girl. They want government help when it comes to controlling females but not when it comes to empowering them. Parents who have failed to establish a trust relationship with their daughters want the government to compel by law the confidences they could not inspire by love.

2. *The Adolescent Family Life Bill* (or "Chastity Bill") would finance programs that encourage teenage sexual abstinence, deny federal support to agencies that offer girls contraceptive or abortion counseling, and encourage girls to give up their babies for adoption.

3. *The Squeal Rule* is not a bill but a Federal Regulation that requires federally financed family planning clinics to notify parents within ten days after a "person" under eighteen receives contraceptives. The regulation is supposedly rooted in parents' concern for their daughters' health. But the risk from birth control pills is one death per hundred thousand users (the risk from the IUD is even less than that), while the risk of death from pregnancy and childbirth among adolescents is more than eleven per hundred thousand.[44]

Here is pedophobia grafted to misogyny. Although one-third of *all* youngsters under seventeen are sexually active,[45] only girls are subjected to parental fervor to restrain their sexuality; unchallenged is boys' freedom to buy condoms or to impregnate their sex partners. The sex role double standard is an old story. What's new is the assertion that For The Sake Of The Family, a young woman's right to privacy takes second place to a father's right to know what his daughter is up to.

Washington columnist Richard Cohen reminds us, "Teenagers who shy away from letting their parents know they are sexually active will not become celibate. They will become pregnant. *Then* their parents will know."

More than half of the clinic patients under eighteen years of age already tell their parents. As for the rest, faced with the requirement of a family confrontation, 25 percent of young women say they would give up getting the contraceptive but only 2 percent would give up sex.[46]

Symbol of the times: On New Year's Day 1982, in New York City the first baby born after midnight weighed five pounds; its mother was fifteen years old. We know a lot about that mother and the other one million girls who get pregnant every year: 80 percent drop out of school, most often because they cannot afford child care; 75 percent require some sort of public subsidy; and teenagers' babies have up to five times greater chance of birth injury and up to three times greater risk of death before age one.[47]

In keeping with the politics of pregnancy (see Chapter Eight), pro-family moralists are willing to sacrifice young girls to the gods of premarital chastity and parental authority. They do not care about the child-mothers or their babies. *They do not care about stopping adolescent reproduction, they care about punishing adolescent sex.* For people who hate out-of-control children, there is no more out-of-control child than a young female who dares to be as sexually free as a man.

Research shows that sex education and the availability of contraception do not increase teen sexual activity, but *do* discourage pregnancy.[48] Yet moralists continue to oppose contraception because they do not want worry-free sex for girls. Pregnancy punishes female sexuality. It puts a girl in her place. It may ruin her life, but—as I heard again and again in Baltimore and since—it serves her right; she had her fun, now she'll pay for it.

The Reverend Dan C. Fore of the Moral Majority claims to be "pro-life," but his words say he's anti-sex: He doesn't want women to be free "to kill the babies and to cover up the sin of fornication."[49] That sanctimonious, moralistic declaration explains the national tragedy of one million children having children every year. To *expose* female sin, contraception is denied and abortion rights threatened. Unmarried girls' babies can be given up for adoption to a "real" family. But first, *the babies must be born to prove the girls have been bad.* And to scare other girls away from sex.

Perhaps, at some foul and twisted psychic core, some people hate children because their very existence is a reminder of the sex act that spawned them.

Perhaps, having lost control of women's sexuality, men need to reassert authority over the means of reproduction through their daughters.

Perhaps women's complicity in punishing their daughters is their way of protecting the standard of the "good woman" that they have bought for themselves with monogamy and "legitimate" motherhood.

In any case, with so much zeal directed toward compulsory pregnancies for girls, one would expect some attention to the destiny of the children that result. But the vast armies of the right retire from battle when it comes to fighting for such things as improved infant nutrition, medical attention, foster child programs, or any of the issues reviewed earlier in this chapter. I remember a political cartoon that sums it up: In the first picture a man is on his knees before a pregnant woman, saying "Miracle of life." In the second picture, the woman's baby is at her side and the same man is saying "Sniveling little welfare cheat."

Faced with this cynical contradiction, Massachusetts Congressman Barney Frank has criticized conservatives for acting as if "life begins at conception and ends at birth."

The epiphany of The Baltimore Connection—that is, recognizing the extent of society's anti-child feelings and the political uses of pedophobia—tears another veil from the smiling face of The Family. We've seen that in our culture, adults by themselves are not considered a family in quite the sense that they become a family when offspring arrive. But how is it possible for a unit that is reified—made real—by the advent of children to be valued and salient unless children are valued and salient? Put another way, our treatment of children betrays our real feelings about families. *This society cannot*

*pretend to hallow The Family, the one institution that suppos-
edly exists expressly for the sake of children, and still tolerate
collective cruelty or disregard of children.*

This is true whether or not your particular family contains
children.

This is true whether or not you happen to value and love
your *own* children.

This is true because 98 percent of American children grow
up in families. Therefore, what happens to children happens
to families.

4

Home Economics: National Policy vs. The Family Interest

WHENEVER I SHOW A VISITOR around New York, I see my city through new eyes. In the same way, we can see our culture fresh by observing how it is presented to recent immigrants.

At the end of the Vietnam War, more than a hundred thousand Vietnamese who had taken refuge in the United States were placed in resettlement camps, where they were given English lessons and orientation courses to prepare them for "life in American society."[1] The men—most of whom had been the business, religious, and political elite of Vietnam—were being prepared for a giant step down the economic ladder: Not only were they directed to blue collar and service occupations, but also to such traditionally female jobs as cashier, nurse's aide, cleaning person, and typist, where they would not compete with unemployed American men who were jobhunting at the same time.

To compensate for this loss of occupational "maleness," the orientation courses assigned the men all the decision-making roles relating to family life, even the roles usually performed in America by women, such as selecting a church and deciding which stores to patronize. In short, what little power was available was given to the Vietnamese man. Furthermore, a bilingual newspaper published by the U.S. Army Psychological Operations Unit advised the immigrant man "not to be frightened by American women who seem 'noisy, aggressive, dominating.' " It reassured him that most women are " 'quiet, content and gentle' and enjoy being taken care of."

Meanwhile, the Vietnamese woman was routed to classes in child care, birth control, sewing, and cooking. Although 86 percent of the women had been employed in Vietnam, and although learning English was touted as *the* key to employment here, most women were discouraged from attending English classes. The few that did attend were taught to say "I am a housewife," regardless of whether back in Vietnam they'd been trained in fishing, farming, or office work. Some camps banned women from English classes because it was assumed they would not have to get work, and because they might learn faster than men who would therefore "lose face."

Only one orientation course covered women's legal rights, realistic work options, and equal family roles, but camp officials "openly disapproved" of it, and scheduled movies and other attractions to compete with it. They claimed the course would "disrupt the Vietnamese family, and make Vietnamese men anxious about resettling in America and having to cope with aggressive women."

How well did this careful sex-role programming prepare the refugees for the realities of "life in American society"? Dismally. The men could not support their families on the work for which they were trained, and within a year, nearly half the women were forced to look for jobs even though they were untrained and illiterate.

PATRIARCHY, CAPITALISM, AND
FAMILY ECONOMICS

The refugees orientation course could be a metaphor for the cultural ethos that rules us all. Those same rigid sex roles and false expectations that led the Vietnamese families into untenable financial straits are taught to every American, not in a six-month crash program, but during a childhood of conditioning and a lifetime of struggle.

To anyone who rebels, it's a shock to discover that *the survival of the patriarchal family ideal is more important to our economic system than the survival of any real family*— more important than any particular family's unpaid bills, untreated illness, or unfed children; more important than the millions of families that are dysfunctional because of it.

Theorists from Friedrich Engels (who posited women as the first "property"), Harriet Taylor, and John Stuart Mill, to such modern thinkers as Zillah R. Eisenstein, Judith Stacey, Jean Bethke Elshtain, and Jane Flax have explored the interaction between patriarchy and capitalism as it affects families.[2] Such writings help one arrive at an opinion on the phenomenon of power, and how it derives from both economic class and gender status. It seems to me that regardless of a man's precise financial circumstances, and regardless of whether strict male dominance obtains behind closed doors, the romantic *idea* of the traditional, ordered *patriarchal family* functions to compensate all men for surrendering some of their freedom in the support of their dependents and submitting to the various indignities of their work lives.

When industrialization took labor out of the home and farm, it eroded family self-sufficiency. In an agricultural society, wrote Kenneth Keniston, "The family, not the breadwinner, produces."[3] Whereas the activities of every member of the family once were economically useful and husband and wife were interdependent partners fulfilling all the family's health and welfare needs, with the rise of industrial capitalism, work and home were separated; families became dependent on labor market conditions, economic growth, money, manufactured goods, other peoples' services, and the good offices of not just the churchman and schoolmarm, but bankers, bosses, government bureaucrats, soldiers, social workers, doctors, and politicians.

Capitalism had different effects on families depending on their class, but the patriarchal payoff was the same. As Philippe Ariés has pointed out, women and children had no life outside the family and school; men had "the city and its urban civilization."[4] And while city and civilization were being radically altered, within the home, male privilege survived economic change unscathed. In the poor family, wife as well as husband became a wage-earner, but because of her sex, her earnings were always lower, supplementary, and subject to the interruptions of child-bearing. On top of her marketplace exploitation, she was expected to fulfill her domestic role, thus doubling her labor while her wifely servitude reassured her husband that he was still the man of the house.

Among the bourgeoisie, from the 1820s onward, the cult of domesticity contributed to the institutionalization of the nuclear family. Cleaning, cooking, child care, and "home-making" became a woman's fulltime job for the first time in history. And for the first time, women did not contribute directly to the economics of the family. As a result, women's newly glorified childrearing role was expanded into a kind of noble craft, that of molding obedient moral children. Mother was sanctified. The wife-companion was romanticized. To her was entrusted the creation of "the home," that refuge of serenity and charm that was to make industrial society tolerable and consumption of capitalism's products necessary.

Summarizing these effects, psychologist Arlene Skolnick writes, "By separating work and family, industrial capitalism both undermined the home and at the same time increased its attraction as the only place where security and emotional release could be found." Furthermore, "The woman was held in the home as hostage to the values that men both cherished and violated in their daily lives."[5]

Whether or not women were employed—and if so, whether they worked for economic need or personal satisfaction—the division of sex roles within the patriarchal family was a social constant. The concept of "women's work" at home provided the model for cheap female wage labor, ensured a wife and mother's free service inside the home, and redefined the family as a unit of consumption, not production.[6] With so much resting on its shoulders, no wonder the traditional family, as Juliet Mitchell puts it, has both "an economic and ideological role under capitalism."[7]

The question of whether capitalism, socialism, or some other system is capable of sustaining families or is responsible for destroying them is not my concern here; my point is that the American economic system rests on the obsolete ideology of family patriarchy—on the domestic power paradigm and the psychic cushion of male dominance—even though strict patriarchal family patterns are present in but a small minority of today's households. Making connections between that obsolete ideology and current family circumstances, this chapter is intended to show that national economic policies affecting families are inadequate because:

a. they are founded on the fiction that the patriarchal stereotype is the norm (and if it isn't, it should be);

b. when a society is fixated on who's in charge, it doesn't always notice who's in trouble (and it stops caring);

c. when families buy into hierarchies of class, race, and sex, they don't make adequate demands on the economic system because they fail to identify their common interests *as families;* and

d. the emphasis on families as consumers has de-legitimated poor families, whereas if families were redefined as *producers* engaged in the production of social attitudes, moral and ethical capacities, mental health, decision-making skills, interpersonal competence, and other human resource development, then *all* families would be valuable and worthy of support in order to protect their "output."

The ultra-right would have us believe that families are in trouble because of humanism, feminism, secular education, or sexual liberation, but the consensus of Americans is that what tears families apart is unemployment, inflation, and financial worries. Seventy-one percent of Americans are "dissatisfied" or only "fairly satisfied" with their family's present standard of living,[8] and when asked the most important problem facing their families, eight out of ten said "the high cost of living."[9] In December 1982, according to Sears, Roebuck, the nation's largest retailer, children frequently asked the stores' Santas to get jobs for out-of-work parents, or to help pay family bills, instead of asking for presents for themselves.[10]

Like many another romance, the romance of the family turns sour when the money runs out. If we really cared about families, we would not let "born again" patriarchs send up moral abstractions as a smokescreen for the scandal of American family economics. Here are a few more *ifs* that clarify what must be done in order for families to be strong, vigorous producers of human resources:

• *HOUSING: If we really cared about families, we would humanize our housing policies and adjust community planning to families' needs.*

We would recognize the impact of housing policies on what happens at home and close the commuting gap between the place of residence and the place of work so that wage-earning activities and family activities could be better integrated, and the separation of the sexes and the separation of young and old would not be ordained by suburban sprawl. We would eliminate the isolation of women, children, and old people; improve public transportation to connect towns with cities; better use underutilized space and people for community needs; create more public gathering places so that families could interact for their social and economic advantage. In cities, we would have a range of apartment sizes and rental rates, some small and cheap enough for the single parent with one child, and some big enough for large families with many children and relatives, or for several single parents and their children to combine forces in comfortable collective living arrangements—rather than force families to double up illegally in public housing apartments, and rather than force young couples to crowd into their parents' homes without ever experiencing privacy or independence.[11]

We don't need a utopian master plan to fix all this, merely an economical, practical one that might allow families to pool their maintenance tasks in one kitchen, one laundry room, and one common room for child supervision, while each family owns its own private space.

In suburbia, we need alternatives to the single-family dwelling. Instead of tearing down old neighborhoods and building tract housing, we could salvage otherwise uneconomically large houses for group living for extended families, or build condominiums or cluster housing and thereby integrate the more than 19 million one-person households[12] into family communities if they so choose. Working parents might be able to employ older singles for child care, solving two problems at once.

If we cared about families, we would not permit anti-child bias in housing. "You can get a place faster if you have an animal," said one mother after months of answering ads and being turned away because of her children.[13] To those who ask, "What about people who *want* to live away from children, do they have any rights? Can't they express their fear of kiddie muggers or their desire for peace and quiet by wanting to live in a child-free community?" the answer must be this: Such people cannot claim rights that infringe on another person's more basic right to fair housing. Such people can ban mugging or excessive noise but they cannot ban an entire group on the *assumption* that all of its members will mug or make noise. Such people are free to harbor stereotyped ideas—whether those stereotypes refer to a group called blacks, Jews, Spanish-speaking folks or families with children—but they cannot make any of these groups pay for their bigotry.

• *JOBS: If we really cared about families, we would have a national employment policy that recognized the centrality of work to family well-being.*

We would impeach a President who dared to blame his economic recession on working women: ". . . ladies, I'm not picking on anyone," said Ronald Reagan, commenting on the cause of high unemployment, "but [it's] because of the increase in women who are working today and two-worker families."[14]

Anyone who cares about families knows that women's employment is not the cause of male unemployment but is often the margin of family survival. Two-worker families are virtually the only families making ends meet today. Furthermore, because of the great number of families being maintained *solely* by women, we have to care about women's unemployment rate at least as much as men's. It is women whose joblessness rose most during the period of which Reagan spoke. Women constitute more than three-fifths of the "discouraged workers" who have given up finding jobs, and black and Hispanic women experience a much higher rate of unemployment than whites of either sex.[15]

There is ample evidence that unemployment—father's or mother's—is bad for families.[16] Each time the unemployment rate rises by one percentage point, there are 318 additional suicides nationwide. In addition, a higher incidence of children's colds, stomachaches, asthma, eczema, injuries, irritability, and suicide attempts is recorded after a parent loses a job. The frequency of family quarrels, adult problem drinking, domestic violence, and abuse also seems to skyrocket;

in Peoria, Illinois, for example, where unemployment reached nearly 16 percent, the number of women seeking shelter from battering husbands almost doubled in two months. Criminologist Elliot Curie observes, "It's hardly accidental that every advanced society with a lower level of violent crime than ours has also historically had a much more effective and humane employment policy."[17] (More on families and work in Chapter Six.)

   • *TAXES: If we really cared about families, we would demand tax policies for families as creative as those that benefit business, because we would see that families too are producers who deserve tax breaks to stimulate their productivity.*[18]

Along with major tax reforms (see page 84), we would propose some immediate changes in tax deductions (which you subtract from your income) and tax credits (which you subtract from your tax bill):

DEDUCTION FOR DEPENDENTS. Right now, you can reduce your taxable income by $1000 per year for each dependent. A "family-conscious" policy would allow an additional $1000 for the first year in which a child is born or adopted or an aged or disabled relative comes to live with the family. This is a reasonable bonus to cover set-up costs and equipment needed to prepare households for new additions.

CHILD-CARE AND DEPENDENT CREDIT. Right now, you can subtract from your tax bill 20 to 30 percent of the expenses for a babysitter, day-care program, or geriatric nurse. If you earn under $10,000, the ceiling on this credit is $720 per year for one dependent, $1440 for two or more. As your income goes up, the tax credit goes down. For families earning $28,000 or more, the credit reaches its minimum: $480 for one child, $960 for two or more.

Not only is the formula needlessly complicated for such a piddling credit, it is hardly a "creditable" gesture of relief. First, if you have two kids and earned less than $10.000 last year, you would have had to spend $4800   services in order to qualify for the full $1440 credit. How many parents earning so little could afford to pay half their wages to a babysitter?

Second, because a credit is subtracted from taxes, not income, if you don't earn enough to pay taxes, you can't take advantage of the credit.

Third, although the government did increase the credit in 1982, the raise is a pittance compared to other inflation adjustments. For instance, in 1976, older people could deduct up to $20,000 received from selling their residence, but by 1981, after three hikes, the IRS was allowing a deduction of up to $125,000. The IRS ought to be similarly realistic about the change in child care costs since 1976.

A family-conscious tax policy would allow a flat tax credit of 50 percent of what you pay a nurse or babysitter. People who owe no taxes would take the credit as a refund. For the specialized costly care required for disabled dependents, the tax credit would double.

EARNED INCOME CREDIT. Right now, if you earn under $5000 a year, you can subtract 10 percent of your earnings from your tax bill—another wan gesture to alleviate strains on the poor. But every dollar you earn over $5000 reduces the credit by a dollar until it disappears. A family-conscious tax policy would increase the base earnings to $10,000, and would expand it further for each child in the family.

MEDICAL DEDUCTIONS. As of the 1983 tax year, you can only deduct medical expenses that amount to 5 percent or more of your adjusted gross income. That means, regardless of the size of your family, if your household earns $30,000, you get no deduction for medical bills until they exceed $1500 (and spending $1500 on doctors takes a hefty slice out of your take-home pay). A family-conscious policy would not punish people for getting sick; it would allow us to deduct all nonelective medical expenses. (Businesses are able to deduct plant damages and depreciate physical equipment; why not us?) At the very least, it would lower the limit to 1 percent and take into account the number of family members being cared for on the household income.

Besides such reforms, a family-conscious tax policy would require some new laws:

TUITION TAX CREDIT FOR NURSERY SCHOOL EXPENSES. Although I do not support it, if conservatives succeed in getting tuition tax credit for private and parochial schools, nursery schools should be included. A working family that exhausts the dependent-care credit on the salary of a babysitter for an infant should still be able to provide an early childhood learning experience to kids who are too young for public education. And they should get the same finanical boost the government gives to families who choose private or parochial education for their school-aged children.

A "KEOGH" FOR CONTINGENCIES. The Internal Revenue Service now permits us to deposit into a Keogh Plan or IRA account a set amount of retirement savings that can be deducted from current income. This encourages self-sufficiency in old age and spares society the burden of supporting people in their nonproductive years. Why not also allow families to deduct from taxable income the money accumulated in savings accounts earmarked for family contingencies that are as inevitable as old age: financing college educations, purchasing a first home, covering emergency medical expenses, or caring for a disabled relative. Not only would this "capital formation" engender family self-sufficiency, the savings would eventually be spent in ways that stimulate the economy, provide jobs, and improve the quality of life.

EXTRACTING CHILD-SUPPORT ARREARS. Despite the "new fatherhood" fervor described in Chapter Nine, mothers end up with custody of children in nine out of ten cases. However, the most recent census study reported that nationwide, only three-fifths of all divorced women with children were awarded child support payments, less than half of those awarded payments were receiving them, and payments averaged 20 percent of the mother's total income or barely $1800 per child per year.[19] In New York, says one official, it's worse than that: Only one supporting father in ten is in compliance.[20]

This financial abandonment of children and their custodial mothers can be rectified in various ways: The courts can put a lien on the wages of the non-paying parent, but that is an expensive system to monitor. The child support could be collected by the, IRS and, just as the IRS penalizes people for tax evasion, it could prosecute for arrears. Through its "Operation Intercept" the Federal government can require that the arrears be subtracted from any tax refund due the father; the trouble is many taxpayers are owed no refund, or could avoid qualifying for a refund by paying less estimated tax or having less withholding tax subtracted. What's more, a new wife might object to the interception of joint income tax refunds for the support of her husband's children.

A better solution would make use of the Social Security system. The rationale already exists: When a father dies, his children are entitled to his Social Security benefits. Why shouldn't the children of an *absent* father be entitled to a portion of his Social Security during his lifetime, if they can get support no other way? The court would attach his Social Security funds to the extent that he is remiss, thus reducing the amount he would get at age sixty-five. This erosion of his old-age benefits might be an incentive for a father to fulfill his financial commitments to his children. However, the Social Security System is already so inadequate to people's retirement needs I wonder whether it could survive if we started taking current deductions for child support from projected future benefits.

Where does this leave us? Until we can devise a foolproof method to guarantee every child support by her or his wage-earning parent, perhaps a small tax on each birth certificate would create a pool of funds for children whose fathers have abandoned them. I realize that many families are so economically strapped that an added fee might represent a real hardship. Yet symbolically if not pragmatically, the birth certificate fee would force new parents to acknowledge the financial realities of childrearing and force society to confront the shameful practice of allowing innocent children to suffer for the sins of delinquent fathers.

• *SINGLE PARENTS: If we really cared about families, we would not make life so hard for families that happen to be maintained by single mothers.*

One out of every five youngsters under eighteen now lives in a one-parent family. If today's trends continue, nearly one out of two children born from now on will spend a significant portion of his or her life in a one-parent family. This concerns me not because I favor marriage but because single parents are more vulnerable to poverty than are people in two-adult households.[21]

That single parent under discussion is usually a woman. Although she usually gets custody of the children, the mother's income declines by 73 percent in the first year after the divorce, while the father's income rises by 42 percent. Since men make 70 percent of the nation's income, and since sex segregation in the work force relegates women to second-class jobs, and since many of those jobs still pay women as though they were supplementary wage earners, the discriminatory job market indirectly penalizes the children of women who are primary wage earners. Women maintaining families have nearly twice as high a rate of unemployment as men .[22] From 1960 to 1981, the number of people in poor families headed by women rose 54 percent. The fact is, a child born into a male-headed family has only one chance in forty of being poor; but in a female-headed family, the odds become one in six. If present trends continue, by the year 2000, "the poverty population would be composed solely of women and their children."[23] That's bad for children. What's bad for women is this Catch-22: If a single mother works, she is said to "neglect" her kids; if she goes on welfare, she's "lazy." As a working woman, she is an inadequate *mother;* as a woman on welfare, she's an unsuccessful *person.* Those no-win self-images added to the economic punishment of low wages or welfare serve as a warning to women who dare to try to survive *un*dependent on a man. *Our system keeps welfare a humiliating, untenable option in order to make attractive women's other economic alternatives: marriage or the female job ghetto.* It's another false choice: soggy asparagus, no asparagus—or collard greens, but not enough to live on.

In two widely read books,[24] George Gilder prescribes women's economic dependence as a necessary incentive for the male work ethic (especially among blacks); in terms of long-term economic progress and the survival of capitalism, says Gilder, patriarchy pays. (A top Republican official told me Nixon's private solution to welfare problems, articulated among friends, was to force women to marry and let their husbands worry about them.)

As Christopher Jencks notes, divorce leaves the typical mother "with less money to support herself and her children than her husband has to support himself alone." Jencks adds that the idea of marrying to get out of poverty "is morally deplorable and leads to a lot of bad marriages."[25] Nevertheless, men in power are pushing traditional family structures to buttress capitalism and patriarchy, while women are paralyzed by Hobson's choices and the havoc that welfare policies wreak on their families.

I'm thinking of someone like Kaye, a single mother from Bethlehem, Pennsylvania. Deserted by her husband during her third pregnancy, she tried to support herself and her children as a "counter girl," earning only twenty dollars more per month than she would have received on welfare. Often she had to choose between food and medicine, between paying rent and buying shoes for her children. One semester her seven-year-old was excluded from gym because she couldn't afford sneakers. Finally, when one child needed eye surgery, Kaye could juggle no more. To qualify for the medical assistance that would help her pay the child's hospital bills, she had to quit her job and go on welfare.

Although she knew it wasn't her fault, and she had no alternative, Kaye was deeply ashamed: "I used to whisper to the supermarket clerk when I paid with food stamps. My kids' friends teased them. Some neighbors called them 'welfare brats.' I sat home with the shades down. Eventually, I felt so inadequate, I lashed out at my children."

Eventually, most parents under economic stress lash out at their children. Is that any way to "save the family"?

The truth is we do not care about saving poor families because they are women's families and children's families. Nine out of ten welfare recipients and seven out of ten food-stamp recipients are women and children.[26] Those are our sleazy welfare "cheats." And more welfare families will materialize from the ranks of the working poor because women like Kaye cannot support their families on what a woman can earn in most women's jobs. And more children will suffer because, with all the cuts in job training programs, AFDC, Medicaid, and food stamps, and the transfer of many social service programs to the states,[27] mothers like Kaye simply cannot produce much in the way of "family life." Let's remember that those federal programs were created in the first place because the state and local governments were inadequate to the task of aleviating extreme social-economic problems.

•   *FAMILY SUBSIDIES: If we really cared about families, we would supplement and support economically troubled households rather than remove children to foster homes or institutions and leave the family's troubles untouched.*

We wouldn't take children out of their homes (unless, of course, parents are abusive) until we had first tried to solve the family's problems with medical care, counseling, emergency homemakers, housing assistance, or extra help with children and old people.

Two of every nine children live in families where one or both parents are sick, disabled, or unemployed. Ten million children are growing up in families with incomes below $7400; more than one and a half million of those with less than $3000 a year.[28] We could subsidize those families of the working poor—not reduce their food stamp and welfare benefits as Reagan did in 1983; we could spend some money to upgrade the parents' job skills, counsel them until they can make it on their own. Most foster families get less money to house children than the average kennel charges to board dogs—yet nearly one *billion* dollars in federal funds are spent yearly for children in out-of-home care.[29] Imagine what that billion dollars could do *in children's own homes.* We could start by raising AFDC payments to the level paid to foster parents. If we believe in family unity, we should not be moving children from home to home as many as eighteen times, and *we should not be spending more on children when they are separated from parents than when they are together.* We should understand that, in most cases, what breaks up families is not moral turpitude but poverty, not lack of love but lack of resources, not failure of will but failure of hope.

Take the example of a Los Angeles family evicted from

their apartment because they couldn't manage the rent. The mother and four-year-old daughter were taken in by one relative; the father and eight-year-old son by another. Because of severe overcrowding, tensions rose in both places. One day, the son brought home a poor report card; the father beat him; the boy ran away, then was picked up by police and placed in a foster home. None of those things might have happened had the family's housing problem been solved with money to put a security deposit on another apartment. Instead, the family split up, a child's and a parent's behavior deteriorated, the child went into foster care, and the costs to family and society were far higher than a security deposit of a few months' subsidized rent.

I'm thinking too, of a Louisville, Kentucky, family: the parents were unemployed but couldn't qualify for public assistance because their older children's meager wages, which counted as household income, made the family ineligible (although it didn't make them solvent). The children had to move out so that their parents could get welfare. In other words, the family had to disband to survive. It's lunacy.

• *RACISM: If we really cared about families, we would care about black families' extra burdens.*

We would not pretend white and black families are in the same boat with enough life jackets to go around.

A black mother is three times more likely to die in childbirth and twice as likely to lose her infant in its first year than is a white mother. Surviving black children are five times more likely to be murdered.[30] In 1981, black families' income was 56 percent of white families' income—the lowest in 15 years. Nearly half of all black families with children under eighteen are maintained by women, and black single mothers are the poorest of the poor.[31] The usual strains of marriage and family life are intensified by black poverty, lack of occupational role models, lower educational levels of the generations emerging from centuries of repression, job bias, lack of seniority, and every kind of "subtle and blatant racism." An unemployed black man in Memphis, Tennessee, pleads, "If you want to help my family, help me get a job and get rid of discrimination."[32] Other minority wage earners might make the same plea.

With so much talk about "threats" to the Family, somebody on the ultra-right might have noticed that the greatest threat to minority families is white racism.

• *COMMONALITY: If we really cared about families, we would take more collective responsibility for the economic and social problems of "other people's families," if not out of plain decency then because of self-interest:*

The adverse circumstances that stunt children's development and tear families apart are not just destructive to those directly affected but are expensive to society as a whole. It costs $134,000, or about $7500 a year, to rear one child from birth to high school graduation within a family setting.[33] But right now, more than eighty-seven thousand children are not in families but in prison, where incarcerating each juvenile offender costs taxpayers $50,000 per year.[34] That's more than six times the cost of family upbringing and more, in one year, than the cost of *four* years of a good college education.

Nevertheless, rather than spend relatively little to help poor parents put their children on an achievement track early in their lives, we watch families "fail." Then we blame the victims, and resentfully pay for their "mistakes." Or as Rep. George Miller, founder of the Select Committee on Children, Youth and Families, puts it, "We choose to fund the failures rather than the successes." For our short-term economies, we leave our own children a legacy of "losers"—other people's children whose contribution to their common future is ignorance, rage, and violence. On a "cost-efficiency" basis, if nothing else, current family-assistance policies are indefensible. In fact, reprehensibly, we are the only Western industrialized country without a coherent family policy. Why?

Marion Wright Edelman, director of the Children's Defense Fund, attributes our national indifference to several myths about families that compound the American ethic of bootstrap individualism:[35]

1. *Myth: Only other people's children have problems.* Fact: Most families have or will experience some form

of hardship or difficulty—learning problems, emotional problems, drug problems, money problems, sexual problems, and
so on. Such problems are not necessarily anyone's "fault."

2. *Myth: Good families are self-sufficient and take care
of their own.* Fact: Every family gets help from "the system"
somewhere along the line: mortgages, tax write-offs, car loans,
credit cards, if not food stamps.

3. *Myth: Families are undermined because professionals
have "taken over" from parents and no one but parents should
take responsibility for children.* Fact: Every family uses professional services for its children. Affluent families just turn
to different professionals: architects to design a child's play-
room, lawyers to set up a child's trust fund, doctors to cure
a child's infection, tutors when children can't keep up in class,
clowns to entertain at a child's birthday party.

4. *Myth: Helping families "encourages dependency."*
Fact: Getting help with the economics of the family is a respectable middle-class habit. We condone it when an executive seeks a better benefit package or a union worker strikes
for better wages. Only when the poor demand more does it
become a symptom of dependency. As Columbia professor
Sheila Kamerman points out, when the government gives help
directly it is very visible and tinged with the stigma of charity,
but when the government gives help indirectly, through tax
policies, it is private and dignified.

Nancy Amidei, head of the Food Research and Action
Center, remarks sarcastically that in conservative Washington,
"people who buy $2000 dresses are viewed as productive
members of society, and those who use food stamps are considered a problem." She has a plan to put matters into proper
focus: "Rich people could be given their tax breaks in the
form of luxury stamps so that when they buy their steak and
lobsters or fancy French wines everyone can see where [our]
tax dollars are going."[36]

5. *Myth: Providing needed services such as health care
or remedial education is too expensive.* Fact: Ignorance is a
lot more expensive than education, and health care is a lot

cheaper than treating malnutrition and disease. Again, to put
things in perspective: We spend more than $21 billion on
tobacco, $26 billion on alcohol, and only $7.5 billion federally
on children and their families.[37] When it comes to basic human
needs, the question is not can we afford to help all kinds of
families, but can we afford not to?

SUPPORTING THE FAMILIES INDUSTRY

In his book *The Zero Sum Society,* M.I.T. economist Lester
C. Thurow offers an economic analysis that I find useful to
explain this sorry state of family economics and to think our
way out of it.

Briefly, Thurow's thesis is this: Competition for economic
resources creates problems. There's a solution to each problem
but reaching it is difficult because economics is a zero sum
game. "Some incomes go up as a result of the solution; but
others go down. Individuals do not sacrifice equally."[38]

A few examples: For tenants to have rent-controlled
apartments, landlords must sacrifice profits, but for landlords
to justify upkeep of their buildings, tenants may have to pay
more. We want clean energy, but solar or other methods may
result in hardship in the coal industry. We like the convenience of word-processing machines, but we know it is offset
by automating some people out of a job. Everything in the
economy is a trade-off, says Thurow. For one person or industry or interest group to get a leg up, another somewhere in
the system has to take a step down. In essence, he says, everyone wants things to improve but no group wants to be the
one that suffers economic losses for the general good. Politicians don't want to have to answer to the losers. Each of us
wants someone else to shoulder the burden of sacrifice while
we protect our own incomes. Obviously, those with the most
to protect also have the greatest power to protect it. Winners,
by definition, are not losers.

As I extrapolate from Thurow's thesis, patriarchy gives
men the most to protect and the greatest power to protect
it. But patriarchy also skews families' economic realities by
making masculine and feminine roles into a zero sum game,

where it is entirely misplaced. It is bad enough when gender competition intrudes in the workplace, but in the home no family can afford to operate on the principle that for one member to win, someone else must lose.

With the Vietnamese immigrants, for instance, it was assumed that if the wife won (gained skills, status, independence), the husband lost (lost face, power, and so on). Actually, however, the wives lost and no one won: The by-product of patriarchal rigidity was family poverty.

Here's an insurance salesman admitting to a home-grown version of this fallacy: "At first, I didn't want my wife to work at all. I wanted her home when I got there. Then, when she started to work, I insisted that we live within *my* means, on *my* salary. Now we both live on both paychecks and I don't know how in the world we would live any other way."[39]

It is now a matter of family survival for sex roles to be divorced from economic decision-making. A woman must be able to improve her status and her family's security without diminishing her husband's manliness. The zero sum mentality must be eliminated from inside each family. The family unit cannot be atomized into competing interests that make all of us losers. Rather than men *vs.* women or parents *vs.* children, each family should be seen as an interlocking enterprise whose members contribute to its fluctuating needs and draw upon its resources in different ways at different times.

The zero sum mentality must be eliminated not only from inside each family but also from the *community* of families. Rather than allow various kinds of families to be pitted against one another (urban *vs.* rural, single-parent *vs.* two-parent families), all families should identify together as an economic *interest group*, like farmers, or as an industry to reckon with, like coal. Despite our differences, families would rally behind issues of common interest just as farmers in the South or Midwest, whether large or small, dairy or produce, have unified around demands that enhance their collective economic destiny.

For instance, although middle-class women may intuitively resent welfare mothers, their family interests are interconnected. When government social services are reduced, government jobs usually held by middle-class women often are eliminated. Thus, cuts in the welfare rolls may lower taxes for the middle-class family, but the wife's being laid off from her job as a social service worker would wipe out any gains.

Just as children should not have to move out so that parents can survive, one family should not have to make its wins on another family's losses. The zero sum game must not operate *inside* families or *among* families, but only between the families constituency and *other* interest groups. Other industries will have to give up some of their winnings so that the family industry can increase its productivity of content, healthy, competent, ethical, contributing, caring citizens. Because other industries are unlikely to do this voluntarily, an intermediary is required. Enter, the government.

Equity Decision-making. With government standing in the middle, says Thurow, competing interests lobby and pressure "to bend decisions" in their favor.[40] Families might be less sophisticated political activists than the farm or tobacco lobby, say I, but who's to claim families are not more entitled to federal supports and subsidies? In any case, it's up to the government to make what Thurow calls an "equity decision." The government must choose who is going to get more economic security and who is going to have to take less. It does this through the exercise of its various functions: levying or repealing taxes, expanding or contracting public expenditures, extending or abolishing regulations. Too often, thanks to "decision-bending," the government comes down on the side of the already powerful. Lockheed, Chrysler, and Harley-Davidson are not allowed to fail; the government intervenes. But Kaye's struggling family and troubled families in Detroit, Denver, and Dallas are left to the fates. This is not only infuriating, it is philosophically and politically inconsistent. Under capitalism, inefficient businesses are supposed to be driven out by productive ones. Yet the U.S. government contradicts the capitalist system by saving dying industries. (Or dying institutions, for that matter. Conservatives are trying to give a whole-blood transfusion to the failing business of patriarchy, while real families suffer pernicious anemia.)

Those rugged individualists who despise government rescue of poor families demand government protection, import quotas, and subsidies if their farming, automobile, trucking, steel, motorcycle, rail, oil or textile interests are threatened. "The same people who oppose special programs for blacks support special programs for textiles," notes Thurow. "Imagine the furor that would arise if we started programs for blacks similar to those now in place for farmers."[41]

That is just what we must do. For families to start winning the zero sum game, we must fight nose to nose with other interest groups. We have to retrain American voters to support such direct subsidies as Aid to Families with Dependent Children, with as much equanimity as they support what Nancy Amidei calls "Aid to Farmers with Dependent Crops"[42]—that is, indirect subsidies hidden in the form of regulations.

Thurow points out that economic discrimination operates most effectively when an individual "cannot easily leave the group in question."[43] Thus, to avoid discrimination, disabled people cannot leave the category of the blind or lame, minorities cannot leave their ethnic or racial group, and, I would add, children cannot leave their families. Justice demands changing the economic circumstances of troubled families, not expecting poor children to change families.

Investing in the Families Industry. To increase industrial efficiency and productivity, Thurow wants government to underwrite research and development for selected companies. He favors this even though federal aid would help those companies become more advanced and profitable than others. There's nothing wrong with a few people becoming highly successful, he says, as long as our tax system redistributes some of their wealth, and they are compelled to share their technological innovations with others in their industry.

This is a fine model for federal investment in the development of families. Let the government jump in and help "inefficient" families become more successful as long as a fair tax system keeps things in check and the helped families share their resources with others in their "industry."

For the funds to underwrite this investment in the diversification and enrichment of the families industry, this nation

must first change its economic priorities; if we have enough
money to spend 24 million dollars *an hour* on defense, we
can find enough money for family development programs.
The cost of *one* MX missile would eradicate poverty in 100,000
female-headed households, says Marian Wright Edelman. And
the cost of nine B-1 bombers would finance Medicaid for all
poor children and pregnant women combined. Of course,
eventually government must make equity decisions taking
income from someone to finance government expenditures
for someone else. But, asks Thurow with zero sum logic, whose
income should go down? There's not much cream to skim
off if, a few years back, the top fifth of all households earned
only $24,000, and $38,000 put a taxpayer in the top 5 percent.
These are not the rich. The rich are people with "so little
taxable income," Thurow explains, "that it is impossible to
promise substantial income tax reductions for the rest of the
population by raising the tax rates of the rich. To tax the
rich it is necessary to change the official definition of
income"[44]—and to close all tax loopholes even if the rest of
us lose a few escape routes too. The lowest 60 percent of
the nation's wage earners will pay more taxes in 1984 than
they did in 1980 but the under 1 percent earning more than
$100,000 will enjoy tax cuts from $4000 to $20,000 per
household.[45] Thurow would tax inherited wealth and instant
wealth at normal rates. (Fifty percent of the great fortunes
derive from inheritance, but taxes collected on that wealth
amount to 0.2 percent on net worth!)

This tax (plus a re-ordering of the nation's budget priorities) would give government the resources to redistribute
to families. But how much is enough? Thurow suggests a
reasonable standard: Every worker should have earnings
equal to the average earnings of today's fully employed males.
These earnings will not be dealt out like a soup kitchen give-
away; government's intervention will fit the American work
ethic. In order for economic minorities—which I take to include poor families and mother-headed families—to catch up
with white male earnings, they must have access to the kind
of jobs that white males occupy. Government must create
those jobs and make them comparable in quality and challenge

to what is available in the private sector. This is more than compassionate: it makes objective economic sense. In 1978, we spent $224 billion on welfare and only $10 billion on subsidized jobs, says Thurow. "How odd that we find it much easier to set up welfare programs to give people money than we do to set up work programs to give people jobs."[46]

If we could remind ourselves that we are subsidizing *our own industry,* families might favor tax redistribution efforts that create a job for every parent who wants one, or provide support services and other transitional aid while families "retool" for greater productivity. We might demand that public funds help sustain the growing "Family Support" movement—grass-roots programs ranging from drop-in counseling centers to parent education courses, drug and alcohol abuse hot lines, classes that teach parents how to play with their kids, havens from the incessant demands of parenting, assertiveness-training, budgeting, stress management programs and information and referral services on everything from natural childbirth to nutrition. We might celebrate these innovative projects by supplementing their meager budgets with federal, state and local contributions, rather than using their existence as an excuse to abandon aid to families.[47] And we might more actively monitor laws, regulations, and policies that have an impact on the family, and research, services, and trends that might help the family prosper.

Bizarre as it is to compare families to businesses, it helps sharpen the logic of saving them collectively. But unlike bankrupt businesses, each family that "fails" is irreplaceable. Therefore well-functioning families are society's *most* invaluable units of production. Although families don't necessarily raise cattle or turn out useful products like wheat, computers, or lumber, they do raise human beings that all of us can live with. They turn out useful people—good future parents, workers and taxpayers, a poet, inventor, a great teacher or leader, or the person your child grows up to love.

If we could make that leap of understanding of our ultimate commonality, all families would have an authentic bond in the struggle for economic survival.

5

Power Struggles
on the Home Front

*If you want to make enemies,
try to change something.*
—Woodrow Wilson

CHANGE DISTURBS the status quo, which in families means the power relations. In this connection, I've noticed how often some woman in my lecture audience—no matter where I speak in the country—will raise her hand and ask, "How can I get my husband to change?"

Because of that recurrent question, and the fact that more than 95 percent of Americans marry at some point in their lives, it seems reasonable to begin with the husband–wife power struggle, although it should be understood that the dynamics under scrutiny apply as well to other cohabiting pairs regardless of sexual orientation or marital status.

Still, I wondered why only women seek advice on spouse "reform" or at least, why they ask the question aloud. The answer seems to be that men have fewer complaints and less desire for change, because when the quirks of both partners are equaled out, women are the ones who tend to give up more freedom, get less satisfaction from the union, and make more accommodations.[1] Sociologist Jessie Bernard found that every marriage is actually two marriages—his and hers—and the two versions "do not always coincide."[2] To put it plainly, the woman's marriage is not as good as the man's. Contrary to the common wisdom, married men are generally happier and healthier than bachelors, but single women are happier and healthier than married women.

When those women ask "How can I get my husband to change?" they do not mean they want him to lose weight or bring home flowers, they want to change *him*, that is, his treatment "of me as a *person*."

The honest answer is maybe she can't.

After the arguments and grief, she may discover that their marriage is founded not on love but on power, a conclusion that announces itself when he responds to her confession of misery. Either he says he'll try to change no matter what the struggle—thereby affirming his love and the importance of her feelings—or he says he will not try to change, thereby exercising his power and revealing that, in his view, the relationship exists solely for his comfort.

The second response is his way of saying "I hold all the cards, honey; take it or leave it." Some women leave it only after trying to rescue the marriage singlehandedly and trying to deny that it means so little to their men. It hurts to face the truth but, warns Frances Lear, "You cannot make a silk purse out of a chauvinist. Nor can you make an attractive partner out of a wife who keeps on fighting when she does not have a fighting chance."[3]

The change-making process is usually precipitated by the woman's altering herself. She works to improve her education, assertiveness, fitness, self-image, career goals, friendships and so on, and before long, she discovers that one partner changing is like one hand clapping: there's movement but no impact. So she asks herself, "Why am I putting up with him?" Which invariably leads to "He ought to change, too." That's when she tries to pick up pointers from others who have survived the marital power struggle. She asks "How can I get him to change?" in order to learn the risks as much as the strategies. And I think she asks it out loud because she senses that it is *everywoman's* question and she knows most women want the same things—more sharing of housework and childrearing, which I give ample space in Chapter 7—and:

- Emotional communication
- Personal autonomy
- Financial independence
- Physical safety

Well, you may ask, don't men want the same things from women? And mightn't some husbands want to change their wives' behavior in these areas? Not quite. Turn them around to make them men's demands and they become skewed, captious, excessive, like a pair of belted trousers demanding suspenders. No, for now, we are talking about women's needs.

EMOTIONAL COMMUNICATION

> I get so sad because we can't really talk to each other.
> He looks at me like I'm crazy, like he just doesn't
> understand a word I'm saying.
>
> —*Working-class wife*[4]

Marriages are suffering what one writer calls a "crisis in intersex conversation."[5] Communication failure, some say, is the single most common reason for divorce today.[6] Here's a real-life example of that failure: The wife is lying in bed with her husband. She is in tears after recounting the details of her terrifying fantasy of his death. He says nothing."I turn to James, then intrude on his perpetual silence and ask, 'What are you thinking . . .' and he admitted (it was an admission because he was incredulous himself at the fact): 'I was thinking about the Knicks. Wondering if they were going to trade Frazier.' "[7]

Maybe it is true that men wish they could talk to their wives about basketball trades, but women's longing for emotional communication borders on terminal heartbreak. One writer claims, "Marriage is the only thing that affords a woman the pleasure of company and the perfect sensation of solitude at the same time."[8] In the end, the solitude isolates men too. After a while, there are no words to describe the words that are missing. Couples talk but they don't connect. You hear them exchanging banal remarks about the weather or the children or the movie they've just seen; they sound like strangers making small talk or blind dates filling the silence until they can go home. Some couples hardly talk at all. You see them sitting with closed faces, side by side in their cars or across a restaurant table, staring at other people or studying their food with unwarranted interest.

I don't recall the source but it was Friedrich Nietzsche, believe it or not, who counseled men,

> When marrying, one should ask oneself this question: Do you believe that you will be able to converse well with this woman into your old age? Everything else in marriage is transitory.

Yet many men marry for sexual desire and women for status (both reasons masquerading as "love"), never once having *made* conversation—that is, created the verbal web between each other's thoughts and feelings. It is only a matter of time, then, before the silence rolls in, like mist off the sea.

Doctors say unless you have an intimate to talk to in later life, "you get sick in the gut or sick in the head."[9] I would say the sickness starts when boys are taught to be stolid and composed while girls are taught to need approval and demonstrations of affection. It is aggravated when boy groups are expected to talk about sports and girl groups to talk about boys, and when men are "supposed" to talk about business and women about babies. Having thus grown up speaking two different languages, they cannot always traverse the communication gap. What's more, although women are taught to marry "up"—in terms of education and class—powerful men are taught to talk *at*, not listen to, their inferiors, including the women they marry.

"It's funny," a friend admitted recently, "if you asked me when I married my husband *why* I was marrying him, I'd have given you the same reasons I have now for divorcing him. The things I want to change about him are the very things that attracted me to him in the first place: his quiet power and his cool way of staying in control of his feelings. In the beginning, I remember thinking, 'this must be what a real man is like.' Then for twelve years, I begged him to talk with me. I would have given anything for him to say, 'How do you feel, honey?' or to just sit around and muse about our lives. He was always too busy. Finally, when I'd get crazy, he'd say, 'Okay, you want to talk, *talk!*' By then I felt like a jerk saying, 'I just want you to say you care . . .'"

This friend has a theory about women like herself who are now dissolving marriages that once seemed ideal. "In the old days, smart girls used their brains to catch strong, confident men who would give us part of their identity. Now that we have our own identity, we're stuck with that hyperrational, self-important, noncommunicative guy." In other words, now that women no longer need derivative male power, we want authentic male love.

PERSONAL AUTONOMY

> Don't walk in front of me, I may not follow.
> Don't walk behind me, I may not lead.
> Just walk beside me and be my friend.
>
> —*Albert Camus*

> Why is this wedding different from most other weddings? This is a wedding of two people. Not one person and one possession. No one but no one can give Karin away. And no one can be given her. She belongs to herself.
>
> —*Gloria Steinem*
> *Wedding toast for Karin Lipper*
> *and Martin Keltz*

To some people, the idea of a wife "belonging to herself" is anathema. Her satisfactions are supposed to be derived through others, her freedom *given* her by permission. "My husband lets me do what I want to do," says Phillis Schlafly.[10] Women with independent dreams are Selfish! Distorted! and Unnatural! These exclamations came to me courtesy of some "pen pals" who were moved to write after seeing me on the *Donahue* show:

> You feminists are trying to change things that shouldn't be tampered with: A Christian woman puts things in the proper perspective, namely
>
> 1. God and the Bible
> 2. Husband

3. Children

4. Herself

—Indiana Housewife

I have served my family 25 years and I'll do it till
the day I die and you humanists will never change
us! A true Christian husband appreciates an unselfish
devoted wife who makes *him* her life. He would
never leave her! Only secular men do that!

—Moral Majority Housewife

Still another correspondent sent me a booklet called *God's
Answer to Women's Lib,* which lists "100 Things to Look for
in Choosing or Becoming an Ideal Wife." For example, a wife
must be

- Christian

- Same race

- Pure Virgin

- Long hair

- Can sew and iron

- Willing to give up separate identity to become married

- Truly desires to do husband's will above that of her
  own

- Takes an interest in husband's interests

- Doesn't give husband backtalk

- Concerned with husband's well-being, puts his interests
  first

- Appreciates husband

- Listens to husband's advice above that of others

- Relies on husband's judgment in all areas of life

- Present and future wants and plans coincide with
  husband's[11]

This regimen of nonpersonhood creates a breed of wife–martyr who eventually will exact a price for her loss of self. Psychologist Noel Hedges found that seemingly happy relationships in which one partner does most of the giving and the other most of the taking "are headed for trouble after the first 18 months."[12]

> Item (from an interview with a working-class wife) "I don't want to be like my mother, just sort of hanging around being a professional mother and grandmother. So I thought I could go to school—you know, take a few courses or something, maybe even be a teacher eventually. But he says I can't and no matter how much I beg, he won't let me."[13]

Just as sex bias in the workplace hurts not just the woman being held down but whole families that depend on her earnings, the attitude that allows a "he won't let me" at home can translate into sexist barriers in the outside world. Conversely, when a wife is autonomous—a functioning individual whose wants and plans are honored even when they don't always "coincide" with her husband's—that egalitarian relationship at home can become a paradigm for other male–female relationships in society and men can get into the habit of dealing with autonomous women.

Young moderns who write equality into their wedding vows may see no big deal in a wife's having ideas and work of her own. But traditional men who are asked to accept that phenomenon at midlife usually have problems. I'm thinking particularly of a man who met his wife when she was a struggling ingenue and he was building stage sets in a summer theater. After a few years, he became a successful cabinetmaker and she quit the stage to become a wife and mother. Now he is forty-five; his career is solid but static while she, at forty, is just coming into her own as a character actress. She looks and feels ten years younger. Suddenly, he's jealous and scared, and she in turn is resentful: "When he went into those other women's homes to build them shelves and cabinets, I wasn't supposed to think twice. But now that I'm building a career for myself, he's worried: Will I get bored with him, will I find someone else? He had no experience loving me as a separate person."

To keep the person we love without losing the person we are. That simple goal was realized in a historic relationship that predates modern consciousness and proves autonomy possible in marriage.

One day in 1850, Henry Blackwell, who owned a hardware store in Cincinnati, cashed a check for a young woman and fell in love. Henry was an abolitionist and a strong supporter of the fledgling women's rights movement, a logical commitment given that his sisters were Elizabeth Blackwell, America's first woman doctor; Emily, another doctor; Anna, a foreign correspondent; and Ellen, a writer. The woman Henry Blackwell chose to love was Lucy Stone—feminist, abolitionist, and lecturer—who stopped into his store en route to the National Women's Rights convention. Their courtship and correspondence lasted for several years, during which they exchanged ideas about the rights and responsibilities of a marriage of equality. These letters are typical:[14]

> I have set out with the determination that my love shall *never fetter you* one iota—that I will never directly or indirectly impair your activity, but that I will compel you ten years hence to acknowledge "My acquaintance with [Henry] had been an advantage to me in every way."
>
> *—Henry Blackwell to Lucy Stone*

> How soon the character of the race would change if pure, and equal, real marriages could take the place of the horrible relations that now bear that sacred name.
>
> *—Lucy Stone to Henry Blackwell*

> I do not want you to forego *one sentiment* of independence, not one attribute of personality. I want only to help you, as best I can, in achieving a really noble & symmetrical Life. I want you also to *help me* to do the same. We *can help* each other I am sure not merely as friends—nor as lovers, but as husband & wife.
>
> *—Henry Blackwell to Lucy Stone*

Lucy and Henry were married on May 1, 1855. Before their wedding ceremony, they stood together and read the protest they had written against the rules and customs of traditional marriage. (Lucy Stone became the first American wife to keep her own name.) Their "emancipated marriage" lasted for nearly forty years. On October 18, 1893, after a full life of activism, love, and motherhood, Lucy died of cancer. Years before, she had written of her wish to live "with a husband and with children and with large freedom, pecuniary freedom, personal freedom and the right to vote." The vote took another twenty-seven years, but Lucy Stone had everything else.

FINANCIAL INDEPENDENCE

I resent not being financially independent, but I've convinced myself that I've been given a grant to support my writing. Some get theirs from the Ford Foundation. I get mine from my husband Howard.
—Leah Fritz

Now all of a sudden, I had to ask him for everything, and he couldn't understand why that bothered me. I felt like I was a charity ward case.
— Working-class wife[15]

Economic *security* is not enough. Children need economic security but women want economic *independence*. Without her own money, a woman has no mobility, no bargaining power, no true freedom. Even if we never spend a penny on ourselves, just knowing we have our own money to spend as we see fit is a measure of adulthood.

By themselves and others, self-sufficient women are more favorably perceived than dependent women. Studies show the "happiest" women are those who hold high-paying jobs and *also* are wives and mothers, and it is their economic independence, not the other factors, that gives them the highest self-esteem.[16] Despite this—and despite polls indicating that a great majority of men find self-sufficient women most appealing[17]—there is not much female economic independence around. While 42 percent of single women have their own credit cards, only 19 percent of married women do; well over 60 percent of single women but only 28 percent of wives have checking and savings accounts in their own names. What's more, about a third of American women lack the basic skills needed to survive on their own economically.[18] If a woman in a bad situation cannot walk out the door and know she will be able to feed and house herself and her children, chances are she won't walk out. She probably won't even make a demand for fairness for fear it will get her thrown out.

There is no delicate way to frame this reality except to say, in most families, *money is power.* Some men wield the power by withholding the truth about how much they earn or where it is invested. Others use money, material things, or vacations as a system of reward and punishment. Even in households where the husband gives the wife his paycheck and she controls the budget and pays the bills, she is powerless unless she controls the source and access to income. Otherwise, dependent women are like children who must behave in order to get their allowance or students who must obey because they cannot afford to go to college on their own.

Studies show that a woman's power in family decision-making increases with her age, education, competence, earnings, and occupational achievement. Her power *decreases* the more children she has, because multiple motherhood domesticates a woman and ties her down. It also decreases as her husband's income increases because men who do not depend at all upon their wives' supplementary earnings can afford to behave high-handedly.[19] How then, can a childlike and powerless woman move toward economic independence? Frequently, the answer lies in the internal struggle that precedes any power struggle between the two partners. If her sense of her own financial ignorance is so entrenched that she cannot begin to function, she may want to start by taking a course in bookkeeping, accounting, or money management. Although I've found that most men start out as mystified by money matters as most women, the men seem to learn by doing; they fake it, make mistakes, or hire experts, while the women are allowed to internalize their "math anxiety" and remain financial innocents.

Once she is ready to come of age as a person and to level out the power relations in a marriage, woman after woman seems to make the same few demands:

• A bank account of her own (echoing Virginia Woolf's "room of one's own")

• The right to cash checks without a husband's permission

• Authority for major spending decisions that affect her, and mutual authority with her husband for those affecting the family unit

• Shared responsibility and/or complete understanding of the household's income tax calculations, insurance policies, investments, other assets, and bookkeeping methods

• For the unemployed housewife, disposable income of her own, over and above the "allowance" her husband gives her for household expenses

• For the wage-earning wife, a policy of pooling both partners' incomes from which household expenses are paid and disposable moneys divided equally, rather than earmarking her earnings for food or rent, and putting her in the position of asking for "his" money for other things

After the "power of the purse" is more equitably distributed, other autocratic behaviors sometimes reform themselves. For example, whereas wives with the least "power" are the most likely to be abused, research shows that wives with the most education, financial autonomy, and job possibilities tend to leave husbands who abuse them.[20] Which brings us to the last and most critical component of the family power struggle, the question of violence, where we begin to expand the discussion beyond the primary adult relationship. In terms of the previously discussed issues of communication, autonomy, and financial independence, most people would argue that to varying degrees, children's immaturity justifies some imbalance of power between parent and child. But regardless of age, when it comes to feeling safe at home every family member has the right to demand equal protection.

PHYSICAL SAFETY

> . . . the American family and the American home
> are perhaps as or more violent than any other single
> American institution or setting . . .
>
> —*Behind Closed Doors*[21]

Violence is the ultimate act of inequality. In marriage, it is the triumph of domination—the male–female power struggle acted out in muscle and blood. Studies show that "husbands tend to kill their wives because of bruised male egos" while the wives who kill tend to do so only after years of being abused.[22] In gross cultural terms, the high incidence of marital violence is the result of conditioning women to be victims and men to equate manliness with force. In *The Second Sex*, Simone de Beauvoir writes, "For a man to feel in his fists his will to self-affirmation is enough to reassure him of his sovereignty."[23] Behavior scientists acknowledge that "the wife abuser, when he feels his dominant role threatened, uses power to maintain it."[24]—just as countries do and parents do when they feel a threat to their dominance.

But let us begin with marriage. For some, the wedding license is a "hitting license": there are estimates that one out of two married women will become a victim of her husband's violence.[25] The families that hurt are not restricted to one class or race: Estimates of the prevalence of domestic abuse range from one household in six up to 60 percent of the nation's 47 million couples.[26]

Dr. Murray A. Straus, director of the Family Violence Research Program at the University of New Hampshire and co-author of *Behind Closed Doors,* stresses four misconceptions that perpetuate this level of violence:

1. *The misconception that men who batter are mentally ill.* The truth is that not one study finds a higher rate of mental disorders among wife beaters. Battery is not a "sick" act; it is merely an extra step along the continuum of normal male dominance behavior as our culture defines it.

2. *The misconception that anger causes men to "lose control."* Straus insists that each batterer is in complete control;

in fact, each has an internal rule as to just how far he will go. One will slap, another will punch, a third will stop when he draws blood or breaks his wife's bones. Since most men are much stronger than most women, if they truly "lost control," more husbands would batter their wives to death. But they don't. They let women heal between beatings.

3. *The misconception that drunkenness causes battery.* In most instances, says Straus, men don't hit because they're drunk, they drink to have an excuse to hit. Later they can say "The *real* me wouldn't do this."

4. *The misconception that violence is idiosyncratic.* It isn't, says Straus, it's systemic; it's something we *learn* and can unlearn with the help of the criminal justice system. Straus and other experts advise a get-tough policy, citing studies that prove mate abuse lessens in jurisdictions where offenders are arrested, not given therapy or counseling.[27]

When Straus testified in Congress, he was asked to limit his remarks to *serious* assault. He responded, "What if one out of six Congressmen got hit, slapped, and punched? Would you limit my testimony on violence in Congress to 'serious assault'?" Straus asserts that our culture tolerates a double standard: We do not permit among strangers one iota of the violence excused in a marriage. Proof of this phenomenon lies in a series of experiments which found that when fights were staged in which a man attacked a woman, 65 percent of the passersby came to her rescue when the pair were said to be strangers, but only 19 percent tried to help when they believed the victim was the assailant's wife.[28]

Marital violence is not only not taken seriously, often it is made into a joke: A "Wife Beater's License" was for sale in vending machines on the New York State Thruway until women protested this "fun" document that entitled a husband to "horsewhip or otherwise manhandle his wife in any way he feels necessary." Making light of abuse more officially, a judge in Kansas ordered a man who was found guilty of wife battery to buy his wife a box of candy.[29]

But family violence is no joke. Of all murders committed

by people acquainted with their victims, sixteen out of every hundred involve family, and half of those are spouse murders.[30] At one city hospital, 70 percent of all emergency room patients were women who had been attacked by their husbands or male "friends."[31]

James Bannon, Executive Deputy Chief of Police in Detroit and a specialist in domestic violence problems, says abuse cases account for a third of all police calls, but cops are reluctant to respond to such calls. This is partly because of the potential danger to those who interfere in volatile disputes, but mostly, police say, it isn't worth the hassle because the victim rarely presses charges. "They don't tell you the same is true of *all* crime victims," says Bannon. He agrees with many other experts that the therapeutic approach to domestic batterers and sexual abusers has been a failure and that the only "appropriate response" is arrest. And in jurisdictions where domestic abuse is taken seriously, 90 percent of the victims press charges. Most importantly, a police action tells all members of society, especially our children, that violence is *not* okay and the system will punish such behavior wherever it occurs.

Maria Marcus, professor of law at Fordham University, contends that police, prosecutors, and judges have resisted taking appropriate action, first, because of the old notion that wives are a man's property, second because of the presumption that the victim has consented or at least "caused the violence," and third, because of the perverse reluctance of authorities to arrest a family wage-earner—thus making women pay for their support with their skins. Marcus agrees that a stronger police response could avoid family homicide, and cites police records that validate her opinion: police were called in to most family violence situations at least once before those situations escalated to homicide; in half the cases where battery eventually culminated in murder, they were called in at least *five* times.[32] Fair warning for authorities who care enough to pay attention.

Sexual abuse is another skeleton in the closet of family life. According to informed estimates, one out of every seven married women in this country has been raped by her husband. Yet only fourteen states allow a woman to charge her husband with rape if they are living together.[33] Again, the concept of wife-as-property permits him to take what he wants from her when he wants it. What is the difference between marital rape and rape? Dr. Kirsti Yllo, a Massachusetts sociologist, answers, "It's the difference between living with the frightening memory of having been raped, and actually living with the rapist."[34] Dr. Yllo defines marital rape as "forced sex without a woman's consent." That may be the physical definition, but the larger truth is that rape is about power, not sex. Whereas loving sex is reciprocal pleasure, rapists as well as victims see rape as an act of violation and humiliation, an expression of a man's deep anger toward all women, a *sexualized* form of battery.[35] Battered wives are at the greatest risk for marital rape. Abusive husbands attack their wives most brutally during pregnancy,[36] as though attacking the very symbol of biological womanhood. The compounding of masculine domination with the desire to hurt and debase what is female makes sexual violence the most virulent kind of power relations, especially when it is "legalized" by marriage or sanctified by parental authority. Straus formulates the paradox in stark terms: "The family is our most loving institution and also the greatest location of risk of assault. In contrast to the outside world, at home you have an astronomical chance of being victimized by violence."[37] Obviously, because of their vulnerability and dependence on adults, children in families are at the greatest risk of victimization.

Violence against one's own children often passes for normal. Not too long ago, I watched a small boy of about three resist being strapped into his seat on an airplane. Obviously, he was afraid. "It's his first flight," his mother told the flight attendant who had come to help. "The seat belt might be too tight," she offered, loosening the buckle. But the child would not be relieved. He cried and squirmed, his face turning red. His father's face also began to darken with anger.

"You know what they do with bad boys on airplanes?" asked the father. "They lock 'em in the overhead bin!"

The boy answered with a wail, his eyes turning desperate behind the tears as the engine revved and the plane took off.

"Shut *up!*" shouted his mother from one side. But the

boy kept pulling at his seat belt and squirming toward the floor, thrashing and gasping for breath.

In a burst of rage, the father released his own seat belt, lunged at the boy, rammed his little shoulders against the seat back, and squeezed the child's face until his cheeks turned yellow-white. *"If you don't stop crying this minute, I'll throw you out the window!"* bellowed the father. Rigid with terror, the little boy stopped crying.

Inevitably, parent power gets results. But this sort of negative parent power leaves casualties behind, while positive parent power leaves some of itself. Power is positive when it creates energy (empowerment), produces light (understanding) or heat (comfort) or forward motion (progress as opposed to restraint). Power is negative when it is oppressive, self-aggrandizing, violent, dependent on size or age, or equated with manhood. ("If a man can't subdue a noisy three-year-old, what kind of man is he?") Negative power destroys trust. Positive empowerment builds trust; it is genderless; it is collaborative; it is power *for*, not power over.

But, someone is sure to say, families cannot allow three-year-olds to refuse to wear seat belts, four-year-olds to decide the menu, or eight-year-olds to spend money at will. Surely parents' greater maturity and the wisdom born of experience entitles adults to exercise authority over children. Yes, of course. Giving children reasonable rules of safety and consideration, guidance, support, and protection, and establishing moral and intellectual standards are the fundamental responsibilities of parenthood. That is what a loving parent or caregiver *does*. But *how* the job is done is the question at issue throughout this book. The parents on the airplane could have loosened the strap slightly, held the boy's hand, explained what would happen during takeoff, distracted him with a book or toy, explored the diagram of the plane that is stored in the front seat pocket; that is to say, they could have used their superior powers to add to his understanding of the world and help him overcome his fear.

In a democratic family, those with superior knowledge and resources (i.e., power) use them to strengthen others in the family. In an authoritarian family, power is used to "tame" and control others, to consolidate power. Let me further explain the difference through some dialogue that might accompany a familiar parent–child power struggle: Six-year-old Susie won't eat her peas. Peas are good for children, but Susie won't even taste them. What's a parent to do?

Negative Parent Power. "You'll stay at that table until you finish every one of those peas!"

"If you don't eat your peas, you may not have dessert."

"Go to your room—and no television tonight!"

"I'm sick and tired of your finicky eating habits! You'll eat what I give you or you won't eat in this house!" (Smack!)

"Open your mouth!" (Forces spoonful of peas into child's mouth.) "You're going to eat this for your own good."

Positive Parent Power. "When you were a baby, you loved mashed baby-food peas. Let's mash them with your fork and see if you still like them that way."

"We don't care if you don't eat peas, but we care if you don't get the special vitamins in peas. We can get other vegetables that have the same vitamins. Which would you like?"

"Maybe you don't like *cooked* peas. Try these sweet peas right from the pod: They're fun to open and you can slide the peas in your mouth right down the peapod chute." (This obviously comes from my overcooked asparagus experience.)

"Let's hide one pea in a spoonful of mashed potatoes and see if it's better that way."

I do not mean to turn this into a parent guidebook, but I consider the resolution of parent–child food fights ideally illustrative of the difference between authority and authoritarianism. The authoritarian parent is saying "You'll eat because I say so and if you defy me, I will use my power to punish you." The democratic parent uses his or her authority—in the sense of knowledge—to introduce information (other vegetables with similar nutrients; the child's own former preferences; other pea choices, and possibilities that might affect the child's taste) and, by example, to teach the child how to negotiate and reason with others. That is empowerment. That is the positive use of parent power.

Also by example, parents or other adults who share all the responsibilities and pleasures of family life teach children how to avoid power struggles in the first place. The original democracy and mutual respect operating between adult male and female—or homosexual partners rearing children, or a single parent and his or her friends—creates the template for all human relations to come. Conversely, when family arrangements are authoritarian, power eclipses love and *violence becomes a solution to being out of control:*

> ITEM: Oberlin, Ohio. The police have arrested the parents of a 3-year-old girl who apparently starved to death after her unemployed father refused to accept welfare.
>
> "The father does not like to accept welfare. [He believes] that he can take care of the children himself," said Police Chief Robert Jones.[38]

QUESTION: If masculine pride—the equation of manhood with the ability to "take care" of a family—is more important than a child's life itself, don't we as a society have to defeat the masculine mystique? In so many cases, it is not feminism that is "destroying the family," but *masculinism.*

> ITEM: WIFE OF PROFESSOR KILLS 2 CHILDREN AND THEN HERSELF WITH A SHOTGUN. A neighbor described her as "a loving and caring mother, not the kind who farmed out her children to others."[39]

QUESTION: What good is it to glorify the "loving, caring mother" role if it forces a woman to choose murder and suicide rather than be "the kind" that asks for help? Isn't it better to make good child-care services available to all overworked parents, rather than have women who are literally killing themselves to measure up to the motherhood ideal?

> ITEM: Two-thirds of reported cases of child molestation are committed by family members or other close friends.

More than 90 percent of those children sexually abused by adult relatives are female and the vast majority of abusers are male. The average age of the victim when incest is initiated is between six and eleven years.[40]

QUESTION: Who will save sexually abused children if "family privacy" becomes a New Right shibboleth and Father bars the door of his castle? To ask that is not to suggest that government belongs in the home or that there is something inherently wrong with family privacy. It is my way of saying that privacy is a desirable goal *until* it becomes a cover for the exploitation of those who are most powerless in the family.

Of all family phenomena, incest—which studies show is overwhelmingly imposed by male adults on female children—underscores the abuses to which power imbalances can lead. Some men cannot see a clear line between patriarchal rule around the house and following Father into his bed when so ordered. For some men, fatherhood means "she's mine, I can do what I want with her." For some men, getting total adoration and service from a daughter is what fatherhood is all about. I heard one father excuse his sexual demands on his child by saying, "Hey, nobody got hurt." I heard another describe his incestuous relationship with his 10-year-old as "just another form of father love."

Think about this telling contradiction: In normal families (where incest would be unthinkable), it is culturally unacceptable for a son to be a "Mama's Boy" but just fine for a daughter to be "Daddy's Girl." Modern psychology almost seems to prescribe a kind of benign eroticism of flirtation and mutual appreciation in father–daughter relations to prime a girl for heterosexual sexuality. Add that "normal" eroticism to those "normal" power imbalances between male and female, and father and child, and you have a fertile field on which father–daughter incest can almost seem normal too.

Ignoring these family politics, the helping professions call incest a sickness and try to cure it; the law calls it a crime and tries to punish it; religion calls it a sin and tries to redeem the poor souls. One by one. Case by case. Misapprehending the causes. Blaming the victim. Marveling that what is considered *depraved* keeps happening in family after family after family. Freudians continue to misread the Oedipus legend as a symbolic description of every child's secret sexual longing for the parent, instead of, as Erich Fromm rightly saw it, "the rebellion of the son against the authority of the father in the patriarchal family."[41] The Oedipal triangle's father–daughter counterpart, the Electra Complex, lets society attribute father-abuse to daughters' "seductive behavior" or else deny it altogether as daughters' "wishful fantasies." In keeping with this psychological reductionism—and in deference to the hierarchy of age-power relations—judges and juries continue to distrust children's testimony, and social workers send children home to their abusers rather than "break up the family." Again, the institution rises above the individual; again family mythology takes precedence over children's safety. And we have yet to locate the cause of incest in the social order that normalizes and validates male supremacy in every other context; so why not in Father's bed?

> *Item:* POLICE SAY COUPLE BEAT BOY TO DEATH "They said they hit him to correct his habit of lying," Detective Michael Kelly said. "A parent may chastise a child within reason, but this went on for four hours. You don't beat a child for four hours."[42]

QUESTION: How long do you beat a child? Would one hour have been within reason? Twenty minutes? What, short of death, *is* a fit punishment for a child's lie? And might a child acquire "his habit of lying" to try to avoid such chastisement? Here too, the answers are less than satisfying. Perhaps it is enough to say that power unleashed in the name of love— "we hit her for her own good"—leaves more terrible wounds than the attack of a stranger. It scars children with a lifetime of confusion between love and pain; it tells them we can force others to do what we want them to do, once we have the power and they don't.

Out of the tragic profusion of family violence, I chose those few newspaper items to illustrate the grimmest fulfillment of family politics. Whether grisly or pitiful, my examples drive at the same point made in the case of Susie and the peas. Very simply, the family is where we either do or do not teach the integration of power into love. It is also "where most people learn the emotional and moral meaning of violence."[43] Sadly, the family classroom is pretty bloody. More than half of all households in one survey reported at least one act of violence.[44] Social scientists have found that "violence toward children is culturally acceptable and even culturally mandated ('spare the rod . . .'),[45] that nearly all parents have used physical punishment at some time in their child's life,[46] and that the most violent children come from the most violent homes, where they have witnessed savage attacks on their mothers or been severely abused themselves.[47]

Much is made of the accelerating brutality of young people's crimes, but *rarely does our concern for dangerous children translate into concern for children in danger.*[48] We fail to make the connection between the use of force on children themselves, and violent antisocial behavior, or the connection between watching father batter mother and the child deducing a link between violence and masculinity. We have yet to learn that reducing family violence is not a matter of learning self-control but of undoing power relations. It is not a question of class or breeding but of hierarchy and politics.

The authors of an eight-year study of family violence conclude that force is "used as a mechanism to control the behavior of family members," and not, as some parents claim, "in the best interests of the child." Frequently, say the researchers, "the conflict between parent and child is one of pure confrontation where *only who wins matters.*" As for marital battery, they go on to say something I wish to emphasize:

> . . . wife beating is much more common in homes where power is concentrated in the hands of the husband. *The least amount of battery occurs in democratic households.*
>
> . . . Inequality may initiate a chain reaction of *power confrontations* running throughout the family.[49]

Typically, the husband hits the wife, she realizes it is too dangerous to retaliate directly, so she hits a child, who in turn hits a younger child, until the youngest child abuses the family pet. There can be no winners in this game of domino dominance. Whether hurting takes the form of verbal abasement, spanking, sexual violence, or pitiless thrashing, what hurts most is the abuse of power that is the betrayal of love.

In my discussion of emotional communication, personal autonomy, financial independence, and physical safety, I bypassed most of the psychodynamics in favor of a narrow focus on the family politics inherent in these problems. With that same perspective, I want to touch on a few other relationships where traditional roles and hierarchies can interfere with family happiness.

Having just said so much about the offense of incest, I want to speak now on behalf of the millions of ordinary families that have suffered from the *sexist sexualization* of normal father–daughter relations. Old-style fathers are locked into old roles: masculinity mentor to sons, sexuality reflector to daughters. One can only hope that the new father (described in Chapter Nine) will not let patriarchal pathologies inhibit the healthy expression of his love for his children nor distort that love into exploitation.

DOUBLE-STANDARD DADDIES

There are two kinds of fathers in traditional households: the fathers of sons and the fathers of daughters. These two kinds of fathers sometimes co-exist in one and the same man. For instance, Daughter's Father kisses his little girl goodnight, strokes her hair, hugs her warmly, then goes into the next room where he becomes Son's Father, who says in a hearty voice, perhaps with a light punch on the boy's shoulder: "Goodnight, Son, see ya in the morning."

Rather than be the best, most loving, most natural father he can be, the double-standard daddy screens his behavior. He relates to girls and boys in different ways according to prescriptive notions of the father's role in facilitating each child's proper sexual identification. With this critical assignment in mind, he infuses male-to-male affection with so many negative innuendoes that father–son love becomes tainted with perversion. Then, of course, he holds back; he's not as demonstrative as he might want to be and he worries about toughening up his son for life in a man's world. Son's Father sees himself as the Master Tutor of his boy's manhood.

I remember interviewing a man who said proudly that he taught his sons to shake hands and not kiss their Dad beyond a certain age. "What age is that?" I asked.

"Three," he said.

On the other side of the ledger, Daughter's Father assumes the sacred trust of training her to be loving and lovable. When she is young and neuter, small and cute, father is lavish with his affection. If she is spunky, father–daughter relations are idyllic and fun-filled. But as she begins physically to resemble a full-grown woman, the idyll ends. Seeing her as a Woman, Daughter's Father loses sight of everything else she is as a person. The double-standard daddy, heir to a cultural attitude that defines women as sexual above all, consciously or unconsciously cools his affection for his own daughter so that their relationship will not seem "provocative." The daughter, prone to the same cultural influences, learns to pull away despite her sense of loss. For instance, one California woman wrote me about her father who diapered and fed her as a baby, then played with her throughout childhood, cuddled and hugged her, was her best friend, helped with her problems—until she became a teenager. "What stings my heart to this very day (I am now 35), is why did my Dad and I stop touching each other then?"

She asked that question of a therapist at the time and was told it was "normal" for fathers and daughters to grow apart when the girl reaches puberty. But she never understood and she never stopped hurting:

> How I wish that doctor or someone would have encouraged me instead to reach out to my Dad, and to work through the feelings that were getting in the way of our showing each other how we really felt. My Dad died when I was 28, and he never knew why I had physically withdrawn from him. I'd give anything to have the memory of having hugged and kissed him goodbye as he went off in the car with my mom . . . a trip from which he never returned.[50]

MATERNAL SEXUALITY

A woman's power over her child is so total during infancy that our culture has evolved the ethic of maternal purity and selflessness to make it tolerable and to keep it detached from female sexuality. Maternal sexuality in particular is said to be "a topic that makes virtually everyone anxious."[51] Women feel guilty, for example, if they experience sexual pleasure from nursing or if they are sexually aware of their children's bodies during diaper changes. Some combination of pop Freudianism and spillover prurience from pornography has corrupted maternal responsiveness. What pornographers have accomplished by eroticizing dominance is to make mothers ashamed of the pleasure they feel at the sight of small children's bodies. But where are the words for that pleasure? Male language for sexual arousal is grossly inadequate to describe a mother's satisfaction with nursing or her thrill at the feel of her baby's skin. One who *feels* does not necessarily *act* on that feeling and in the case of most parents—mothers *and* fathers—sexual awareness and sensual appreciation of our children, whatever their age, is a far cry from sexual abuse. The first is a love trip, the second is a power trip. Only the pornographers pretend there's no difference.

THE MOTHER/DAUGHTER DEAL

In the past, the way daughters honored mothers best was by reproducing their mothering. Conversely, daughters defied both motherlove and motherpower if they did not choose to become mothers like their mothers—if they found another way to be women. My own experience speaks directly to this point.

My mother died when I was fifteen. Twenty years later, I saw what bereavement and self-pity had veiled: In some ironic way, my mother had mothered me best by dying. Had she lived, I would not have gone away to college, then lived alone, traveled, learned to support myself, taken risks. I loved my mother too much to have rebelled against her. At fifteen, I was well on my way to becoming a homebody, a port in the storm not a rocker of boats.

As I watch other mothers and daughters be women together, I wonder how we would have been had she lived. In the quiescent 1950s, could I have absorbed her generous temperament without at the same time absorbing her habit of self-abnegation? Through the defiant 1960s and 70s, would I have criticized her for playing it safe? Would I have held her responsible for her own suffering? Would I have forgiven her for giving too much of her life to my father and me? Would she have forgiven my ingratitude? Could I have explained that I loved her without wanting to be like her? I've known a few mother–daughter relationships that effortlessly weave camaraderie across the gap, but many more that are held together only by dutiful phone calls and obligatory visits as daughters try to be less enslaved by love and less afraid of power while their mothers remind them of what they were supposed to be, and still more allow themselves to be pitted against each other in the patriarchal competition for youth and beauty. I wonder how my mother and I might have fared.

Today, like every woman who is not only a daughter but the mother of daughters, I am caught in a triangle more eternal than the lover's bind. I want to be different from my mother without negating what she was. I want to be different from my mother without then asking my daughters to be just like "new improved me." I have chosen to be an involved, even intrusive mother despite the fact that I owe my independent strengths to *less* mothering. I do not believe this to be a contradiction. In my early years, a mother's death was one of the only reasons a girl was given her freedom. But today, with our own fuller lives, we mothers are learning to mark our mothering success by our daughters' lengthening flight. When they need us, we are fiercely there. But we do not *need* them to need us—or to become us. And we don't have to die to let them go.

DECODING DEPENDENCY

All parents have a favorite stage of child development. I've heard it said that God made babies cute so that their parents would put up with the endless demands of infancy, yet I will confess that adorableness aside, infancy was my least favorite

stage. I prefer adolescence, when our children became opin-
ionated, impassioned, and funny, like old friends who are suddenly inspired to reveal their true selves. What's more, I feel
more useful now than I did when the children were young.

I know a woman who feels just the reverse. She says infancy was her favorite time because serving her babies' vital
needs was daily proof that she was important. She admits she
never thought of herself as an independent adult until she
had a baby depending on her—which makes sense to anyone
who has ever noticed how much status men draw from having
women dependent on them.

I'm not saying that nonverbal communication or minister-
ing to a baby cannot be a kind of meaningful interchange.
But for many of us, there is scant gratification in being needed
by someone who is so totally powerless. A passion for infancy
may reveal a desire to exercise some control in a world that
disapproves of women in authority. The risk for a woman
who considers her helpless children her "job" is that the children's growth toward self-sufficiency may be experienced as
a refutation of the mother's indispensability, and she may unconsciously sabotage their growth as a result. How much better if parents could respond to their babies' needs without
feeling that they are irreplaceable or omnipotent. The work
of feeding, bathing, burping, or diapering does not draw upon
everyone's best talents; some people are better at it than others. In any case, neither child care nor the power accruing
from children's dependency should be confused with love.

SECOND CHILDHOOD

Let's say you are 32 and becoming forty is still an abstraction.
You can only try to imagine how it will feel. But when your
children turn nine or twelve, you have a thousand points of
reference that can enhance your capacity for empathy in ways
a thirty-two-year-old cannot empathize with the pre-forty jit-
ters. Your child is uniquely nine or twelve, but because you've
been past all those landmarks that she or he is encountering,
you experience an observed second childhood—a kind of a
second chance—this time knowing what comes next.

Unfortunately though, just as fraternity men who suffered

the worst initiation rites sometimes are the most sadistic when it comes to paddling next year's pledges, parents who remember a painful childhood sometimes seem to take revenge on their kids. Rather than try to resolve our childhood powerlessness through our children, we can use our power over the present to improve our children's childhood. In short, whenever possible we can choose empathy over authority.

MOTHERING A SON

While a father is a boy's direct model for male adulthood—and, we hope, a warm and involved one—a mother also helps him define his manhood. She does this partly by teaching him to share the world with women and by reminding him that he cannot "hate girls" because she is one of them. In the psychoanalytic view, a boy must reject his mother in order to become a man; emancipated from womanly care, he can orient himself toward male achievement. As the mother of a son, I do not accept that alienation from me is necessary for his discovery of himself. As a woman, I will not cooperate in demeaning womanly things so that he can be proud to be a man. I like to think the women in my son's future are counting on me.

POWER STRUGGLE AND THE STEPFAMILY

More than 35 million people now live in stepfamilies, including seven million children, or one child in six. If this "fastest growing social phenomenon" continues, as many as half of today's children will live in stepfamilies sometime in their lives.[52] Yet the persistence of a "wicked stepmother" mentality sours many of these relationships from the start. Emily Visher, co-founder of the Stepfamily Association of America, says that's why, despite a potential market of 35 million purchasers, there are no greeting cards wishing "Happy Birthday, Dear Stepchild." At the same time, the typical stepmother today is the younger woman dad married to replace the older first wife. No wonder the kids are encouraged by mom #1 to resent her.

Needless to say, the special problems of stepfamilies are

considerably more serious than a lack of a Hallmark card and less soluble than the problems of *The Brady Bunch*. It's hard to blend disparate families who have lived by different rules. Jealousies develop among stepchildren and between children and the new spouse. There is anger when money needed by the new family goes to one spouse's children from the old family. There is hurt at the recurring evidence of a past history shared with the first family and forever closed from the new spouse. Some children feel ashamed of their parents' divorce or hide the fact that they shuttle between two households in a shared custody arrangement. Others are made uncomfortable by the affection shown by partners in the new marriage, or by the stepparent's eagerness to be liked, or worst of all, by the arrival of a baby—living proof that the newly constituted family is a fact.

A father feels guilty about spending every day with his stepchildren while his own kids, in the custody of their mother, hunger for more time with him. A young childless woman suddenly has four adolescents in her life because she married their father. A long-time wife suddenly has no husband, or has a new husband who doesn't care about her kids. Stepparents and biological parents disagree on discipline, spending money or nutrition. And so it goes for children whose family is famil*ies* and for adults whose vital human connections enlarge geometrically with each new alliance.

To therapists, stepfamilies may present convoluted psychological dilemmas; to me, they are the Rubic's cube of family politics. But beyond the complex interactions is one stunning surprise: The stepfamily configuration seems to *increase* the power of the child. That is to say, compared to other parents, remarried parents seem more desirous of their child's approval, more alert to the child's emotional state, and more sensitive in their parent–child relations. Perhaps this is the result of heightened empathy for the child's suffering, perhaps it is a guilt reaction; in either case, it gives the child a potent weapon—the power to disrupt the new household and come between the parent and the new spouse.

Whereas in theory any child can become an irritant sufficient to divide his or her parents, in an intact family most parents would feel perfectly justified in uniting to correct the child's behavior. In stepfamilies, the parent already fears that his or her child feels betrayed. A clear alliance with the new spouse against the child would be the *coup de grâce*. At the same time, the parent is not likely to combine forces with the other parent, the ex, because of the jealous reaction of the new spouse, as well as the residue of hostility felt toward the ex. So the child is in this odd position of control, wielding the power to hurt by being hurt, to divide his or her parent's loyalties, to punish the adults who have "destroyed" the child's *real* family.

This set of power relations explains why studies find that satisfaction decreases in second marriages in proportion to the number of children in the stepfamily, and is worse when there are older children involved rather than younger ones.[53] Not only are younger children more adaptable to changed circumstances, they are less capable of manipulating the social system of the household. One suspects that the older child's power to hurt and disrupt can feel like well-deserved compensation for the sorrow, anger, and powerlessness the child experienced during the parents' divorce. Furthermore, the child's heightened *visibility,* or affect, was probably presaged by events during the divorce process. If children are objectified in court, used as weapons of revenge and humiliation, fought over like property or the spoils of battle, it is no surprise that they begin to "use" themselves in strategies of emotional blackmail.

We all know that power corrupts. In this chapter, I have tried to show that family power struggles corrupt absolutely. The cast of characters may change—parents, stepparents, live-in relatives, cohabiting friends, adult or child—but the politics remain the same.

6

Too Many Trade-Offs:
When Work and
Family Clash

• You're a single mother working the four-to-midnight shift. You've used up all your sick leave and personal days but tonight your daughter is performing in the eighth grade production of *Romeo and Juliet.* Do you go to work or to school?

• You've been promoted to branch manager, but the branch is in South America. Your wife is starting law school after ten years of full-time motherhood, and the kids have finally made friends in the neighborhood where you moved the family for your last job transfer. Do you uproot them again?

• Your brilliant advertising campaign increased sales dramatically. The boss wants to give you a raise that would put you ahead of your husband, a man with old-fashioned ideas about male supremacy, who never wanted you to work in the first place. Do you take the raise?

WHEN I HEAR such job–family conflicts, I think of the classic holdup line: "Your money or your life!" For wage-earners who are also spouses and parents, the threat is: Your job or your child! Your raise or your marriage! Your promotion or your family's happiness! Take your pick. You're going to be robbed one way or the other.

In the above cases, the single mother had to explain to her broken-hearted child that she couldn't afford a theater ticket that could cost both of them her job. The executive, fearing the company would otherwise question his career commitment, allowed himself and his family to be relocated. After two months in South America, at loose ends and with disgruntled children on her hands, the wife had a nervous breakdown and the company had to spend $12,000 to bring the family back. (Wives of transferred managers, it seems, "suffer more frequently from depression and related illnesses than other people," and children in such families show similar symptoms plus academic difficulties, drug use, and even suicide.[1]) Afraid of wounding her husband's ego, the advertising genius rejected the raise, and continued refusing increases and bonuses until after her husband died. As a widow, she was "free" to earn what she deserved.

Although Freud said happiness is composed of love *and* work, reality often forces us to choose love *or* work. In traditional families, women have been expected to concentrate on love and men on work, but lately the division of spheres and sex-typed competencies seems increasingly absurd. Both women and men work for the same reasons—for economic need and for personal satisfaction—and at the same time, both sexes consider the family the most important element in their lives, which would explain why job–family conflicts account for as much as a quarter of all working people's major problems.[2]

With most married couples living on two paychecks, with more than half of all American mothers in the labor force and a half million more entering each year, with 32 million children having employed moms and more than four million women supporting their families by themselves,[3] the *love or money* alternative has become an utterly false choice. Yet many of the either/or trade-offs demanded by current working conditions seem founded on those outdated sex role dichotomies, and most employers continue assuming that workers will rob their personal lives to pay for their economic survival *rather than upset traditional male–female power relations.* And many of us do just that.

The choice boils down to "your money or your life" because workplace realities have been allowed to imitate patriarchal family politics, in which love and power are sex-linked and mutually exclusive. Keep that thesis in mind as we discuss the effects on families of sex discrimination in employment, the work ethic in America, sex role strain, and the problem of child care.

SEX DISCRIMINATION

The persistence of unequal treatment in the workplace robs virtually every family that has a woman in it. A nationwide poll taken in 1982 found that most American women "feel they do not have equal opportunities with men"[4] and the facts bear out their feeling. Women earn an average of 59 cents for every dollar earned by men working comparable hours; women are concentrated in low-paying dead-end jobs; the majority of women workers have endured some form of sexual harassment—suggestive comments, leers, fondling, and worse[5]—in order to keep their jobs; and averaging all age groups, full-time working women with college degrees earn less yearly income than men with just an eighth-grade education.[6] Those facts cheat families of the earnings potential of their female wage-earner whether she is sole support of her children or a team-earner with her husband.

This is particularly crucial now that working wives contribute up to 38 percent of their families' income, often keeping the household above the poverty line and sustaining the family unit when unemployment strikes the husband.[7] Economist Rudolph G. Penner calls the two-parent family "a private safety net that supplements public programs."[8] Sex discrimination (unequal pay and job segregation) weakens the female portion of the safety net, sometimes riddling it with holes and imperiling the entire family. Yet government's equal-opportunity efforts have slackened to the point of inaction and today's working women are expected to remain silent about discrimination. Those who file a complaint under anti-bias laws are open to ridicule and reprisals, not to mention years of litigation. Here, the holdup threat is "if you don't want this job the way it is, there are plenty of women who do. And besides, you should be at home where you belong."

As long as women are still assumed to be in charge of love, employers can say they are lucky to get work. As long as women's work opportunities are limited, men will have primacy in the job market, the two-income family will remain an inadequate solution to family economics, and the New Right can claim that women workers might as well go back to the kitchen and let us pay men enough to support their families alone. As long as the patriarchal family is assumed to be the norm, there will be no urgency to the problem of sex discrimination and its effects on women's families.

In addition to causing families economic hardships, "the segregation of women in low-paying and low-status jobs . . . sets the stage for male dominance and a traditional division of labor in marriage."[9] Indeed, some men who enjoy the financial contribution of a wage-earning wife simultaneously use the fact of women's secondary job status to justify the patriarchal order at home.

"We are not equal," said one man married for twelve years. "My role is primary to hers . . . at no time has she been able, nor do I think she will be able, to assume the total management of the family."

Labor Pains. "Discrimination against women because of their childrearing capacities is one of the most prevalent and problematic types of employment discrimination,"[10] writes legal scholar Nancy Erickson. Yet, odd as it sounds, in the mid-1970s, the Supreme Court ruled that employers who discriminate on the basis of pregnancy were not necessarily discriminating against *women,* they were only distinguishing "pregnant people" from nonpregnant people.[11]

In 1977, I testified before the U.S. Senate subcommittee on labor in support of a bill to prohibit job-related pregnancy discrimination:

> I find it profoundly symbolic that I am appearing before a committee of fifteen men who will report to a legislative body of one hundred men because of a decision handed down by a court comprised of nine men—on an issue that affects millions of *women.* . . . I have the feeling that if men could get pregnant, we wouldn't be struggling for this legislation. If men could get pregnant, maternity benefits would be as sacrosanct as the G.I. Bill.

Employers have trouble understanding that women serve their country by giving their bodies to childbirth at least as significantly as men do by giving their bodies to defense. Finally in 1978 Congress passed an amendment to Title VII of the Civil Rights Act prohibiting discrimination "on the basis of pregnancy, childbirth or related medical conditions," and at last working women have some guarantees and entitlements.[12]

Now, if you're a pregnant working woman, married or not, you must be allowed to continue on the job as long as you are physically able, and to return to work after delivery as soon as you can and want to. To the extent that your company provides benefits for other disabilities, it must grant you sick leave and disability pay for your pregnancy-related problems, including abortion complications. You can use accumulated sick leave for maternity absences. You cannot be fired for having an abortion, nor can you be forced out because your employer considers pregnant women unsightly. Your job or a comparable one must be available when you return from maternity leave and your seniority protected.

It's true that none of these benefits is guaranteed by law; employers are only required to apply them to pregnancy when they apply to other disabling conditions. Nevertheless, this is a giant improvement over 1901, when the president of Barnard College was promptly fired upon the news of her pregnancy. In 1981, when the current president of Barnard was pregnant, she was called a role model for young women everywhere. Then, again, she was married; shortly thereafter, a pregnant Long Island schoolteacher still had to fight to keep her job because she was single.

At any given time, there are one and a half million pregnant workers, and more than eight in ten working women are of childbearing age.[13] Patronizing concern for a woman's biology does not inspire equal treatment in the workplace. It inspires comments such as a colleague directed some years ago to Congresswoman Pat Schroeder. "How can you be both a lawmaker and a mother?" he asked ingenuously.

"Because I have a brain and a uterus," she said. "And I use both."

Too often though, a woman is still asked to choose between brain and uterus, between being productive and reproductive—between her money and her life.

Unsafe at Any Salary. In certain jobs, exposure to industrial substances forces a woman worker into untenable choices. Some employers refuse to hire women of childbearing age— or demand proof of sterility as a condition of employment. If a job exposes workers to lead, vinyl chloride, radioactivity, or anesthetic gases that might be hazardous to the worker, her developing fetus, or nursing infant, companies refuse to subject themselves to later claims by the mother or deformed child. Faced with such a policy, one woman had her tubes tied rather than lose her job at a lead storage battery plant. Another signed a waiver of her rights without fully understanding the health risks.

There is a growing body of evidence that what harms a woman's reproductive system also harms a man's. Therefore, negotiating various compromises with workers who might be willing to take reproductive risks is a delusion—and a disservice to the health of the human species. If ours were truly a pro-family society, we would insist that the only rational and legal solution is a safe workplace. The burden must be placed on the employer to devise a health standard that protects every working man or woman. And in 1980, it was: that is when a full set of Guidelines on Employment Discrimination and Reproductive Hazards was issued by the United States government. But one week after President Reagan took office, the guidelines were withdrawn, and today business is again able to make workers choose between cancer, brown lung, or genetic defects, and a living wage.[14]

A society truly committed to The Family would never tolerate such a choice.

THE WORK ETHIC

Chief executive officers of the 1300 largest U.S. corporations typically work 60 to 70 hours a week, travel six to 10 days a month and give up their weekends for business meetings. On their way to the top, many relocated six or more times. . . . Corporate leaders are resigned to the hard grind. Most believe a successful career requires personal sacrifices, and most put their jobs before their families or themselves.

—The Wall Street Journal[15]

Diane is the 40-year-old college-educated wife of a successful executive in a large Midwest corporation. Her own needs and happiness come second to those of her husband, and third and fourth to those of their two children.

—The New York Times[16]

The all-American work ethic, destructive enough by itself, also packs a gender double standard that strip-mines the natural resources of both parents. It has taught us that as their earnings and success increase, men become "more manly," while women become "less feminine." This perverse cultural dynamic gives fathers an *incentive* to stay away from their families and kill themselves at work, while coercing mothers to limit their career commitment, which in turn limits their wages and shortchanges their families. The trade-off here is, "Your sex norm or your salary."

The toll the work ethic takes on men is well-known: ulcers, heart disease, hypertension, alcoholism, and premature death. Despite all their pressures, fully 80 percent of male executives do not discuss their problems with anyone (only 12 percent turn to their wives, eight percent to friends or associates).[17] Successful men cannot afford to ask for help; they're supposed to solve problems, not have them.

We needn't belabor the ironies: In the act of proving himself a Big Man, he becomes an absent husband and incidental father. By providing so "manfully" for his family's future, he doesn't survive to share it.

"It is sobering to note the rising number of women who are millionaires . . . widows of the successful men who followed the logic of their vision to their grave," writes Daniel Maguire. "The work ethic as it is championed and lived in this nation is not pro-family."[18]

While "workaholism" is bad for men, work-deprivation

may be bad for women. Some researchers go as far as saying a meaningful paid job may be "a kind of preventive medicine . . . to protect women from psychiatric symptoms" and to reduce the likelihood of menopausal difficulties.[19]

"People who occupy powerful roles have fewer symptoms of distress than those who are powerless," observes one sex role psychologist.[20] Dual-career couples often seem happier than spouses in one-career families; for the wife this may be because earning money has been found to increase women's power in marriage by ensuring them a say in how it is spent and other family decisions.[21] Thus, whatever stress may be caused by a woman's role deviation or role overload seems to be dramatically outweighed by the advantages. In plain words, work is directly related to both equality and mental health. This doesn't mean all women (or all people) must have paid jobs to be sane or equal human beings, but it does mean that those who need or want to be employed must feel it is *sex role appropriate* to do so and to prosper.

SEX ROLE SECTARIANISM

> I come from a long line of male chauvinists in a
> very traditional family. To rebel against my back-
> ground, I didn't shoot dope—I married a working
> woman.
>
> —*Joe Bologna*

Despite more than a decade of women's job progress and men's somewhat increased presence in the family, there has not yet been a full integration of both roles for both sexes because there has not been a full cultural synthesis of the love/work dichotomy. It is still true that *a woman's work molds itself to her family while a man's family molds itself to his work.*[22] As long as the husband's work automatically comes first, he remains part of the working wife's problems.

One can see this most plainly in a body of research that reveals what causes the greatest work–family conflict for the average white woman. It is not the demands of her children but her husband's unfavorable attitude toward her having a job outside the home—and well over half of all employed women believe their husbands disapprove. (For black women, husbands' attitudes seem less important.)[23]

Role Strain and Overload. Women bend over backward to fulfill all their roles without inconveniencing men. In fact, they think their jobs cause far more inconvenience than *men* do. In one study, one wife in four said her husband was bothered by having her away from home so much, but only one husband in a hundred made that complaint; one wife out of five said her husband was upset that the house wasn't as clean as before she took a job, but *none* of the husbands reported being upset.[24]

Sex role strain is alive and well because so many women are still overdosing on the feminine mystique, still confusing their personal identity with a clean house, still fearing male disapproval and doing penance for stepping out of the domestic sphere. For all her new earning power, the nontraditional woman remains trapped by tradition: "She does not want to feel that her husband is deprived of advantages he would have obtained if he had married a 'true woman.' " (Simone de Beauvoir).[25]

Men seem to want it both ways: Studies show they prefer competent partners with "feminine" values; a wife "who combines career and family in a compromise fashion."[26] In two-career situations, divorce is not caused by a wife's employment says political scientist Andrew Hacker, but by "husbands who still expect to hold the center stage."[27] Husbands may accept a wage-earner wife, writes Caroline Bird, but they still want household hegemony:

A breadwinner expects the meals to be served when he is ready to eat them. He expects that she will listen when he wants to talk and shush the children when he wants to sleep. When she has a job of her own she may not be able to adjust to his timetable. Even worse, he may discover that she has something else she would rather do. . . . [He is] startled and ashamed to admit a sense of loss when the phone rings for her—and that the conversation is so interesting that she leaves their dinner to cool. . . . [Men] are used to being scolded by their wives for leaving the dinner for an important phone call for themselves, but the reverse is inconceivable.[28]

Who Comes First? If all else were equal, each spouse would be similarly influenced by the career of the other in terms of mutual ambition, job crises, making sacrifices. But when it comes to tolerating odd work schedules or accepting a job transfer or deciding whose career merits moving to another city for better opportunities, most wives (even avowed feminists) tend to subordinate themselves to their husbands.[29]

And why not? Thanks to historic male favoritism, his job offer is probably where the money is, whereas following her interests would result in a financial loss. So his career continues to come first, which compounds his advancement, which is how patriarchy begets patriarchy.

Sad to report, most men don't want a woman "on top," no matter how much her success would enrich the family unit and the men themselves. Sex role sectarianism is so rigid that four in ten Americans of both sexes still do not approve of a wife's earning more money than her husband. What's more, the higher the wife's earnings (especially if she works in a nontraditional job), the greater the probability that the husband will suffer premature death from heart disease and the couple will experience physical and psychological abuse, sex problems, separation, and divorce.[30] Here, the disturbance of traditional male–female power relations takes on the trappings of a full-scale tragedy. Rather than be the cause of celebration, one partner's increasing success becomes the cause of family decay, *if that partner is female.* Money is power, and power is so culturally masculine that husbands, and often wives themselves, cannot reconcile themselves to a woman's having it. Even when the husband is unemployed and the wife's earnings are keeping the wolf from the family's door, both adults are tormented by the sex role "inappropriateness" of living off a woman's labor. It's a no-win dilemma: Do they starve to save his self-image or does she save them and feel guilty, earn enough for subsistence but not prosper so much that she threatens their *identities*—he as breadwinner, she as supplementary? My question: Why can't they just do the best they can without regard for who is doing how much? Why can't they be an earnings *team*, a family *unit?*

The answer is depressing. I think it is not true that Americans want financially secure *families;* what we really want is financially successful *men* who then exercise the power to take care of women and children. That is a very different thing.

In a 1976–77 poll, seventy percent of *Harvard Business Review* subscribers said a wife should go to dull parties to advance a husband's career, but only 45 percent felt a husband should do the same for a wife's career. Patriarchy breeds patriarchy and legitimates patriarchy: Studies show that most people judge the social standing of a couple by the husband's occupation only; his wife's occupation, however impressive, either has no effect or, if she is very much more successful than he, depresses the status of her husband.[31]

Although working-class women—and most black women —have historically worked outside their homes for reasons of family survival, and although few would choose to give up paid work to become full-time housewives, most have simultaneously clung to the traditional housewife mindset and the housekeeper *role* at home.[32] Presumably, they need both the mindset and the role to validate their cultural femininity, and to affirm their husbands' place at the head of the family. Thus, many men have been able to accept the idea of their wives' working not just because of the needed dollars, but because the wives have neutralized the "masculine" *power* of work by also fulfilling the "feminine" work of *love.* The wife's superhuman housekeeping efforts have taken the onus off her wage-earning role and ensured the continuation of domestic tranquillity.

Who Has It Harder? In their work situations, professional women report far more negative experiences than professional men—from sexual harassment to less influence and challenge on the job. In their personal lives, the women far more than the men felt guilty and emotionally overextended in terms of their obligations and other people's demands on them. Then the double-whammy is compounded because these conflicts between family and job reduce the women's job satisfaction even further.[33]

Having an employed spouse enables both husbands and wives to take career chances and be more choosy about their jobs. Assuming he can overcome his discomfort with sex role imperatives, a man who is unhappy with his job can quit and coast for a while on his wife's earnings while he seeks something better. In fact, men living in two-paycheck marriages not only change jobs more often, they take longer vacations and work 14 percent fewer hours than traditional breadwinners.[34] So there is clearly something to be gained from role-free teamwork. But what do men do with those extra hours?

Unlike the top executives studied by *The Wall Street Journal*, six out of ten more-average working fathers say they *do* have enough time for themselves. But more than six out of ten working mothers say they do *not* have enough time.[35] Working mothers meet the extra demands of job, house and child care by cutting down on their sleep and eliminating leisure activities. As we will see in the next chapter, help from their husbands is "minor."[36]

When asked the single biggest disadvantage of the two-career family, professional working wives said "too much to do," while husbands said, "not enough time together"[37]—a critical difference. Likewise, a study tapping a broader sample of Americans found that more men complained of too many hours of work and of conflicts between work and leisure, but more women complained of fatigue and irritability and of conflicts between job and family schedules.[38] Since it is wives who put in more total worktime (job plus housework), why is it husbands who feel more work pressures and a greater tug between work and leisure?

Graham L. Staines, a Rutgers University psychologist and a co-author of the latter study, says that men complain about excessive hours partly because they tend to work longer job hours each week than women. But he further speculates that men complain about work–leisure conflicts because they are more likely to experience their family life and home chores as *leisure-like* (i.e., being a child's playmate or athletic coach or puttering with repairs) and thus to see their time on the job as time away from recreation. Women complain about schedule conflicts and fatigue because they are more likely to experience family life in *work-like* terms since they are expected to take responsibility for the unpleasant routine (like laundry or meals), or for rigidly scheduled activities that cannot be postponed (such as watching a child in a school play).

In short, says Staines, "more men than women feel 'my job stops me from having fun at home,' while more women than men feel 'my job stops me from attending to family responsibilities.' "

This difference is disturbing on several counts. First, it reaffirms that The Family does not exist as a uniformly satisfying experience even in households "equalized" by the presence of two full-time wage-earners. Instead, "family" is more positive for most men than most women: When Dad comes home from work he has fun but when Mom comes home from work, she has more work.

Second, what passes for the new "liberated" two-career family reveals itself to be a three-career family: The wife does two jobs, paid work and family work, while the husband does one. Thus, the supposed equality signaled by the rising number of employed wives and mothers may actually signify an alarming increase in overworked women.

Third, I worry because women complain about fatigue and schedule conflicts instead of complaining about men's not doing their share, or about employers' continuing to operate as if every worker has a wife at home. The female sex role imperative has expanded to allow women to "have it all" as long as they can *do it all.*

Mothers First. Several years ago, when tennis star Margaret Court accepted an unctuous bouquet of roses and a stunning defeat from over-the-hill men's champion Bobby Riggs, *The New York Times'* report of the match included the following revelation:

> Mrs. Court's Mother's Day began on an ominous note when her 14-month-old son, Danny, threw her only pair of tennis sneakers into the toilet of their hotel room.[39]

The image was funny but its implications were as infuriating as they were prototypical. How could an athlete psych herself for major competition if a toddler was underfoot? What coolheaded pro bounds onto the courts in soggy sneakers? Would a baby be allowed to disturb a *man* before such a match? If someone else had entertained Danny on his mother's big day, might she have beaten Bobby Riggs the way Billie Jean King did with no toddler to distract her?

Whoever we are and whatever we have to do, once we are mothers, it is virtually impossible for us to be excused from the care of our children. We are supposed to be mothers first and tennis pros second, mothers above all, persons only incidentally. And because that ideal is so thoroughly internalized, we swallow our fury, fish the sneakers from the toilet, and go on with the game of being all things to all people.

The Everything Cult. Women of the 1980s are supposed to want Everything—professional success, marriage, children, community status, travel, glamor, money, beauty, family life. But having it all means *adding* roles, not altering those we already play with such difficulty. If having it all really was a new frontier of freedom (i.e., more is better), men would want *in* on nurturing, preparing food, and staying home. But that's not what "all" means. It doesn't mean men doing more, it means "letting" women do what men do without changing what men do. Let the little woman redesign her life plan, build a career, have children, return to work straight from the hospital, go to business school, be a coal miner, break down all the barriers: Women's job progress has been proven safe for men. "So long as married women were able or willing to assume the primary responsibility for the home along with a job outside the home," says Carl Degler, "the traditional family was in no danger."[40]

The Everything Cult operating in a traditional culture makes labor market work a cheerful "extra," not a firm entitlement for women. It swings with the times. In the past, it wasn't enough to be a career woman; that was sterile and suspect. Now it isn't enough to be a housewife or mother; that is boring. Doing it all is better, *as long as nothing changes but a woman's demands upon herself.* No wonder the women with the worst coronary problems are not single, childless careerists, the ones who presumably work "like men," but married women with children and jobs[41]—the women who are trying to do it all. By themselves.

There are other alternatives: a climate of consciousness that encourages a blend of people's public and private commitments, a more humanized workplace, and a personal life that functions like a balance beam—tipping responsively to the changing weight of family or job demands but always recovering its equilibrium. For this to happen, and for work–family conflicts to disappear, two rock-ribbed institutions must change: the whole concept of children's care, and the way the workplace works.

CHILD CARE

Who Will Raise the Children? That question was the forthright title of a book about new options for fathers.[42] It is also the question all parents, politicians, and policymakers must answer in urgent seriousness now that less than half of American mothers spend all day at home. Who will raise the children? The alternatives are obvious:

1. The full-time at-home caregiver. Not only is this arrangement growing less common and more economically impractical, it also may be psychologically problematic in terms of isolation of the stay-home parent and understimulation of the child. In any event, it is workable only if voluntarily chosen by an adult positively inclined to domesticity and children, and this is so whether the full-time at-home caregiver is the child's parent or some other loving, significant person in the child's life.

2. The combination of part-time mother and part-time father. Desirable and beneficial especially during a family's early formative years, this arrangement affords young children adequate time with both parents (or other meaningful caregivers in the family unit), and gives parents a healthy balance of the love–work continuum. However, it requires massive reorganization of the workplace to develop the part-time option (see page 137), union-management cooperation, and an end to the equation of masculinity with a paid, full-time career.

3. The paid housekeeper-babysitter. Many variables complicate this plan: the family's ability to pay; parents' skill at screening applicants; the child's response to the surrogate who may change several times over the years; availability of competent, nurturant caregivers who affirmatively choose child-care work; problems of absenteeism, turnover, and no backup coverage. This could change if child caregiving were recognized as the important profession it is.

4. Patchwork quilt solutions. When parents work different shifts, kids see both parents, but parents don't see each other. Marriage and family life is disrupted.[43] Other kinds of make-shift pieced-together coverage by relatives, neighbors, and teenagers is often an imposition and does not guarantee dependability, adequate child-care skills, or a pleasant attitude. Unless child care arrangements are relatively permanent and regularized, a child can feel like everybody's burden.

5. Nursery school. Although it may be ideal for the child's social and cognitive development, nursery school is not always a realistic option. Many schools have long waiting lists for admission. They're not always open during full workday hours, which causes difficult logistics for pickup and delivery. Further, since nursery schools usually accept only children aged three and over, they're of no use to parents of infants. And of course, they are usually too expensive for most families to afford.

6. Family day care. The luck of the draw is such that sometimes your child buys into a home full of love and warmth, sometimes crowding, neglect, and abuse. (Better licensing procedures could improve this.)

7. Group child care. Although common and highly successful in most European countries, U.S. child-care centers are so underfunded that their potential for excellence is unknown, and likely to remain so as long as right-wing slander gives group care a bad name.[44]

Scare words such as "communism," "mind control," and "government intrusion into the family" have deflected people from discovering that child-care services can exist to supplement and support the family, not to replace it. Since 1971, when Richard Nixon vetoed the comprehensive child-care bill saying it would "sovietize" the American family, no new legislation has succeeded. Being spared sovietization has put as many as seven million "latchkey" children on the streets or at home alone, and has made child care a very costly problem for working parents. Some families pay "in the foregone earnings and missed career opportunities of a parent, usually of the mother who stays home to care for children. Some pay in complicated work schedules or nightwork. Others pay in money, energy, time, and consistency of parenting styles. But for all families, the costs are high," declare researchers studying the strains on working families.[45]

Besides the obvious disadvantages to millions of children whose needs are unmet, lack of good child care remains the major stumbling block between working women and equal employment opportunity,[46] and therefore a serious handicap to family wellbeing and economic security. Good child care. What does that mean?

According to an extensive survey of parents, seven features make a center "good": nutritious meals, careful supervision, cleanliness, educational activities, discipline, room to play, and a dependable, loving staff.[47] Despite the common impression that anything but full-time mothercare will harm child development, one study found that children in good centers with a small teacher–child ratio matured faster and had better-developed learning and social skills than children reared entirely at home.[48] Since much intellectual development takes place before age six, it is not surprising that disadvantaged children who were in Head Start preschool programs are far less likely to need special education classes later, and have "higher math and reading scores than their peers." Unfortunately, Head Start reaches only one in five of our neediest children.[49]

Nationwide, licensed child-care centers can accommodate only 10 percent of the children of working mothers, yet under Reagan, federal support for child-care programs was cut by a fourth, hundreds of thousands of families lost child-care services and a large number of the working poor had to leave their children entirely untended—some as young as seven, and 10 percent aged three or younger![50] Typical of the sad stories resulting from child-care cuts, was that of a working mother in Wichita, Kansas. Her two toddlers were disqualified from a public child-care center because she was earning "too much." But since she wasn't earning enough to afford private child care, her only solution was to leave the children in her car while she worked.[51] The choice: work or good child care. Your money or your life.

Not only is there great need for child-care services—and evidence that they do *no harm*[52]—but most people whose children actually experience such services are "very satisfied,"[53] and there are some who see very positive byproducts. For instance, if divorce is straining a parent–child relationship, "a good day care facility can provide important emotional support," and for children with absent fathers, a male caregiver at a child-care center may offer a child his or her only experience with a male in a nurturant role.[54] To make up your own mind about the advantages and disadvantages of group child care visit local facilities, consult one of the recently published child-care guidebooks,[55] or contact your local Day Care Council for information or referrals.

I do not believe that institutionalized child care is the only answer to work–family conflicts; but I believe the option must be available to families whenever they cannot manage alone. I also favor the promotion of other options. Two or three children of working parents can be cared for by a full-time homemaker who already is watching her or his own youngster, or by a team of senior citizens who offer diverse skills (and who can spell each other when one is exhausted), or by a live-in college student in return for room and board, or by responsible teenagers who might be paid the minimum wage to pick up young children after school and be their companion until parents get home.

Although many children do just fine, and even enjoy coming home to an empty house, one study found that "latchkey" kids have more nightmares and greater fears than supervised children. Profiles of some of the victims of Atlanta's child murders indicate that they were from single-parent families whose parents worked nights. Since recreational centers had been closed by the city in austerity moves, the children had no place to go after school.[56] In the absence of afterschool centers, apartment houses can convert empty basements into supervised group playrooms; communities can organize a network of households that display an "open house" sticker to designate a safe harbor for any child who feels threatened on the streets or for kids whose regular babysitter is temporarily unavailable. Other stay-home people can give their phone numbers to children as contact points to relieve the anxiety of working parents who are not permitted to take or make personal phone calls on the job.

Why am I making such a fuss about child care? Because it seems to epitomize the central issues raised in this book. The split between love and power—or between love and work—allows most men, whether legislators, economists, employment specialists, or fathers, to ignore the problem of caring for children. Children are lumped into the love sphere, the female sphere. Therefore, few men ever experience the direct *connection between the responsibilities of love and depletion of power.* In *Kramer vs. Kramer,* the career drive of an advertising up-and-comer hit a brick wall when the needs of his five-year-old had to come first. Work–family conflicts— the trade-offs of your money or your life, your job or your child—would not be forced upon women with such sanguine disregard if men experienced the same career stalls caused by the-buck-stops-here responsibility for children. Children would be better off if the *care* aspect of life were not so relentlessly privatized and feminized. In sum, child care is an employment issue *and* a family issue, not "just" a women's issue. Child care is an issue of power as well as love.

HOW THE IDEOLOGY OF CHILD CARE MUST CHANGE

To answer right-wing critics and clarify why child care is our *collective* responsibility, I like to bring up the subject of public roads. Most public roads are paved, well-lit, clearly marked with printed signs, traffic signals, painted lines, and safety zones. To use the roadways, streets, parkways, thruways, highways, and freeways of this nation, you need no special papers: A car with Connecticut or California plates is as entitled to travel the Massachusetts Turnpike as a car registered in Boston. You don't have to be rich. Most roads are free and where a toll is charged, it is not prohibitive. You don't have to be poor either, despite the fact that roads (like welfare) are financed with public funds.

Many people who worry about energy depletion and pollution support public transit over private cars yet they pay for these highways. Not every American owns an automobile, drives to work, makes a living in trucking or takes vacations in a camper yet the nation's roads are there for them and all of us when we need them. Our roads attest to a democracy's commitment to open access, interstate reciprocity, and improved quality of life for all.

In the same spirit, a nation that recognizes its obligation to help people get their cars or trucks from place to place without undue cost or hardship should be willing to help people get their children from infancy to school age without undue cost or hardship. Many people could not get to work each day without roads, and many cannot work at all without reliable care for their children.

Just as one needs no means test to qualify for entry onto roads built with public funds, need should not be the criterion for a child to enter a publicly funded child-care center. If there were enough spaces for every child, preschool education would be seen as essential developmental stimulation and about as "sovietized" as kindergarten or first grade. Peer socialization would be considered family enrichment for all, not a handout for the poor. One should not have to be rich to afford adequate child care, although some centers (like some roads) might charge a token fee (toll) to finance improvement of their facilities or equipment. No one asks you if you plan to use a road yourself before taking your taxes for "public works." Who cares if you or I get around on foot, by train, or if we are teamsters or chauffeurs? Roads are not matters of personal privilege but of public good.

Similarly, child care is a public good deserving our tax support whether we have six children or none, whether our kids are under five or over twenty-one, whether we choose to send our toddlers to a private nursery school with a tuition as high as Harvard's, or keep them at home. No parent should be unable to work for fear of leaving a child unsupervised, and no child should slip between the cracks because a place and a person cannot be found to love and watch over her or him. Child-care centers, like roads, should be there for us when we need them. A strong child care network would attest to our democratic commitment to open access, interfamily reciprocity, and an improved quality of life for all.

If we can do it for cars, we can do it for kids.

HOW THE WORKPLACE MUST CHANGE

In addition to child-care services, there are workplace innovations that would make it easier for parents to keep love and work integrated. These are not off-the-wall dreams but reasonable alterations in the way offices, stores, factories, and service organizations function, and most have already proved effective someplace in the country. Because each has been embellished and cost-analyzed elsewhere,[57] I present them here as a brief blueprint for change in the hope that activist readers will target one or more ideas for their own workplace.

Flexible Schedules. Under "flexitime," all employees must be at work during a "core period" but may arrive and leave when convenient as long as they fulfill a weekly total. This flexibility allows parents to spend more time with their children before and after school. It also saves the time usually wasted in rush-hour commuting, and facilitates doing family errands during merchants' business hours. The hitch: studies show that men use flexitime to add to their leisure; women use it to do more family chores.[58] (See Chapter Seven.)

Part-time Work. A sixteen to thirty-two-hour permanent part-time work week suits many parents and should not be considered solely a working *mother's* option. At present, more than 20 percent of all workers are part-timers. Experience shows that they are less prone to unemployment. However, they also receive less frequent salary increases.[59] It is essential that part-timers be taken seriously as workers and that they receive pro-rated retirement, insurance, health, and vacation benefits.

For management, the advantage of part-time workers is reduced overtime and absenteeism and higher productivity.[60] For the good of both workers and management, part-time work could be supplemented with take-home work in such areas as research, writing, planning, bookkeeping, or computer technology on a small scale.

Compressed Work Weeks. In 1980, nearly two million workers chose to gain free time by working four ten-hour days or three twelve-hour days instead of the "normal" five-day week.[61] Since the definition of "normal" presupposed male workers with wives at home cooking dinner and watching the kids, normal isn't necessarily normal anymore.

Job Sharing. When two workers share one position, they increase their flexibility 100 percent. They can switch time slots or cover for each other in emergencies with no loss of pay or efficiency. Bank tellers, clergy, teachers, social workers, copywriters, bus drivers, journalists, engineers, city planners, and factory workers are among the growing tribe of job-sharers. Advantages for employers: Because people working four hours put out at the top of their energy level, they tend to be more productive, doing up to 80 percent of the job in 50 percent of the time.[62]

Drawbacks for employees: Some companies fail to recognize job-sharers' career dedication; it is hard to promote one job-sharer but not the other; many single parents cannot exist on partial income and benefits.

Cafeteria-style Benefit Plans. Since benefits can account for up to 30 percent of your compensation,[63] why shouldn't you be able to choose only what you and your family need? For instance, if you are covered by your spouse's medical insurance, you might take full life insurance instead. If you have young children, you could elect orthodonture coverage and relinquish some retirement money. If you are putting a child through college, you might trade vacation time for cash.

In one survey,[64] only 8 percent of companies said they offer cafeteria benefits, but 62 percent said they favor the idea because it is cheaper for employers to pay for only what each employee requires instead of providing to everyone what is wanted by just a few.

Alternatives to Layoffs. Since women (and minority men) were often the last to be hired in certain occupations, they're the first to be fired when layoffs become necessary. This may be fair on seniority grounds, but it is unfair in that it perpetuates past discrimination and has a disparate impact on single-parent families who need the work the most.

Rather than fire senior workers *or* vulnerable new groups, employers should explore alternatives, such as early retire-

ment bonuses, natural attrition, and work-sharing. Almost anything is better than layoffs when families are home waiting
for a paycheck.

Due to the cultural primacy of the male breadwinner,
unemployment used to produce more psychological distress
in husbands than in wives,[65] but recent studies indicate that
being without a job is "about as traumatic an experience for
women who are in the labor force as it is for men,"[66] and
we've already mentioned the deleterious effects of parental
joblessness on children.

Transfer Policies. Of the great many employees trans-
ferred each year, more than a fifth of those with working
spouses are reluctant to relocate.[67] Corporations can help
spouses find new jobs when their wives or husbands are trans-
ferred as well as easing the move with salary boosts, reimburse-
ment of travel and moving expenses, and psychological counseling. Company policies in these areas vary considerably at
present.[68]

Should all enticements fail, the employee must suffer no
career forfeiture for deciding to reject the transfer. Not everyone has to move onward and upward.

Nepotism Revised. Family relations should carry neither
privilege nor penalty. Some companies consider employees
who are married to each other to be "a corporate time bomb"
if their jobs involve trade secrets, bidding for work, competition for clients or sales, or insider trading information.[69] Although it is legal to ban the employment of two mates, it is
not rational. Can anyone prove husbands and wives are less
trustworthy or more easily corruptible than two best friends
working for the same company?

Parental Leaves. Besides maternity leave for childbirth,
which now averages six to eight weeks,[70] employers should
give mothers *and* fathers time for a childrearing head start
with a newborn or adopted child. In Sweden, all new parents
are entitled to up to nine months off at 90 percent of their
pay, continued vesting in pension and health plans, and guaranteed reinstatement to the same or a comparable job. Swedish government and business leaders recognize that early intimacy and parent–child bonding are good for Sweden, that

it pays off in worker loyalty and happier, better members of society. In the United States, fewer than one in ten companies gives paternity leaves. As far as I know, the most generous employer is the Ford Foundation which offers its employees eight paid and eighteen unpaid weeks of child-care leave.

Working parents should also be able to take paid sick leave and personal days in full- or half-day units to care for a sick child. (In Sweden, parental insurance replaces wages for up to sixty days' absence per child per illness *or* per illness of the child's usual caregiver.)

Employer-sponsored Child Care. During World War II, when industry needed women workers, hundreds of companies operated showplace child-care centers and women brought their children to work. Today, such facilities exist at some twenty corporations, one hundred hospitals, two hundred military installations, and at least one suburban office park complex.[71] Now that sponsors (whether one company or a consortium of employers) can get tax credit for child-care-center construction and operating expenses, such services should be commonplace either on-site or off. (If the center is at the workplace, children must be picked up on days when their parents are too sick to go to work.)

If full-scale centers are not feasible, companies should maintain recreation facilities for afterschool hours and school vacations staffed by teachers who want to earn extra money after work. Small firms, such as doctors' offices, should allow employees to bring babies to work when regular child-care arrangements collapse.

Child-care services should be available to working parents within the cafeteria-style benefit program, or partly subsidized by the employer and partly paid by the employee on a sliding-fee scale pegged to income. And all companies should reimburse employees for child-care expenses incurred while they are away from home on business.

Given American values, the best motive for establishing corporate child-care centers is the profit motive. The center operated by a Texas medical equipment manufacturer, for example, charges fifteen dollars per week per child, is open 6:30 A.M. to 6:00 P.M. for infants through age six, and is utilized by the children of janitors and executives alike. The center has reduced labor turnover by 23 percent, saved fifteen thousand hours in absenteeism, and helped the company attract the largest pool of qualified applicants it has ever had.[72]

Instead of or in addition to a child care center, employers can sponsor a "Section 129 Plan" (named after Section 129 of the Internal Revenue Code), to which workers may contribute a portion of their salary on a *pre-tax* basis. This tax-saving plan then reimburses the workers' child care costs, up to 100 percent of those costs. If your employer sponsors such a plan, you can contribute an amount up to the lower of the earned incomes in your family—yours or your spouse's. Suppose you earn $20,000, your spouse earns $15,000, and child care services cost your family $5000 annually. With a Section 129 plan, you could contribute $5000, have an adjusted gross income of $15,000, subtract two exemptions, and pay Federal taxes on only $13,000. Your employer also saves Social Security taxes which it pays on your lowered adjusted gross income.

Parenthood Seminars. Exxon, Bankers Trust, Texas Commerce Bank, Philip Morris and American Express are among the companies that have begun sponsoring parent education courses, on company time, to help employees learn to balance their family and work more effectively. Corporate officers as well as clerks find they often share the same parenting strains—from difficulty leaving a youngster in the morning to problems decompressing after a day's work—and the opportunity to learn from each other, as well as from the seminar leader, relieves much of the stress.[73]

If we really cared about families—not the patriarchal construct but the *people* in families—such people-pleasing workplace innovations as those described would be as sacrosanct as a cost-of-living increase. Employers would understand that they can help families in two ways: by giving us money *and* by giving us time. In one major study, nearly half of all parents queried said they would sacrifice earnings for more family time.[74] Because of the time their work demands, 70 percent of women executives in another study said they are not having children and 63 percent said they have to sacrifice their marriages, friendships, and leisure.[75] Why should we always have to *sacrifice?*

7

Just Housework

Cleaning your house while your kids
are still growing,
Is like shoveling the walk before
it stops snowing

Phyllis Diller's
Housekeeping Hints

Housekeeping ain't no joke.

Little Women
Louisa May Alcott

ON THE ONE HAND, housework *is* a joke, because the tasks involved are considered trivial. Other jobs may offer morbid comedy material—such as undertaker and sanitation worker—or suggest sexual double entendres—such as nurse, doctor, psychiatrist, or stewardess—but they are acknowledged to be *real* jobs that just happen to have the potential for funny side-effects. Only the housewife is intrinsically silly because her labor isn't seen as real work. Not only are all women supposed to be born equipped to do it, but how demanding could it be if housewives have time for soap operas, coffee klatches, romance novels, being bored, secret drinking, and the latest dirty joke—housewife prostitution rings?

People laugh at a woman who is inept at housework because housework is supposed to "come natural" to a woman. God, it's the *least* she can do. Men who do housework well can't be *real* men, therefore they are funny, like Felix, the neat partner of *The Odd Couple*. In cartoons and TV commercials, men shown doing housework almost invariably do it badly. That's funny the way Albert Einstein's failing arithmetic is funny: Housework is the only activity at which men are allowed to be consistently inept because they are thought to be so competent at everything else. For a man to be "all thumbs" sewing on a shirt button is safely "masculine" comedy.

On the other hand, Louisa May Alcott was right. "Housework ain't no joke." In fact, polls and studies suggest *it is the major source of family arguments be-*

tween parents and children,[1] *and the primary cause of domestic violence.*[2] Conflicts related to cooking, cleaning, and home repairs more often lead to physical abuse between spouses than do conflicts about sex, social activities, money, or children.

A refusal to do housework signals feminist rebellion for women, and resistance to "women's liberation" for men. As for children, the little ones want to clean and cook to prove they're grown up, and the older ones refuse to clean and cook—also to prove they're grown up. More than a third of all parents of children over six complain about their offspring's not doing chores.[3]

When a housewife takes a paying job, getting someone else to do housework is a financial problem. For the single parent or two working parents, finding time to do housework is a logistical problem. The full-time housewife feels defensive because so many women have abandoned housework for paid work. The wage-earning wife feels overwhelmed because she puts in a "double day"—on the job and then at home.

To conservatives, the traditional housewife—a woman serving her man and children—is a political symbol, a glorified archetype in their pantheon of Good Americans. To radical economists, housework confounds their critique of capitalism until it is seen as the one form of labor linked both to production and reproduction. To progressives, especially couples committed to egalitarian family life, housework is the last battleground for equity.

In all, we are dealing with a deadly serious subject whose ramifications, elaborated recently in three comprehensive books,[4] are practical, economic, psychological, and ideological. Perhaps more than any other issue of family politics, apart from abortion and pregnancy, housework is that "intimate frontier" on which love and power are equally coercive.

TIME: WHOSE WORK IS NEVER DONE?

A hundred years ago, workers spent about 45 percent of their lives on the job; today the figure is 15 percent.[5] What do we do with the other 85 percent of our time? Some of it, of course, is spent in childhood, adolescence, and old age; the rest, presumably, in sleep, leisure activities, studies, sports, hobbies—and housework.

Heidi I. Hartmann, a staff member of the National Research Council of the National Academy of Sciences, says, "Time spent on housework [is] a measure of power relations in the home."[6] Obviously, in the single-parent family, what is gained by being able to make independent decisions is lost in having no other adult with whom to share the housework— or even fight about it. However, in two-adult homes, the way housework time is allocated tells us something important about who exercises power—power over free time and free labor, if nothing else. Here's what the studies show:

• In homes where the wife is not employed, the average total time spent doing housework each day is eleven hours and six minutes (less for childless couples; more for very large families).[7]

• In homes where the wife *is* employed, the total time spent on housework averages eight hours and 42 minutes per day, more or less depending on number of kids.

Within these totals, how much housework time is contributed by women, men, and children?

• Women who are homemakers spend more than eight hours per day on house and family work.[8]

• Women who are employed spend just under five hours on house and family work.

• Men spend about an hour and a half a day on house and family work *whether their wives are homemakers or employed.*[9]

• Children spend about as much time on housework as do men.

In other words, on the average wives do 70 percent of the housework while husbands and children each do 15 percent.

Dr. Lenora Cole Alexander, director of the U.S. Labor Department's Women's Bureau, elicited groans from the audience at a conference on "Women, Work and the Family" when she reported that although more than half of all married couples are dual wage-earners, only about one couple in ten shares the housework. Is it fair or just that women assist men with a large part of their formerly exclusive provider role but men do not assist women in what remains their mostly exclusive housekeeper role? Clearly it's not fair, but injustice tends to persist when it is to the advantage of one group to perpetuate it. In terms of housework, most men's paltry time contribution is a measure of the disagreeable nature of most housework, and of men's continuing power to consign disagreeable tasks to women.

A nationwide marketing survey[10] identified four groups of husbands:

• Those who believe in the traditional division of labor and do not help around the house (39 percent)

• Those who believe the man should help but whose actions suggest they do not follow through (33 percent)

• Those who have ambivalent attitudes but say they do help with the housework (15 percent)

• Those who regularly perform household chores and have little difficulty adjusting to the role (13 percent)

If this survey is accurate, nearly three out of four American husbands either do nothing or barely lift a finger. And if so, Heidi Hartmann may be right in her suspicion that husbands constitute a "net drain on the family resources . . . that is, husbands may require more housework than they contribute." She makes the case from another direction: A single mother with two children spends considerably *less* time on housework than a woman with one child and one husband. The difference—about eight fewer hours a week—"could be interpreted as the amount of increased housework caused by the husband's presence."[11]

Off the beaten research track, Sheila Kamerman, Columbia University family policy expert, has found a small trend "toward increased sharing and role equity in the home."[12] And Joseph H. Pleck, of the Wellesley College Center for Research on Women, has identified complex issues such as wives' resistence to husbands' household help, the effect of husbands' involvement on marital satisfaction, and the impact of increased father care on children's sex role conditioning.[13] When studies show a decrease in employed women's housework time, says Pleck, it is usually not because their husbands are doing more but because the women are doing less, either as a result of greater career commitment or smaller family size and thus less time needed for preschool child care, or because of reduced housekeeping standards and more reliance on convenience foods.

Moreover, virtually every time study has found widespread evidence of the traditional sex role division of labor whether the woman is employed or not. "It is still the mother who does the shopping, prepares the meals, cleans the house, takes the children for check-ups and stays home when the children are sick," and it is still Dad who takes care of the car, home repairs, and yard work.[14] Although one study found no variation in this housework behavior among minorities, Harriette P. McAdoo of Howard University says she sees more sharing and fewer sex-typed roles in black two-career families.[15]

I was intrigued by yet another marketing survey[16] in which a thousand married men (half married to employed women) made these claims:

- 70 percent cook

- 56 percent help with major grocery shopping

- 47 percent vacuum floors

- 41 percent wash dishes

The survey does not say whether men cook, vacuum, and wash at the direction of their wives or whether they assume primary responsibility for these chores. It doesn't say what the men mean by "cook." Are they slicing tomatoes while their wives turn out four-course feasts, or are they producing a full meal solo or side-by-side? When 47 percent of the husbands say they vacuum, does that mean they do all the floors all the time? When they say they "help" or "wash dishes" is that every day, often, sometimes, or on Mother's Day?

In my experience, most men cannot find in their own kitchen what most women can find in a stranger's kitchen. Kitchens are not yet male psychic turf. I remember reading a report of The American Home Economics Association to the effect that men married to homemakers spend six minutes per day in the kitchen; men with employed wives spend twelve minutes. In 1982, nearly one in four supermarket shoppers was a man, but of the married men in the previously mentioned study, 75 percent who went marketing *used a shopping list prepared by their wives.*[17]

Housework is physical and mental, personal and political. Doing it is one burden; *remembering* what must be done is another. Both doing and remembering housework take one away from other things, therefore housework is not trivial; it steals one's life. That is why most women are not content to have men "help" in the doing. The buck stops with the one who makes the shopping list, the one who says "It is my *job* to remember."

THE PSYCHODYNAMICS OF HOUSEWORK

It is a proud moment in a woman's life to reign supreme within four walls, to be the one to whom all questions of domestic pleasure and economy are referred.

—*Elizabeth Cady Stanton*[18]

Few tasks are more like the torture of Sisyphus than housework with its endless repetition: the clean becomes soiled, the soiled is made clean, over and over, day after day. The housewife wears herself out marking time: she makes nothing, she simply perpetuates the present.

—*Simone de Beauvoir*[19]

I have too many fantasies to be a housewife.

—*Marilyn Monroe*[20]

Viciousness in the kitchen!

—*Sylvia Plath*[21]

Women's feelings about housework are as varied and self-disclosing as a Rorshach test. The "glad housewife"[22] revels in solitude, cherishes her self-directed work schedule, her "long-simmering soups," and the feeling of pleasing others. The "sad housewife" experiences solitude as "loneliness," housework as "monotony," and her schedule as "fragmentation."[23] (Some homemakers suffer from agoraphobia, otherwise called "housewife's disease," "the trauma of eventlessness," or fear of leaving the house.[24]) The "mad housewife"— immortalized by novelist Sue Kaufman,[25] described by de Beauvoir as "angry," "manic," "harsh," "distracted and disfigured by cares," and by Freud as "hysterical,"—is mad because *she* wants a wife.[26] The mad housewife is Sylvia Plath's purveyor of viciousness or Marge Piercy's angry women in Peoria, Providence, Big Sur, and Dallas, who burn dinner in silent revenge for what has become of their lives.[27]

What accounts for these divergent approaches to housework? First, *personal preference:* Some people love to putter with sauces and spices, others cook just to eat; one friend looks forward to shining silver, another gave away her sterling service for twelve rather than mount one more assault on the tarnish.

Second, we have to take into account *material conditions:* Does the housekeeper have enough money to run the house? Access to basic appliances, such as a washing machine or, for a large family, a dishwasher? The health and strength for the physical labor? Enough time to do the job?

Third, a woman's psychological attitude toward housework depends on how much she has internalized traditional *sex role ideology.* When marriage pronounces a couple "man and wife," he is pronounced a person and she, a role. Actually, she's been rehearsing for her role since childhood. Our culture surrounds every little girl with toy dishes, dolls, and mini-mops just to be sure she knows it is her destiny to feed and care for others. Advertising continues the brainwashing: A stained sink is evidence of failed femininity, "good coffee is grounds for marriage," bad coffee will drive a husband to refuse his wife's brew but take a second cup "from another woman's pot." Guilt, inadequacy, and competitive social rituals bully women into domesticity. It makes you wonder: If women's role is so "natural," why must girls be so relentlessly programmed to do it?

Does the glad housewife enjoy housework because she's *supposed* to? Barbara Ehrenreich speculates that some women do not use housework to fulfill the "feminine" role, but to subvert it: Compulsive housecleaning allows a woman to retreat from family members' more demanding personal services. "Can't you see I'm trying to (wax this floor, vacuum the rug, clean the windows)? You'll just have to get (some apple juice, a beer, your left sneaker) yourself."[28] Is she unconsciously competing with her neighbors for Best Wife Award, or proving to *her* mother that she too can keep a nice house? Does she equate a "nice house" with a "good girl"? Is she intimidated by the housewives on TV?

Televised Housework. The more people watch TV, the more they tend to accept sex role stereotypes as reality.[29] Since housewives can watch television while they do their chores, it's no surprise that up to 58 percent of daytime viewers are women. And what they're seeing, for instance in TV commercials,—and accepting as reality—are three restrictive female roles:[30]

1. maternal care of the family—"preparing and serving meals, grocery shopping, laundry, child care, and care of pets."

2. housekeeping care of the dwelling, furniture, and equipment—"mopping and waxing floors, dishwashing, dusting, vacuuming, oven cleaning and toilet bowl cleaning." (At night, when many more men are watching, housekeeping commercials drop to 10 percent of the total, so men get few TV reminders of all the work to be done around the house.)

3. aesthetic care of herself—feminine hygiene, soap, shampoo, make-up, and so on.

Notice in all three roles, the emphasis is on *care*. Care is the quintessential female activity. The wife cares for everyone (and for her own attractiveness), and in return her husband "takes care" of her. Oddly enough, all this caregiving does not make women experts even at female specialties. Housekeeping commercials show men "demonstrating to naive women technological products such as dishwashers or scientifi-

cally developed cleansing agents." Men are the authoritative
salespersons, repairmen, technical experts, and announcer
voices reassuring the housewife at home that product X will
make her better at her job. If all the men shown *teaching*
women housework ever actually *did* housework, we would
be halfway to equality.

Most curiously, say researchers, children in commercials
are almost never seen performing household chores. "Children appear to exist primarily to be fed and doctored, get
their clothes muddy, and dirty up the house. There is little
indication of parent-child interaction, except in mothers' services to small children."[31]

The family image that results is not a cohesive, participa-
tory social unit but a bunch of atomized, demanding individuals who are served and serviced by the woman of the house.
Because of such potent and insistent commercial messages,
many women are trapped in a sex role prison that denies
parole on the grounds of ring around the collar.

The Power of Power. Finally, women's attitudes toward
housework depend most of all on what one might call "the
power quotient"—whether or not a person feels some control
over her circumstances.

The mad housewife is mad because she resents her economic dependence or feels otherwise powerless to operate
freely in her environment. She experiences her role as subordinate to her mate's by virtue of some unseen authority: "It
seems like I do everything. It's just taken for granted that
I'm supposed to get it all done—as if it were natural."[32] The
mad housewife senses she is living vicariously for and through
her husband and children. The sad housewife suffers from
"the problem that has no name."[33] Her powerlessness is felt
as victimization. She is the one to whom everyone turns for
service and succor. Being needed in this way doesn't make
her feel powerful; it makes her feel oppressed.

The glad housewife is glad because the power quotient
registers positively for her. Whether she can buy household
help or does everything herself, she feels she's her own boss
and runs her own shop. To some degree, power and autonomy
can compensate for economic dependency. In traditional fam-

ilies, the sex role division of labor "rewards" the housewife with a *separate sphere* in which she operates without supervision. Psychologically, the glad housewife, as Elizabeth Cady Stanton put it, feels she "reigns supreme" if she is given control over the children, the money the husband brings home (or the welfare check), the way the house is organized, and the interplay among the family, church, school, and community.

Some housewives are "grateful" for whatever "help" they get from their husbands, since they believe housework, by rights, is not a man's responsibility. Others are happy having a husband who is largely absent from the home, one who works long hours or steers clear of domestic matters. Although the traditional housewife accepts the husband as her ultimate authority, explains sociologist Rose L. Cozer, "in an authoritarian relationship, the one thing that is worse than a nonparticipating husband is a meddling husband." Like any worker subject to a boss, the traditional housewife benefits when she cannot be observed and commanded. Therefore, says Cozer, keeping housework a distinct female separate sphere "increases her freedom and diminishes her husband's control."[34]

All of which leads to a conclusion less dour and more exciting than perhaps anticipated: *Both the politics and the psychodynamics of housework have the capacity to radicalize women.* Isolated nuclear-family housework often deadens the spirit, but it can also give the sad housewife time to think, read, organize. The glad housewife who knows the satisfactions of autonomy in her sphere can logically extrapolate to other settings in which she might be similarly rewarded. And the mad housewife who experiences her powerlessness red hot and clear, and is not lulled by compensatory household authority, can proceed headlong into rebellion.

It is no accident then that the current wave of feminist consciousness is striving to make housework a solidarity issue across lines of class and race. *Other than our biological sisterhood, housework is the one utterly shared phenomenon of the female condition,* not only in this country but around the world. Almost all women have known housewifely responsibility for dirt, meals, and/or children, and housewifely feelings of being overburdened, unappreciated, continuously interrupted, and physically exhausted. Even with hired help, the wife and not the husband usually assumes responsibility for hiring, firing, supplies and work assignments, of the household employee. The "maid" is not said to be doing *the work of the family,* she is seen as a housewife-substitute.

Why can't housework shed its feminine gender? Why can't women get their *heads* out of housework even when their hands are free? Why can't we just divide housework between women and men and be done with it?

The simplest answer lies in male psychology and men's power to keep things as they are.

Housework and the Man Problem

> Few problems confronting women . . . could not be solved
> if one were willing to create a whole host of difficulties for men.
>
> —*Eli Ginzburg*
> Columbia University

> Housework is the hardest work in the world. That's why men won't do it.
>
> —*Edna Ferber*
> So Big

My husband can never understand why so many men insist that their wives stay home and serve them and thus become the kind of dull, harassed drudges that the men never would have married in the first place. After transforming his bright young bride into a matronly household servant, the guy leaves her because he says he's "outgrown" her. Yet it never occurs to him to share the drudgery and thus also share the growth when drudgery is done.

None of it makes sense. In her study of working-class attitudes, Lillian Rubin asked, "Whose life would you say is easier—a man's or a woman's?" Most men thought men's lives are harder than women's. Yet no man wanted to change places with his wife.

"I couldn't stand being home every day, taking care of the house or sick kids or stuff like that. But that's because

I'm a man. Men aren't supposed to do things like that,
but it's what women are supposed to be doing. It's natural
for them, so they don't mind it."[35]

In response, Rubin comments: "Few women would agree
that they 'don't mind it.' They may believe it's their job, and
it's what they *ought* to want to do. They may be frightened
at the thought of having to support a family; they may even
prefer the tasks of housewifery to a job once held that was
dull and constricting. But no woman reacts with repugnance
to the idea of changing places with her husband."

Among middle-class males, nearly 60 percent of teenage
boys and 35 percent of adult men said they think homemaking
has more advantages than other jobs, but only 22 percent
of the boys and 10 percent of the men would want to *be*
homemakers if they had enough money to choose any job
in the world.[36]

Male resistance to housework is not restricted to any particular age group, economic class, or political persuasion. In
her now classic essay, "The Politics of Housework,"[37] Pat Mainardi analyzes the behavior of radical, progressive men who
claim to prefer "liberated women," but who evade housework
as insistently as any male chauvinist.

Because they lack the sex role brainwashing that trains
women to tolerate service and drudgery, Mainardi says all
men "recognize the essential fact of housework right from
the very beginning. Which is that it stinks." Instead of citing
politically "incorrect" sexist arguments about housework being women's work, more sophisticated men trot out ultrara-
tional excuses: housework is too trivial to argue about, you
do it better anyway, show me how and I'll do it, answer a
million questions about it and I'll do it, our standards are different, you won't like my style, I hate it more than you do, how
can I accomplish great things if I have to do housework, et
cetera and so on, each line delivered with the impatience
of a headmaster lecturing a dimwitted student.

Taking dead aim, Mainardi tells the housewife: "The measure of your oppression is his resistance."

Here is how that resistance might develop when an aver-

age traditional man is confronted with his wife's request that
he take more responsibility with the housework:

He says he's set in his ways and too old to change now.
She says anyone flexible enough to have gone from a crewcut
to flowing hair and a full beard is capable of making other
kinds of adjustments, such as hanging up his own clothes, or
figuring out how to get a dirty four-year-old clean.

He says she married him knowing the way he is; she
agreed to become his wife under those conditions and she
can't change the rules in the middle of the game. She says
people grow, their needs change. That's why ballplayers rene-
gotiate their contracts. That's why constitutions have amendments.

He asks her to be "normal" like Margie, Sue, or Helen
instead of getting off on this "women's lib" stuff. She tells
him Margie is having an affair, Sue is saving up to leave her
husband, Helen is a closet lesbian and anyway, none of them
is living with him. What's more, after all these years, how
dare he slap her with a label, or compare her to the neighbors.

He says if trying to make her happy is just going to make
him unhappy, the two of them will be no better off. She answers that she can't believe ironing his own shirts will put
him in despair, but in any event, if someone has to be the
happier partner, by now it's her turn.

He says he *could* do a lot of the things she does around
the house, but since she does them so much better it would
be inefficient for him to take over. She says efficiency hasn't
been her favorite criterion since Mussolini made the trains
run on time; however, she'll be glad to teach him all her
techniques and she'll be patient while he makes mistakes.

He guesses *anyone* can learn to measure fabric softener
and fold towels. Sure he'll pitch in if his doing the laundry
gives her extra time to be with the kids, but not if she's just
going to "fritter away" those hours. She says that what women
need most is time for themselves; she wants uninterrupted
time that belongs only to her.

He says fine, she can sit around and daydream, get a job
God bless her, go back to school, start her own business. Whatever makes her happy is okay with him—as long as one, she's

got dinner ready when *he* comes home from work; two, she's available to go away with him on *his* business trips; and three, her activities don't embarrass him.

He ends this speech with the three words overwrought women hate most: "What's for dinner?" She says, "I don't know, what are *you* making?" And finally, she says, if he will not change his behavior, she will change her address—in other words, move out.

The debate fires up on economic issues. He says he earns the money, dammit; when she supports the family, then she can come back to him with her bill of particulars. She says he wouldn't be able to work and prosper if she didn't manage the house, kids, laundry, meals, and social life. He says she's certainly making a big fuss over a simple division of labor. She answers, if he was living with a male roommate, would he tell the roommate to do the cleaning, cooking, shopping, and washing while he took charge of an occasional leaky faucet, put up the storm windows, and conquered the crabgrass? Would he argue for a division of labor based on his roommate's size, height, or paycheck—or wouldn't he be fair and split the chores down the middle. As his female roommate, she asks no more.

And so it goes until compromise ends and intransigence sets in. Which propels her to move from talk to action. She starts doing things, or she stops doing things, as the case may be. Let's say she stops picking up his socks from the spot where he has dropped them nightly for nineteen years. Or she leaves the house for evening school without first putting a roast in the oven and taping the kids' bedtime instructions to the bathroom mirror. She stops keeping track of his dental appointments. Or starts leaving the babysitter arrangements up to him. Whatever it is, her actions feel dangerous to her because they *are*. Every move is a challenge to the balance of power: She is profaning the divine right of kings; she is making a revolution.

Men's oppression of women in housework, in reproduction, and in the labor market are connected by the sinews of patriarchal politics. All these oppressions ensure women's powerlessness by keeping women dependent on men. Heidi Hartmann explains:

> Dependence is simultaneously a psychological and political-economic relationship. Male-dominated trade unions and professional associations, for example, have excluded women from skilled employment and reduced their opportunities to support themselves. The denial of abortions to women similarly reinforces women's dependence on men. . . . Their control of women's labor power is the lever that allows men to benefit from women's provision of personal and household services, including relief from childrearing and many unpleasant tasks. . . . Patriarchy's material base is men's control of women's labor, both in the household and in the labor market; the division of labor by gender tends to benefit men.[38]

Okay, the men problem makes sense on a genderwide basis in that *all* men benefit from *all* women's free labor at home and cheap labor in the marketplace. But it still doesn't make sense for each *individual* man to prefer that his wife serve him at home if she could be earning for them both outside the home. (Nor does it make sense for him to tolerate job-market sex segregation and low female wages if those conditions penalize *his* wife when she does get a job.) None of it makes sense until we acknowledge three simple but crucial facts:

1. how very pleasant and habit-forming it can be to receive personal services at your convenience

2. how intensely someone can hate the unrelieved mess of housework, especially if he is unaccustomed to doing it

3. how much power men would lose if women were no longer dependent upon them

The underlying point is, men do not want to do housework because in our society *a man's maleness is compromised both by his having to do "women's work," and by his not having a woman doing it for him.* Thorsten Veblen put it this way in 1899:[39] A man gains status from the "conspicuous consumption" of a woman's labor time in the service of his needs. Conversely, a man loses status (or social "masculinity") when his woman's household work is reduced. This would explain why male science and technology are relatively uninterested in devising ways to increase household labor efficiency. (A simple change such as larger capacity dishwashers, for instance. If dishes never had to be put away in the cupboard at all, it would mean a saving of many hours of labor per month.) Throughout American history, men have ensured their hegemony by re-emphasizing women's family functions, not relieving them. Ann R. Markusen of the University of California, Berkeley, contends that this lack of interest in household efficiency reinforces the illusion that only men do *real* work requiring the attention of technology. Further, says Markusen, for a man in a patriarchal household, the personal service of a wife who tailors family activities to the husband's needs, a wife who is flexible about scheduling meals, provides home-cooked food and handmade amenities, may outweigh all considerations of efficient labor.[40]

The average man's conscious resistance to the inconveniences of doing housework is buttressed by an unconscious resistance that originates in the psychoplasm of his boyhood. By age three or four he learned that certain tasks are "appropriate" to his sex and doing them well makes him a "real boy," while certain tasks are not, and doing them well makes him a "sissy." This sex-role imperative is impressed upon him by parents, peers, teachers, children's books, and television, which sex-type his toys (trucks, yes; dolls, no), his fantasy play ("boys can't be nurses"), his emotions ("big boys don't cry"), his interests (math, yes; poetry, no), and his participation in housework ("help Daddy take out the garbage while Sister sets the table").

Researchers studying adults' responses to domestic space—to their own living rooms, kitchens, and so on—attribute men's attitudes to their early sex-role training.[41] In this study, more men than women mentioned features of home design, building, and decoration, suggesting an attempt, say the scientists, "to achieve power and mastery over an environment from which they normally disenfranchise themselves. It is the language of participation through control," and it recalls children's play activities in which boys are introduced to "the manly trades of engineering, mathematics, and design through experience with building blocks." With respect to the kitchen, women mentioned cooking, washing, and tidiness, while men more often mentioned *eating*. The researchers concluded that men experience the kitchen as an area of satisfaction and pleasure; for women it is a job site.

The man problem becomes a family problem when it telegraphs those same sex role imperatives to children. Despite strides in feminist consciousness and nonsexist education, more than six out of ten children still think "it's the mother's job and not the father's to cook and clean."[42] Children will not believe otherwise until they see fathers doing their share around the house.

Housework as Family Work

With grease and with grime from corner to center,
Forever at war and forever alert,
No rest for a day lest the enemy enter,
I spend my whole life in a struggle with dirt.
CHORUS: *Oh, life is a toil and love is a trouble*
Beauty will fade and riches will flee,
Pleasures they dwindle and prices they double,
And nothing is as I would wish it to be.

—*The Housewife's Lament*
(folksong)

Let's face it. Just because great love and interdependence exist within families doesn't mean there is always, in Hartmann's words, "a unity of interests." And when conflict centers on the "uneven responsibilities and rewards of the two sexes," the family becomes a "locus of struggle."[43]

In the conventional patriarchal family, what makes life comfortable for the man (and children) is the housework that makes life hard for the woman. Those who wax sentimental about old-fashioned Thanksgivings, for instance, are clearly not viewing the event through the eyes of the housewife who dusted from cellar to attic, made up beds for visiting relatives, went marketing five times in three days, cooked for a week, polished every glass, set the table, served the meal, cleared the table, washed the dishes, and put the house to rights again.

Holidays and every day, that cherished thing known as "family life" is purchased with a woman's time and labor. Warm family memories rest on a network of chores she accomplished, responsibilities she remembered, get-togethers she organized, messes she cleared away, rooms she made welcoming, food she cooked to please. The rest of the family adds the conversation, games, laughter, stories—the seeds of family closeness. But seeds cannot be planted unless the earth has been plowed and cultivated. Like plowing, housework makes the ground ready for the germination of family life. The kids will not invite a teacher home if beer cans litter the living room. The family isn't likely to have breakfast together if somebody didn't remember to buy eggs, milk, or muffins. Housework maintains an orderly setting in which family life can flourish.

If one person on a farm is solely responsible for all the plowing, it stands to reason that she will have a different relationship to the planting and the harvest. For one thing, she will be tired when the others are just beginning. Then too, she will feel separate and estranged for having worked alone before they got there. And, if her plowed field is taken for granted, she will be bitter.

The alternatives are obvious: Either everyone plows as well as plants so that the pleasures of the harvest are more fully shared, or an outside person is paid to do the plowing so that everyone in the family can start even, and together sow the seeds of family life.

I've described many examples of shared housework in the pages of my previous book, *Growing Up Free*. So, rather than review family sharing, I want to explore the more radical alternative to housewife oppression—professionalizing housework.

WHY NOT THE BEST?

The idea of hiring experts to perform housekeeping tasks has been disdained by both women and men with more passion than seems warranted:

Excuse #1: "Who can afford it?"

While financial limitations obviously provide a valid reason not to hire outside help, for some families it is really a matter of financial *priorities*—sexist financial priorities. A man will hire a painter because he'll be "damned if I'm going to spend my weekends on a ladder," but he "can't afford" laundry service so his wife needn't spend her weekends sorting, folding and pressing.

Excuse #2: "I would never hire some *other* woman to do my family's dirty work."

The same housewife who says this—and I've heard it time and again—does not hesitate to call the Roto-Rooter man when her family's drains are clogged. Major dirt, dirt in pipes or cesspools, can be assigned to professionals, but minor dirt— dustballs, soiled clothes, grimy floors, greasy pots—belongs to the housewife. It is her personal responsibility. It is almost her *fault*. In any case, it is private. Whereas the exterior of a house can need a paint job without shaming the man who lives inside, a pile of dirty dishes or unwashed laundry causes the housewife personal humiliation. The man of the house might be too busy to paint the house, but the woman of the house is assumed to have *only* the house on her mind. The peeling paint does not peel away the man's essential identity. The dirty dishes *do* somehow besmirch the woman's worth as a person. In fact, any family member's dirt casts a shadow on the woman of the house; she is responsible for everyone's neatness and cleanliness.

Linking a woman to her family's wastes and messes assures that she will not expose her personal decay to a stranger's eyes. (Hence the joke about cleaning for the maid.) Linking femininity to cleanliness assures that she will keep her household's imperfections to herself in order to protect her very femaleness. In other words, she will continue to do her own housework.

Excuse #3: "It's silly to pay some woman to do my housework when she'll just have to pay another woman to do hers."

Let's answer this excuse with a short trip into history. In pre-industrial America, wage labor was rare. The typical family was self-sustaining: The wife canned, cooked, made cloth, sewed, baked, and nursed the sick. The husband worked in or near the home, whether as a shopkeeper, artisan, or farmer; he also raised vegetables, chickens, and pigs, milked cows, hunted for game, shoed the horses, built the house and barn, and repaired whatever broke.

Today, the average man goes out to one job, brings home a wage, and the wage pays for products and services that replace his skills. A supermarket supplies the food he used to grow, raise, or hunt. A dairy delivers the milk he once squeezed from his cows. Cars have made his horse obsolete and an auto mechanic does his maintenance. His house is built by experts, its repairs parceled out to plumbers, electricians, roofers, tilesetters, and the like. Of course, he acknowledges, the specialists are far more efficient than any one man could be. The average American man is no longer a do-it-yourselfer *unless he wants to be.*

Meanwhile, in post-industrial America, *the housewife is still doing it herself,* whether she wants to or not. Although some of her chores have been simplified by modern equipment, for the most part "efficiency"—that hallowed aim for men's labor—is a minor consideration for the housewife. She has a vacuum cleaner as well as a broom, but she is still doing the floors. She buys butter instead of churning it, buys bread instead of baking it, but she is still in charge of stocking the house with bread and butter, and she is still the one who butters the children's bread. She may not be making the clothes but she is still expected to wash, iron, and mend them. She has access to miracle drugs and a private pediatrician but she is still on call (or expected to stay home from work) if a child is sick.

Comparatively speaking, the effects of "progress" mean

less to women. Despite convenience foods and labor-saving technology, today's housewife actually spends the same or more time at her chores as did women forty or fifty years ago.[44] This is because of our heightened standards of cleanliness—for instance, people use to wear a shirt for a week, not a day—and the modern ideal of "creative" homemaking (we need twenty ways to make chicken, not two). What's more, while the paid workday has been shortened through collective bargaining and automation, the housewife's workday has remained spread out over her total waking hours.

Although labor itself is genderless, most jobs are still sex-typed in many people's minds and jobs done mostly by men are better paid than jobs done mostly by women. Because men's time has become more valuable than women's (in money terms) we are willing to pay for the "man's work" husbands once did for their families, but we expect wives to keep doing "woman's work" free. But think about it: If our society professionalized housework the way we have professionalized men's chores, would women's time and labor be worth more in the labor market? Why is it okay to hire someone to *fix* the toilet if the husband can't/won't, but not okay to hire someone to *clean* the toilet if the wife can't/won't? Husbands do not make the excuse, "It's silly to pay some man to do my plumbing when that plumber will just have to hire another man to do his carpentry," because he will and he does, and that's called commerce. However Art Buchwald can write, "Behind every liberated woman there is another woman who has to do the dirty work for her,"[45] because housework is still considered *her* work, and because no woman is ever "liberated" until a man decides housework is his dirty work too.

Excuse #4: "You can't get good cleaning women nowadays, so I might as well do it myself."

As in the last two excuses, the assumption is the houseworker is always a woman—and indeed 98 percent *are*. If housework were professionalized, more men would enter the field—which is what must happen to speed its transition from semi-slavery to a respected occupation, and to save family women from exploitation in unpaid work they may not choose to do as the price of admission to their own homes. A century ago, half of all employed women were household workers; now they total only 3 percent and today, a black domestic worker is likely to be middle-aged, under-educated, and a cleaning woman; a white domestic is usually young, better-educated, and a babysitter.[46] But the reason why cleaning help is inadequate is not because household workers are black or female but because, at barest minimum wage, the job attracts only the unskilled: illiterates, illegal immigrants, people who have no other choice. Then too, housework attracts unskilled labor because it is thought of as unskilled labor. The idea is *any* woman can do it, since *every* woman does it, and does it free. (If every man fixed his own pipes at home, the plumber who hired himself out would have trouble convincing customers his services were worth $17 an hour.)

Given the privacy of housework, it remains difficult to assess its skill levels or establish a standard of excellence. As long as housewives are resigned to "I might as well do it myself," people will never fully appreciate what "it" is, or be able to justify paying upgraded wages to those who do "it" for others.

Household Specialist: The World's Newest Profession

In a 1949 article entitled "Women are Household Slaves,"[47] Edith Mendel Stern wrote:

> The role of the housewife is . . . analogous to that of the president of a corporation who would not only determine policies and make overall plans but also spend the major part of his time and energy in such activities as sweeping the plant and oiling the machines.

That's the problem. Housework is treated as a single job, even though a different kind of intelligence is called upon for each of its components. A simple-minded task such as loading the dishwasher (a five-year-old's job) requires less judgment than is needed to decide which colors and fabrics ought not to be washed in hot water with white clothes. It takes very little skill to make a neat bed, but considerable practice to iron a blouse. It takes basic literacy to cook from a recipe, but a lot of experience or talent to cook without one. It takes some budget sense and design flair for home decorating and gracious entertaining, but a vast array of skills to rear and socialize a child.

When all these jobs are lumped together and demanded of one "housewife," it's a wonder any of them is done well. The same will be true of an outside person hired as an all-purpose houseworker. But if we separate the tasks and establish standards for their performance, then, after deciding which skills they can develop sufficiently themselves, a family could hire only those housework experts it needs.

In our family, for instance, no one goes to a barber or hairdresser—I've always cut my husband's and children's hair myself—but we have shirts laundered out of the house. A neighborhood with many employed couples and single parents could share the services of a few specialists. A gifted cook might prepare and freeze five weeknight main dishes for each family. Someone deft with a needle might contract with each family for several hours of mending per month. An efficient shopper might do the weekly marketing for several families. In big cities, a communal shopper with a car could go to the wholesale markets to buy produce, meat, fish, and cheese at hefty discounts. His or her service fee might bring the food up to full price but families would save the time and hassle.

If James D. Robinson III, Chairman of the Board of American Express, can call the growing service economy "an all-American phenomenon,"[48] the rest of us can insist there's nothing *un*-American about de-privatized housework. Already, innovative services called "Renta Yenta," "Homemakers For Hire," and "Support Systems" charge from $8 to $25 an hour to organize closets, do gift-shopping, clean the garage, or manage family finances. Already, one in four meals is eaten out of the house,[49] a practical solution for singles but financially prohibitive for families for whom in-house delivery of meals and housework services is the best answer. "Today this is an accepted practice in public buildings," says sociologist Jessie Bernard. "A firm specializing in cleaning, well-equipped with the most efficient appliances, staffed with trained employees, contracts to keep a building in good shape."[50] It should not be such a major step to extend such services to apartments and houses—if sexist family politics could be swept aside.

Business depends on outside personnel consultants to increase morale, systems analysts to increase productivity, legal specialists for tax problems, relocation specialists to move executives, outside doctors and psychologists for special employee care. In many ways, the household is a family's business. If one or both parents are generating capital to run the enterprise, it is only reasonable that operating costs and special expenses would be incurred in the process of increasing the efficiency and productivity of the family unit.

I am not counseling the depersonalization of everything; let's be clear about that. Research suggests that families who farm out *all* household production lose something in cohesiveness.[51] I've said that everyone in the family should do some of the housework (plowing), but by the same token, families that cannot manage certain tasks alone should have the option of hiring a domestic specialist. For that to happen, *housework must be given a monetary value.* Then people of either sex who choose to do their family's housework for nothing would know what their labor is worth, and people who are paid to do others' household jobs could command a reasonable wage pegged to each job's skills.

The Economic Value of Housework. The contradictions tell the story:

• A few years back, Funk and Wagnalls Dictionary defined a housewife as "one who doesn't work for a living," at the same time that a Chase Manhattan Bank study found that housewives work up to 99 hours a week at twelve different tasks.[52]

• The U.S. Department of Labor, which classifies jobs according to their skill levels, gives hotel clerks and parking lot attendants a higher rating than homemakers and child-care workers. Yet a 1981 analysis of the kinds of work a typical homemaker does—cleaning, counseling, teaching, cooking, decorating, budgeting—came up with a dollar value of $41,277.08 (which buys three or four hotel clerks.)[53]

• According to traditionalists, being a housewife is the noblest calling for women, and a talent that comes "naturally" to females. I suspect they would also call being a soldier the noblest calling for men, and one that comes naturally to males. Assuming this parallel, we might ask why the United States spends billions to train and equip the supposedly instinctual warrior while no funds are allocated to basic training for the supposedly instinctual housewife.

• *Quote of the Month:* When asked why she didn't stay in the kitchen where she belonged, Bea Farber, harness racing's most successful woman driver, said, "Honey, you show me how to earn over $600,000 a year in the kitchen, and I'm on my way."[54]

• *Quote of the Year:* "MYTH: Most women who live in the suburbs are housewives. FACT: Most women who live in the suburbs work."[55]

The point is, the housewife is culturally extolled but economically valueless. She's "just a housewife." She doesn't "work." If she dies, her functions as helpmeet, lover, homemaker, and mother cannot be duplicated for any amount of money. In that sense, she's priceless. But when the widower replaces her services, the wage he pays is substandard and the person he hires is often ill-equipped. Thus, the same work that was so revered and priceless when done "for love" becomes nearly worthless when done for money.

Looking at it the other way around suggests *The Sound of Music* syndrome: A woman who works as a housekeeper, as Maria did for the Baron von Trapp and his children, receives a wage—a pittance, but a wage. When they marry, she becomes, in John Stuart Mill's words, "his bondservant."[56] The services continue but the market value disappears. No other working person but the housewife is expected to put in forty hours of work plus overtime each week in return for room and board. No other worker is asked to consider money for food, housing, kids' clothes, and medicine her "spending money." No other worker toils into the night, on weekends, through illness and vacation (when her chores are just relocated to a trailer or summer cottage), gets no sick pay, disability insurance, or retirement benefits (other than what her husband links to his), or qualifies for Social Security benefits only if she was married to her husband for at least ten years. Yet these are facts of life for the homemaker, and these facts have taught women of every social class that the marriage contract is no guarantee of lifelong security for house-wives. Laws that make husbands responsible for support tend to benefit not wives, but creditors. A wife cannot use these laws to compel a husband to support her. She can only sue for separation or divorce. And despite cries of rage from ex-husbands, only 14 percent are ordered to pay alimony and less than half of these remit payments regularly.[57] So the full-time homemaker risks *all* on her husband and his largesse— which means she is only one man away from welfare.

When she is widowed, deserted by her husband, or thrown onto the job market when he is unemployed, a house-wife learns the hard economic truth: Her decades of budget-ing, mediating, managing, creating, decision-making, nurtur-ing, and physical exertion elicit a sentence that chills the soul. "Aha," says the job interviewer, "I see you haven't worked in years."

No use answering, "But I followed the rules; I worked for my family." That may wave banners at a Moral Majority convention but it doesn't wash in the personnel office.

And no use blaming the women's movement. Feminists don't denigrate housework; in fact, it is feminists who say housework is so important that men should do it, too. And if men *did* it, the United States would probably have an Undersecretary of Housework in the Department of the Interior and multimillion-dollar housework research budgets that rival the space program. Because we do not have such things doesn't mean housework is unimportant. Many modern thinkers have agreed with Charlotte Perkins Gilman, who wrote:

> The labor of women in the house certainly enables men to produce more wealth than they otherwise could, and in this way women are economic factors in society.[58]

I've heard others argue that the housewife is an economic burden on the community because "all she does is assure continued domestic service for one man." But that is not all she does by any means. Women's unpaid work in the home serves capitalism well (which is why conservatives idealize the housewife): Free housework lowers a family's cost of living, thus lowering the wage demands of the employed husband, thus contributing to corporate profit margins.

Economist John Kenneth Galbraith goes so far as to say the American economy hangs on the housewife's apron strings.[59] The economy needs someone to run individual households that need individual toasters, refrigerators, bathtubs, and Barbie dolls. Where would business be without the housewife? Yet once she has consumed, and trained a new generation of consumers, her economic contribution seems to vanish. Few recognize that the housewife manufactures *products:* clean and wearable clothing, healthy meals, emotional and physical healing, more competent and humanized children, family transportation services, financial and bookkeeping services, and the creation of an environment as palpable in its way as is an architect's. Given this more realistic perspective, how can housework's product be acknowledged and rewarded?

GOVERNMENT SOLUTIONS

We could make housework visible by giving it a dollar value and coding it into the Gross National Product. Economists have estimated that unpaid housework would increase the GNP by up to 48 percent.[60] How would we arrive at a dollar value for housework? One way is the "opportunity cost" method, which says the housewife is worth what she could have earned if she spent x years in paid employment instead of at home. This approach is fraught with difficulties because each woman's mythical earnings would be contingent on too many individual variables: age, education, market conditions, degree of sex discrimination in her chosen field, and so on. A second method would simply evaluate the housewife's services at whatever is the going rate for a full-time domestic, a method whose defects are obvious. The best approach, the "replacement cost" or "market value" method, assumes the housewife is worth what it would cost to replace her many diverse services in the labor market:

> *Replacement cost* equals *hours* spent at a given task multiplied by the *market wage* for that skill.

The market wage would be a national average obtained from the Bureau of Labor Statistics.

For argument's sake, if a professional cook earns an average of $8 an hour, and if the average housewife spends 10 hours a week cooking, then each housewife is worth $80 a week as a cook. Add similar computations for the hours housewives spend at each of their other tasks and you arrive at the total "replacement value"—or the economic value of housework.

At current wage rates, this formula would probably yield a dollar value for housework that is somewhat lower than the $41,277.08 mentioned earlier. But it would be considerably higher than the $6417 arrived at by government economists in 1972,[60] possibly higher than her own husband's salary, and certainly higher than most housewives value *themselves.*

In a 1981 poll,[61] men said the job of homemaker was worth $12,700, and women said it was worth $13,800. Within this group of women, homemakers priced themselves lower ($13,700) than did working women, who considered homemakers worth $14,000; family traditionalists said housework was a $19,600 job, but *feminists* as a group gave housewives the highest value of all: $21,500.

The idea of "replacement value" has a respectable legal precedent. It is recognized in court for purposes of compensating a surviving child or husband for loss of household services and consortium if a housewife is killed in an accident. Insurance companies have accepted that a full-time homemaker is worth between $11,000 and $13,000 per year.[62] Why should women have to die to be worth that kind of money?

If a "replacement value" figure were legitimated on a broad scale, housework *as work* would be economically quantifiable, regardless of the sex of the homemaker. Not only could divorcing couples use the figure to evaluate the housewife's contribution in order to make an equitable division of property, but all homemakers could use it as an earnings equivalency to establish:

• Social Security in their own names not hinged to their husbands'

• Disability insurance coverage (at this writing not a single insurer will write a policy on the fulltime housewife)

• Individual Retirement Accounts that are portable in and out of marriage or the workplace (and not dependent on a husband's generosity, as is now the case)[63]

Who is going to finance the Social Security and disability contributions that are normally paid in by an employer? The husband? Taking it from his paycheck would be an untenable hardship in most families, and would create no more independence for the housewife than would sleight of hand. "No," says University of Iowa professor, Nancy R. Hauserman, a lawyer and expert on the economics of housework. "We, as a society, would pick up the tab collectively. After all, we are the same society that told women 'it is your role to be a dependent adult.' We ought to pay for it." As utopian as the proposal of housewives' Social Security sounds, it is no more unreasonable than asking all Americans to finance unemployment insurance for people who aren't working at all. If taxpayers' funds *were* paid into homemakers' Social Security accounts, men might lose some of their enthusiasm for privatized housework. (Each man may enjoy his own wife's unpaid services, but he's not about to underwrite the next guy's.)

Finally, says Kathleen Newland, of the Worldwatch Institute, "Perhaps the most effective thing a government can do to encourage equality in private life is to enforce equality in the public sphere of paid employment. If women continue to be cast in secondary roles in the labor force, it will seem natural for them to shoulder most of the responsibility at home."[65]

WORKPLACE SOLUTIONS

The workplace changes spelled out in the previous chapter would make all the difference: *flexible work schedules* so family people can come in late (get the housework done in the morning, and miss rush-hour traffic), or leave early (to pick up kids, or get to the cleaner's before it closes); *paired jobs* that permit two homemakers to split one paid job; *resumé credit for transferable skills* acquired through homemaking; on-site *child care;* as well as *upgrading paid household workers* with training, pay escalation for experience, and a work contract including benefits and obligations.

EDUCATIONAL SOLUTIONS

If schools taught housework as *survival skills,* everyone would know how to make a bed (boys learn "hospital corners" for the army; they can learn it for their families); scour a sink; sweep; use a stove safely, cook basic meals, and clean up after themselves (so they don't become men who wait for some woman to come home and "feed" them); launder, iron, mend, balance a checkbook, and do basic home maintenance and repairs (so a grown woman doesn't have to sit in the dark waiting for a man to come home and flick on the circuit-breaker switch).

Schools ought to offer children hot lunches (for health's sake, as well as to accommodate busy homemakers and working parents who cannot be home at noon); schedule parent-teacher conferences before or after parents' working hours; and become sensitive to sexist assumptions (don't assign kids to have their *mothers* bake brownies or their *fathers* help them make kites). It is not the school's business to determine which parent should fulfill what household role.

COMMUNITY SOLUTIONS

As mentioned in Chapter Four, we need to rethink cities, suburbs, and spatial design. Single-family houses, isolated housing developments, and their separation from the workplace are not desirable for those who must spend hours chauffeuring, stuck inside, shopping in sterile stores or limited to the company of children. A nonpatriarchal restructuring of community design would reduce the conflict of interests within a family; that is, the woman would not have to stay home to assure that the husband and children can function.

Why not have family cafeterias built into every housing complex; child-care available at an hourly rate (such tot lots are popular in department stores in Sweden to permit shoppers to move about unencumbered by small children); delivery and repair services that schedule definite appointments instead of expecting the housewife to wait at home all day; evening hours for medical and dental offices; Displaced Homemaker Centers to counsel, train, and find jobs for older women who are "displaced" from the traditional housewife role by divorce or the death of a supporting husband (several centers opened in the 1970s but under Reagan, federal and state funding has evaporated.)

On a more individual scale, why not institute Dr. Jessie Hartline's plan: Two homemakers employ each other by exchanging services and salaries, thus entering the job market perfectly legally, and becoming eligible for Social Security, workers' compensation, Individual Retirement Accounts, and health insurance.

Why not form two-family cooperatives for adults who can work flexible hours (such as part-timers, self-employed business people or artists, homemakers and students). The four adults split a twelve-hour day into four three-hour duty segments; each gets nine hours off, and all share the two households' laundry, cleaning, cooking, shopping, and child care equally. The slight loss of privacy is more than made up for in the luxury of nine hours of free time every day.

Or establish non-profit "havens"—a room in an office or someone else's house that can be rented by the hour so the harried homemaker can have a refuge for quiet reverie, writing, reading, napping: the legendary room of one's own.

All this and more is possible if the "just a housewife" mentality is supplanted by housework justice.

8

The Politics of Pregnancy and Motherhood

MY FEELINGS ABOUT FAMILY are luxury items, like truffles and limousines; not every woman can afford them. I have the luxury of my satisfactions because of two facts: (1) nobody forced me to have my children, and (2) society considers me a "respectable" mother. But another kind of motherhood, not so readily acknowledged, is equally real. We grow mawkish about Mom on Mother's Day and clap for the "mother of seven" or the Mother of the Year, but watch the applause fade if the woman has no husband, is not white-skinned, or happens to be a lesbian or a teenager. Certain mothers aren't "right" for the part. As for the traditional heroine—the married, moral, fulltime mother—no one is rushing to sit next to her at a dinner party or to publish her memoirs. Show me a woman who starts talking about her day at home with the kids, and I'll show you a man whose eyes have glazed over. As a male college instructor put it, "The only thing worse than being with a group of women is being with a group of pregnant women."[1]

TWO-FACED IDEAL

Although the average woman spends only one-seventh of her lifespan either pregnant, nursing, or caring for preschool children,[2] it is *as mothers* that all women are defined. Motherhood is sacred. But only when it happens to married women. Children are precious. But only when they're born after the wedding. Mothers and children who fail to fulfill these criteria are not sacred and precious, they are "unwed mothers" and "illegitimate children" (nearly one in five births).[3] Unclaimed by men, they are nonpersons.

Under the Social Security Act, for instance, when a male wage-earner dies, mothers' insurance and children's benefits are payable to his legal widow and surviving children. Unwed spouses get nothing and "illegitimate" children can collect only if they can prove paternity *and* dependence. (Natural or adopted children are assumed dependent simply because they are children. Illegitimate children, I suppose, are assumed to be self-supporting.)

The original rationale for mothers' insurance was to subsidize the surviving parent so she could stay home and give her full attention to her child. By upholding the denial of mothers' insurance benefits to unwed mothers,[4] the United States Supreme Court has shown itself willing to deprive certain children of the celebrated benefits of full-time mothering. Moreover, by disqualifying unwed mothers, the Court has in effect disqualified these women *as* mothers, invalidating their cultural "femininity" and devaluing their children's needs. In other words, if society thinks full-time mothering is important enough to underwrite with insurance, why isn't it important for *all* children.

Here's another example of double-standard motherhood: Reproductive technology is said to be a boon for infertile women who want to become mothers. However, it is men who decide *which* women are permitted to become mothers. U.S. government guidelines require in vitro fertilization to be used only for married couples.[5] In 1982, the California sperm bank that stores and dispenses the sperm of "geniuses" tightened its screening procedures after learning that a woman they impregnated was unmarried.[6] Although she was a psychologist and thus ostensibly a worthy match for the sperm of a computer scientist, an unwed mother is, by definition, unfit to bear a genius. (The morals of the sperm donor were not open to scrutiny.)

A third example: Remember the eleven-year-old rape victim who was forced to bear her child when Judge Donald Halstead refused to allow her to have an abortion (see page

49)? After giving birth, she lost custody of the baby because everyone agreed she was too young to care for it.[7] Not too young to rape. Not too young for compulsory pregnancy. But finally, too young to care for the baby her body was barely old enough to produce.

"Adoption not abortion!" shout the Right to Life marchers, as if the scars left by an unwanted pregnancy and birth on the life of an eleven-year-old can be healed by wrenching her baby from her and giving it to a "real" family.

Finally there is the racist double standard of motherhood: While poor black women are threatened with welfare cutoffs and forced sterilization if they become pregnant, middle-class white women are pressured to reproduce. Poor women are accused of having babies just to qualify for welfare—as if $14 a day for a mother and child is a bonanza—and at the same time, educated young wives and women executives are warned not to postpone childbirth until the biological clock runs out.

For the privileged classes, pro-pregnancy propaganda is everywhere. *Vogue* photographs Jill Clayburgh's belly. *Time* runs a seven-page feature on "The New Baby Boom" with pictures and comments from celebrities over thirty who've had babies without sacrificing their careers. Sissy Spacek, Donna Summer, Sandy Duncan, Faye Dunaway, Ursula Andress, Jaclyn Smith, and assorted lesser-known actresses, agents, anchorwomen, physicians, architects, lawyers, writers, and editors are among the chic "new madonnas" pictured in designer maternity clothes or working at full tilt after childbirth.[8] As one newspaper columnist noted, "Making motherhood fashionable is just another way of getting back to the same old trap of making women feel they are nothing if not mothers."[9] So we've come full circle in less than ten years.

One day back in the early 1970s, I interviewed several mothers at a local playground. "I feel defensive," said one. "I always imagine you feminists are looking at me and thinking, 'Is that all she can do?'" A pregnant woman, pushing a toddler on the swing, nodded. "In her day my grandmother hid her pregnancy out of modesty. I feel I should hide mine because it labels me unliberated." "I'm not sure I want science to disprove the maternal instinct or fathers to get paternity leave," said a third mother. "What will be left for us to be special about?" Another added, "I wish we could just be mothers like our mothers, and stop thinking about it so much."

In the Seventies, everyone seemed to be thinking about motherhood. Childless women and veteran mothers, feminists and nonfeminists, women with men and without had begun to talk seriously about the old have-a-baby imperative and the new why-have-a-baby backlash, about the realities of daily child care and the costs and rewards of modern motherhood. Although most feminists were careful to emphasize that the goal was to make motherhood an option, not an imperative, some women felt threatened by the very idea of choice. Becoming a mother had always been synonymous with becoming a woman. We were of the generation that pitied childless women and believed being a mommy was the one certain route to respect and maturity.

Throughout the Seventies, all those givens of my generation and my mother's were re-examined. All over the country, ordinary women began talking more honestly to one another about the motherhood experience. Many young women approached the question of childbearing with a rigorous analysis once thought inappropriate for such "natural" acts. By 1980, nearly nine out of ten Americans thought there was "nothing wrong" with having no children.[10] Many recent books have explored the option of nonparenthood as well as the wonders, frustrations, and significance of childrearing.[11] Keen feminist thinkers have written brilliant analyses of the *institution* of motherhood, questioning, for example, whether the mother–child relationship is the ultimate model for love between two human beings, or whether it is the ultimate paradigm for dominance and oppression; whether motherlove can be pure if it arises from a relationship of inherent inequality; whether feminist ambivalence toward motherhood makes non-mothers unsupportive of women who are mothers—the tough issues, the questions that could not be asked just a few years ago. Motherhood's choices and trade-offs have been illuminated, publicly and among friends, in published and spoken testimony, and the unromantic realities—of single mothers, working mothers, stepmothers, mothers with shared custody, lesbian mothers, disabled mothers, adoptive mothers, poor mothers—have been given new visibility. I had begun to believe it possible to demythify motherhood and enable women to make their procreative decisions without coercion or value judgments in one direction or the other. And then, a year or so ago, the pro-motherhood campaign started gathering steam, fueled by "pro-family" bromides on the right and maternity chic in the media. Suddenly, real women's ambivalence and honest deliberations are being displaced by misty-eyed celebrities patting their bellies. Headlines warn ominously[12]:

- "THE MEDICAL RISKS OF WAITING"

- "FETAL HEALTH: A NEW VIEW EMERGES"

- "STUDY SHOWS FEMALE FERTILITY DROPS SHARPLY AFTER AGE 30"

- "NEW TIME FACTOR FOR WOMEN WHO DEFER PREGNANCY"

- "WOMEN RECONSIDER CHILDBEARING OVER 30"

A month after these stories were splashed across the newspapers and television, reports on followup research found the infertility warnings "misleading" and called the initial findings "a false alarm,"[13] but the rebuttal was reported so quietly that nobody seemed to notice it. The truth about motherhood is always hard to come by, but especially when pregnancy is In.

The New York Times Magazine followed up a report called "Voices from the Postfeminist Generation" with a cover story one month later on "Careers and the Lure of Motherhood," and story in the daily paper two months after that, entitled, "Mothers Who Shift Back From Jobs to Homemaking."[14] *The Wall Street Journal* found "disruption in corporations and law firms caused by the wave of pregnancies at the managerial and professional levels," which Phyllis Schlafly declared was proof that every woman has "baby hunger" after all.[15]

Whatever the angle, the new message is this: Real women *should* have babies, successful women *are* having babies, and even feminists *want* to have babies. Schlafly is saying women are choosing babies *instead* of worldly accomplishment; the subtle upscale opinion-makers tell women they can have worldly accomplishment *and* babies. Either way, what are you waiting for?

In any culture, the keystone of family politics is the promotion of motherhood for the "right" kind of woman—the woman of racially and socioeconomically "superior" stock. Hitler awarded the Mutterkreuz (Mother's Cross) to the most fertile Aryan women.[16] With the genetic precision of an orchid breeder, he matched the tall, elite German princes of his S.S. with pure-blooded, fair-haired *fraüleins* whose duty was to mother the master race. In post-revolutionary Russia, Stalin outlawed abortion and promoted women's "right" to a family and "duty" to bear children. The Stalinist press glorified the family, called abortion "selfishness" and associated it with promiscuity—"all key elements of current 'right-to-life' rhetoric."[17]

And now, in the United States, right-wing fundamentalists campaign outright for large families and full-time motherhood, while the more sophisticated appeal to professional women couches the pro-pregnancy line in the alluring promise, "You can do it all." Underneath, writes Gloria Steinem, these advocates share a common anxiety about "the decline of the white birthrate to a low unprecedented in American history—even producing too few 'adoptable' white infants to meet the demand." Thus, abortion is presented to the white middle class "as the symbolic beginning of some horrifying future. It will destroy marriage and morality by removing the inevitability of childbearing as the only goal of sex and as God's will; it will endanger the birth of future people like them. . . ."[18]

COMPETING INTERESTS, CONFLICTING RIGHTS

Traditionalists tend to favor parents' rights over children's rights *unless the parent in question is a woman.* The U.S.

Supreme Court has ruled that states may not take children away from their parents without "clear and convincing evidence" that the parents are unfit; supposedly *parents* are given every benefit of the doubt, even in cases of child abuse. But, in practice, *mothers* lose custody of their children for the slightest deviation from the "norm."

Just recently, a woman disabled in a car crash lost custody of her four-year-old to an "intact" family who babysat with the boy after her accident; she had never been charged with neglect or abuse.[19] A divorced woman who lived with a man without marriage lost custody of her child because she was "living in sin," and a working mother lost custody to her ex-husband because he could offer the child his stay-home second wife.[20] A lesbian mother (many of them, actually) lost custody because of her sexual preference[21]—and the child went to live with a father whose sexual practices, though hetero, for all anyone knows may be utterly bizarre. A woman who said "hell" during her custody hearing lost her four children because the judge did not approve of a mother using "construction site language."[22] A woman active in radical politics stands to lose custody of her daughter on the grounds that her political activities are detrimental to the child—although officials acknowledge that the child "is unquestionably well cared for."[23] After a white woman gave birth to an "illegitimate and racially mixed baby," she was declared "an unfit mother" and she lost custody of her first child, a white-skinned boy, to her ex-husband.[24]

If the measure for such Solomonic decisions was always the best interests of the child, one might excuse the system's mistakes. But it is only a measure of Solomon's *power:* The issue does not become whether a woman is a good or a bad mother but rather whether she is a "respectable" or a "deviate" woman. Is it in the interest of the state, The Family, or the child to remove it from its own mother's custody if her only crime is nonconformity? Whose interests are being served? Since a mother loses her rights not by mothering poorly but by violating patriarchal rules for *women,* then "parent's rights" are but a subterfuge for *men's* power and not to be confused with mother's rights, such as they are.

Questions of competing interests or conflicting rights are often knotty. When the choice is between the human rights of an adult woman and of an incomplete embryo, people should be free to make a religious claim that they are equal. However, one cannot make a *legal* claim that they are equal without severely curtailing the rights of the woman. Consider the legal dilemmas that would have to be faced if the ultra-right wins and the fetus is given the status of a "person" under the law:[25]

• Does a fetus need a passport in order to travel inside a woman who is going abroad? How is its "identity" established in the absence of a photograph, distinguishing marks, or a birthdate?

• Does concern for the fetus' health compromise a woman's constitutional right to travel?

• If a zygote (fertilized egg) is guaranteed life, should women of childbearing age be forced to take monthly pregnancy tests to ascertain whether there is a life to protect?

• If a pregnant woman smokes, drinks, drives, or skis, is she liable for endangering the health of the fetus?

• If a "test tube baby" (an embryo fertilized in a glass dish) is found to be developing abnormally and is discarded, should the laboratory scientists be open to a murder charge?

• Could a woman cancer patient who needs radiation therapy be prevented from treatment because of fetus rights?

• Could a woman be barred in advance from strenuous employment on the chance she might be pregnant?

• If a woman dies in childbirth after being denied an abortion, do her husband and surviving children have the right to sue the state for her wrongful death?

• If a prescribed contraceptive fails and a carrier of genetic disease has a seriously handicapped child, can the parents sue for "wrongful birth"?

• If a pregnancy would endanger a woman's health, can she refuse to have sex with her husband on the grounds that abstinence is the only sure contraceptive, once abortion is outlawed?

• Since abortion is known to be safer than childbirth, can a pregnant woman who is at risk sue for abortion to ensure her own safety? Can't any citizen refuse state-directed compulsory risk-taking—except when there is a military draft? Does the government have the right to draft women for compulsory motherhood?

Despite such complexities, a vocal contingent of conservatives are intent upon outlawing abortion by declaring the fetus a person. In 1981, a Senate subcommittee was arrogant enough to hold hearings on "when life begins," an issue that has evaded every major philosopher since Aristotle.[26] The three major Western faiths are far from unanimous on the issue. Many Protestant writers make a religious case for abortion. For more than four thousand years, Jewish law has never considered abortion murder. And the Catholic Church sanctioned abortion for eighteen centuries.[27] As for twentieth-century scientists, most have called the question of "when life begins" metaphysical, theological, philosophical, but unanswerable by science.[28]

In its 1973 abortion decision, the Supreme Court sidestepped the question and addressed only the issue of Constitutional rights. The Court ruled that the woman's rights are paramount in early pregnancy and the fetus' rights become more "compelling" as the pregnancy progresses.[29] Passing years have proven that judgment as reasonable and workable as any proposed before or since. The alternative is not equal rights for fetuses but a blanket reversal of the rights of women.

PRO-PREGNANCY POLITICS

The highly charged word "pro-life" describes a position that is merely pro-pregnancy, and is in fact anti-woman, anti-family, and anti-child.

Many pro-pregnancy advocates do not care what damage

the pregnancy does to a woman's body or whether the gestat-
ing fetus may be defective; they call amniocentesis (the in
utero test for Down's Syndrome) "a conspiracy to threaten
healthy fetuses," and some do not care if the pregnancy was
the result of rape or incest, or if it leads to a woman's death
in childbirth.[30] The pregnancy is the client. The pregnancy
is both the punishment for autonomous female sexuality and
the ultimate woman-tamer. Since the capacity for pregnancy
is the major difference between women and men, when controlled by men it can become the great *un*equalizer.

Somehow, pro-pregnancy people can rationalize the suicides of little girls like Melissa Putney, pregnant in the eighth
grade, who knelt on a Maryland railroad track, made the sign
of the cross and let an Amtrak train put her out of her misery.[31]
Somehow, they can brush aside reminders of the women killed
and injured from illegal abortions; they don't care about the
inevitable return of back-alley profiteering, or the blackmail
and extortion fed by women's desperation. To them, all unwilling mothers are sinful. The life of a fully grown woman is
secondary. The "pro-life" forces are only interested in "innocent life," referring, oddly, only to those that have never lived.
This philosophical loophole allows them to support capital
punishment, wars, and nuclear bombs at the same time as
they favor a constitutional amendment protecting fetuses.
They manage to be "pro-life" and pro-death simultaneously.

But ultimately, their utmost inhumanity is directed not
at unwilling mothers but at unwanted children. Researchers
specializing in family violence have found that "deformed,
defective, retarded, *unwanted,* or *unplanned* children have
the highest risk of being battered." Rather than admit that
those children would be at risk, the pro-pregnancy people
claim The Family is at risk unless the government coerces
every pregnant woman to term. But how does forcing a raped
eleven-year-old to have a baby create a family? How can it
be that forcing a forty-year-old mother of five to have a sixth
child is good for her family? And whose family is "threatened"
when a poor woman chooses to have an abortion instead of
bearing a malnourished baby?

No, families are not the issue; compulsory pregnancy is

the issue. Abortion represents a woman's refusal to mother, and mothering is what traditional men believe all women *should* do. Abortion doesn't threaten the family, it threatens the patriarchy. As in the marketplace, the person who controls the labor controls the product. By retaining control over pregnancy, traditionalist men retain power over women and children. Most men wouldn't dream of forcing any man to take a job he didn't want; they understand that the unwilling producer often sabotages the product. Yet they would force millions of girls and women to bear children and take on a job commitment of nearly two decades' duration even if the "product" is a person and the sabotage is utter neglect.

People who decry government involvement in business contend, at the same time, that the state has a bonafide interest in pregnancy. People who object that the national 55-mile-per-hour speed limit is not a safety measure but an invasion of privacy[33] are the same people who contend that pregnancy is not a private matter. People who protest occupational safety regulations insist staying pregnant is a health safety measure, when in fact, abortion is twenty-six times safer than childbirth.[34] Even setting aside the health factor, the idea that a speed limit is an invasion of privacy, and a compulsory pregnancy isn't, suggests the level of reason in this debate.

The centerpiece of the pro-pregnancy agenda is the reversal of the Supreme Court's 1973 decision, and passage of one or more of the following:[35]

• *The Human Life Amendment* to the U.S. Constitution (HLA) would declare the fetus a person with the 14th Amendment protection that American *women* have never fully secured for themselves. Thus, a fertilized egg would have more rights than the woman in whose body it exists.

• *The Human Life Statute* (HLS) is a kind of fast-food HLA. It contains the same fetus-personhood provisions, but because it is a bill and not a Constitutional Amendment, it could be passed by a simple majority vote of the Congress rather than the more complex ratification process. The HLS goes even further than the HLA in that it would ban the pill and the IUD, make it a crime for a woman to cross state lines to seek an abortion, and prohibit medical schools from teaching abortion methods.

• *The Human Life Federalism (or Hatch) Amendment* would remove the Supreme Court's 1973 abortion rights guarantee and give both Congress and the states power to restrict abortion—as long as the states are *more* restrictive than the Congress. On June 28, 1983, a simplified version of this amendment was defeated by a vote of 50–49 in the Senate (a two-thirds vote was necessary for passage).

• *The Hatfield-Hyde Bill* would permanently prohibit federal financing of abortion and would authorize a direct appeal to the U.S. Supreme Court if any federal district judge struck down a state law that restricts abortion.

While these major federal proposals are pending, local pro-pregnancy groups all over the country have been obstructing women's legal access to abortion by:

• eliminating abortion coverage from health insurance

• requiring hospitalization rather than a simple clinic procedure for second-trimester abortions

• imposing a twenty-four-hour waiting period

• creating cumbersome paperwork requirements

• requiring additional (and costly) doctor visits

• forcing all teenagers to get parental consent

• forcing doctors to show women color photos of fetuses, to warn patients of severe emotional repercussions of abortion, and to describe the potential dangers of every medical procedure involved so that a woman can give "informed consent." (If every graphic detail of gallstone surgery were forced upon you, you might not consent to that operation either, no matter how life-threatening your condition.)

• requiring abortion clinics to be separated from all family-planning facilities, thus creating an abortion ghetto and disturbing the integral relationship between abortion and contraceptive education.

These restrictions were declared unconstitutional in a sweeping Supreme Court decision handed down in June 1983. But continuing harassment and firebombing of abortion clinics, plus the withdrawal of federal funds for poor women's abortions, still interfere with women's private decision about whether to mother or not. And it could get worse. If "human life" legislation passes, abortion would be a federal crime for the first time. If you're a woman, you would not be allowed to take the pill or use an IUD that prevents implantation of a fertilized egg. If you had a miscarriage that seemed "suspicious," you could be tried for murder. You would not be allowed to have an abortion even if you had been exposed to thalidomide or dangerous radiation known to result in fetal deformities. You would not be permitted to have amniocentesis. You would have to have your baby even if you were impregnated by your own father, or if you conceived because your husband raped and beat you, or if you are too weak to withstand a pregnancy or too poor to feed the children you already have.

WHO'S IN CHARGE OF MOTHERHOOD?

I said I had the luxury of positive feelings about family because I'm considered "respectable" (i.e. married) and because nobody forced me to have my children. Let me put that somewhat more dramatically. If I had to name one question that exposes the power relations inherent in family politics, it would be "who's in charge of motherhood?" In sum, an absolutely rudimentary power rests with whomever decides: a) who mothers, b) whether to mother, and c) when to mother.

a. *Who* mothers pertains to previously mentioned issues of race, class, gradations of women's worth, and "legitimacy"— all of which are determined by men or by religions and governments run by men.

b. *Whether* to mother pertains to the decision only a woman can make about the use of her very life for reproduction: the use of her body's blood and strength to sustain nine months of pregnancy, and the use of her life's energy and time to rear a child for nearly two decades. A man, if he is a fully involved parent, bases his decision to father only on the second of those considerations: the commitment of his energy and time. If he is a fair-minded man, he makes his determination only *after* a woman has agreed to the use of her body.

Ellen Ross points out that although contraception is usually thought of as a "family decision," it is often an area of dispute between a couple.[36] Some men seem to want more than their say. Recent court cases center on the demand for notification of the fetus' father before a woman can have an abortion.[37] In other words, some men want to retain control of whether women mother. They don't want the child-care responsibilities of motherhood, but they want the last word on the decision that determines the use of women's bodies. Why?

Does that control compensate the man for not actually creating life within *his* body? Is the power to impose mandatory motherhood his last-ditch means of putting a woman in her "place" by chaining her to her biology? Is power over women's bodies man's belated revenge against his mother for having absolute power over his body in infancy? Or is it an unconscious resistance to the idea that, as easily as his mother birthed him, she could have decided not to?

During the 1981 hearings on the Human Life Statute (page 185), North Carolina Senator John P. East wondered aloud whether his own mother would have considered aborting him if she'd known he was going to get polio when he was twenty-four years old;[38] the very idea of a woman controlling a man's destiny appalls him. Men tend to think of abortion in terms of themselves as the fetus, says Andrea Dworkin; women think of themselves as the uterus.[39] Perhaps men want to ensure their own birth retroactively, by controlling whether women mother.

In one of his columns, Russell Baker takes off on the familiar claim that the world might have been cheated of many of its geniuses had abortion been available in say, Beethoven's time.[40] Although Baker doesn't point out that techniques for inducing miscarriage have been in use since at least the fourth century,[41] he does say that the half-dozen geniuses lost to abortion are "negligible compared with the hordes we've lost to wars and automobile accidents." Which reminded me of the Catholic Archbishop who once said the Vatican would have been much more outraged if America had dropped contraceptives on Japan than it was when we dropped atomic bombs.[42]

If men seem less troubled by lives lost to manmade weapons and manmade machines than by lives lost to far fewer— but *woman*-controlled—abortions, might the crucial difference be the issue of men retaining *power over women?* What's more, since medicine (still overwhelmingly male) has been more successful at making pregnancy safe than making contraception safe, can we speculate that men are more interested in having women reproduce than in enabling women to decide not to?

c. *When* to mother pertains to family planning and abortion, reproductive activity that has obsessed Christian moral consciousness, as Mary Daly wrote, "in a manner totally disproportionate to its feeble political concern."[43]

More than six in ten people and seven in ten *women* (Catholics included) believe legal abortion should be available to every women.[44] As for the vocal minority of compulsory-pregnancy fanatics, I leave it to others to persuade them of the compelling case for contraception and abortion as issues of women's sexual and reproductive freedom. Here I want to make one of the key points of this book: that *a woman's decision about when to mother has as much to do with children's welfare as it does with women's right to choose.*

If you want to decode the current political debate, you need to understand that "pro-life" is anti-family, while pro-choice is pro-child. Pro-choice is pro-child because, as has been proven in countless data on abuse, a woman who has chosen when and how often she mothers is far more likely to be a loving and caring mother. Given how demanding motherhood is under the best of circumstances, I want every mother to be able to undertake it with, at minimum, the running start of a loving, caring enthusiasm. Thus, for the sake of children (as well as for the integrity of women), I want us to be free to determine the timing of our motherhood.

I have done my mothering in the best of circumstances; yet it has been incredibly demanding work. I cannot imagine how I would have done it if even one complication were added: if I hadn't been ready for it; if I hadn't had their father at my side; if my employer hadn't allowed me to juggle my work schedule; if I was disabled or my child was handicapped; if I was a lesbian living in fear of having my children taken away; if we couldn't have afforded babysitters, cleaning help, nursery school, doctors. . . . I think about the women who mother without help and under all those complicating conditions and I fall silent. Their motherhood is heroism, and nothing less.

Although the new right tries to equate abortion with hedonism and promiscuity, fully two-thirds of the abortions performed before the procedure was "legalized" were obtained by *married women with children.* [45] In my opinion, these were responsible mothers who chose not to stretch their strength and resources, mothers who refused to shortchange the children they already had.

In 1980, there were one and a half million abortions. [46] As far as I am concerned, that figure represents one and a half million women who knew they were not ready for the enormous task of rearing children. As Adrian Ruth Walter says:

> The tragedy of this country is not "abortion on demand" as President Reagan put it . . . but a situation where one pregnant woman in four thinks it better *not* to bring her child into the world.
>
> Instead of attacking the symptom of abortion, it would be better if all . . . worked to make this a world where children had a chance to grow up in a safe environment; where their mothers earn more than 59 cents on

the dollar; where they would not be discriminated against because of race, sex or poverty; where a nuclear holocaust would not seem more probable every day. . . .

Meanwhile, for a quarter of all pregnant women, not having their babies seems to them to be their only option.[47]

In that sense, I see abortion as an expression of respect for motherhood. Almost any biological female *can* reproduce. Only human females have the brainpower to decide whether they *should* reproduce. To deny women that decision-making power is to reduce us to animals. And to deny children mothers who have consciously and willfully chosen to have them is to reduce motherhood to breeding. If we care about children, there can be no other motherhood but woman-controlled motherhood—and since there's not very much of it around, we have to ask how much Americans really care about children. Again, it is a question of power and love: Do we want to protect men's power over women and childbirth, or do we want to protect children's right to be loved?

9

The New Father

HAVE YOU EVER WONDERED why there are so many men in the "right-to-life" movement and so few in child care? Or why a man who testifies so passionately about "unborn babies" is usually mute about babies already born and living in sickness and poverty? I attribute these contradictions to the fact that on public issues men act as men and not as fathers. They are protecting their power, not expressing their love of children.

It's as if masculinist thinking divides life into dualities—power/love, work/housework—so that men can take the half that suits them. In the case of children, men have divided them into the concept and the reality. Men are in charge of the concept of the child (they decide when life begins, or which child is "legitimate"), while women are in charge of the reality (three meals a day, fevers, snowsuits, bathtimes, and diapers). As men become more familiar with the reality—through deeper forms of fatherhood—they tend to discover that many of their concepts were wrong. The fully involved and sensitized father comes to see all children as fresh and fragile little lives needing daily care, rather than as symbols of patriarchal survival.

How much of each man's essential identity is based on the fact of his being a father? When was the last time you read a profile of a male leader or business mogul that included a paragraph about how he manages to be both a father and a mogul? Or when have you ever heard a male expert introduced to an audience as a "husband and father"? Probably never. Yet time and again, family credentials follow women's names in the newspaper, or precede female speakers to the lecturn. "And here she is," I am introduced, "editor, writer, and wife and mother of three . . ." Are those words simply part of my relevant biography, or are they added like a disclaimer on the label of a dangerous drug? Would the audience be less likely to tolerate a dose of feminist opinion without the palliative of a family connection—do they imagine my motherhood *tames* me.

I often think, on the contrary, how much motherhood has radicalized me, how it has grounded me in the gritty earth of human needs. Similarly, I wish that groups of men (and women) cared as much about each man's fathering and considered it as crucial a measure of his character and his humanity as motherhood is for a woman. The trouble is, for most men, the father part of their sense and sensibility shuts down the minute they leave the house. Our duality-ridden culture has let them believe that children are irrelevant to life in a "man's world."

One of my lecture experiences cast a new light on my thinking about fathers and the love/power dichotomy. As a faculty member was introducing me to a college audience, the hushed hall was pierced by the screech of a child imitating a fire engine siren. All heads turned toward the back of the hall where a man was trying to silence a small child, who responded to each "Shhhhhh!" with a shrill "Wrrrooooeeee." When I approached the microphone, the audience's giggles now punctuating each shriek, the father—unable to quiet his child—nervously hustled toward the exit, babe in arms.

"Please stay," I called after him. "If the baby continues squealing, I'll just speak louder and the audience will listen harder. We've learned to work, think, speak, and listen over the noise of male technology—the air conditioners, phones, jet planes, stock tickers, photocopiers, and word processors— surely we can tolerate the sound of one baby." Motherhood had taught me that babies tire of making noise eventually. Experience reminded me how often, though, *mothers* exempt themselves from public events for fear their children will disturb. I told that father he reminded me of all of the world's mothers driven from halls of learning because they care for children, and I told the audience, "We must help parents remain in our midst. We will ask father and baby to stay." The crowd roared its approval. The father returned to his seat. I began my speech and in minutes the baby was asleep.

A few days later, my husband and I attended a concert in Manhattan. When a baby started mewing in the balcony, the mother carried it from the concert hall but the father stayed put. When more fathers are caregivers and more mothers are in control of the podium, perhaps family needs will be accommodated in public life.

The trouble is, most people don't even notice. The separate spheres permit men to ignore what happens to children, knowing there is always a mother to care. As I've noted before, the limitations of traditional fatherhood have come to seem so utterly "normal" that we don't hear them in the very words we use and how we use them. For example, "to father" a child refers to the momentary act of impregnation; "to mother" a child means to succor and sacrifice. It means leaving the concert hall, it means giving up power over your own freedom. Describing nurturant males as men who "mother"[1] is a modern turn of speech that proves the emotional emptiness of the word "father." Somehow, when we watch a man intensively care for a child, we cannot say "look at how he fathers that child" without feeling as though we have misrepresented the scene. Needing to say "he mothers" is like needing to say "the sisters showed real brotherhood." With the growth of a new sisterhood among women and a new fatherhood among men, those words may enter common usage with a refreshed meaning.

Social scientists say that a child who grows up without a mother is suffering maternal "deprivation" (which the dictionary defines as "loss, dispossession, bereavement"). Life without father, however, is merely called father "absence" ("a state of being away"). The difference between *deprivation* and *absence* has allowed men to walk out on their families and be bad guys at worst, while women who do so are monsters. As

Juliet Mitchell put it, "present or absent, 'The Father' always has his place."[2] It will take a new generation of fathers to give that place real meaning and see father absence as children's deprivation.

When a man is the "head of household," our society calls the family "traditional," but when a woman is the "head of household," the family is called "matriarchal" (as in the Moynihan Report[3] on what's "wrong" with black families in America). In America, patriarchy means "power of *men.*" Matriarchy has come to mean "power of *mothers.*" Patriarchy is the name of an entire social system in which men rule over women. Matriarchy is the name of a house without a man presided over by a mother acting like a father.

What we are really saying with common language usage is that men who care for children are imitation mothers, and women who have the power to take care of families are imitation fathers. Family politics has so poisoned the cultural well that parents cannot overtly love their children or overtly use their power for their children without running the risk of compromising their gender identity.

CAREGIVING AND CARETAKING:
A MATTER OF CONTROL

> *Item:* Two little girls are playing house. Karen is the mother, Kathy is the grandmother. "An' who can be the father?" asks Karen. "No one," answers Kathy. "You don't need a father."[4]

If fathers sometimes seem expendable, it is because so many of them make themselves so extraneous to family life. Children come to associate men with the world of work, offices uniforms, money, cars—and only incidentally with the home— and they associate women (employed or not) with family roles, child care, feelings, housework, and cooking. Thus, they learn the double standard of care: Mothers *give* care; fathers *take* care . . . They take the care that mothers give. Studies show, for instance, blue-collar men get not only household services but far more emotional support from their wives than the wives get from the men—and when all is said and done, the wives are the more depressed.[5]

At the same time as women have always taken care of men, writes Harvard psychologist Carol Gilligan, "men in their theories of psychological development, as in their economic arrangements, have tended to devalue that care."[6] Contrary to the popular belief that women have the greater dependency needs, men's (noneconomic) dependency needs are far more insatiable. It's just that they are masked by the "normalcy" of women's caring for men and providing emotional support in the process of fulfilling the feminine role. During childhood, both boys and girls get this care and support from their mothers, but girls lose mothercare when they live with men, while men keep getting maternal support from their wives or girlfriends.

It is considered so "natural" that women give care and men and children take it, that women seem "unnatural" when they want some for themselves. In addition to devaluing women's care, and depriving women of emotional support from men, the imbalance is disguised by another linguistic trick: We turn reality on its head and say that *men* "take care of" women and children. Man's financial support is thus posed as an equalization of women's *caring behavior,* although the felt experience and rewards are completely different.

Rather than result in a simple division of labor, sex specialization in caring atrophies men's capacity to give comfort, thereby eliminating a major source from which women and children can *get* comfort. Furthermore, sex specialization in caring is not fair to children. Men trade support for women's caregiving (although it is far from an even trade), but children lose in the bargain. Women may excuse men's uncaring because they are "taken care of," but children should not have to have only one parent caring for them if they have two living parents. Sex-specialized caring imperils children because it is contingent on parents' sex role choreography rather than children's needs.

This is especially true for children of divorce, who tend to spend most of their time with their mothers. (Joint custody is acceptable in half the states but is still very much the exception.[7]) Their fathers are not just routinely undemonstrative men, they often become little more than weekend visitors and signatures on the child support check. Or else, sad to say, they are "obstinately" delinquent on their payments (of those fathers ordered to pay child support, 51 percent pay little or nothing at all).[8] As if refusing to underwrite mother-power, they force their ex-wives to go on welfare at the expense of their children. Having lost the day-to-day control over their children and the caregiving services of their wives, the men cut off their "caretaking."

Although most parents try to assure children the divorce was not their fault, kids believe otherwise. One boy said, "Look, I know the real reason [for the divorce] is that I broke my nose twice and Daddy didn't want to pay any more medical bills, so he left." Feelings of father abandonment are aggravated if the child's mother has a series of relationships with men to whom the child becomes attached, only to lose them when the romance fades. For such children, *a man who cares* becomes a more and more elusive grail.

Kramer vs. Kramer mined the truth about the long-neglected theme of single parenthood but reversed the statistical reality of who leaves whom: Hollywood found the one story that made the mother the "heavy."

Nevertheless, the emotional residue the film leaves behind is lasting and radical: *Kramer vs. Kramer* subversively taught us what real fatherhood feels like, and what happens to a man who feels it. It showed us that a father who is deeply involved in his child's everyday life, a father who is forced to be the buck-stops-here parent, to give routine and constant care, to *be* there, to witness the heart-stopping injuries, not just hear about them later—that kind of father is unable to let his child go. (It is my hunch that such a father would not be so quick to send his child to war either.)

Film critic Molly Haskel points out that "Hollywood has habitually developed a lump in its collective throat at the spectacle of macho man dwindling into a puddle of compassion over a child." But in its recent releases—*Kramer vs. Kramer, Ordinary People, Carbon Copy, Paternity, On Golden Pond,* and *Missing*—the child in question is always a boy, another version of the male-bonding films of the Seventies, notes Haskel. "The man-to-manness of the bond certifies the virility of the new parenting."[9]

The observation is well taken. But in *Kramer vs. Kramer* Dustin Hoffman did not fight for his son just to win a buddy, or to keep the boy from Meryl Streep. He fought because *he could not imagine life without his child.* He could not go back to fathering the way he used to, the way most men are fathers, and certainly not the way most men with visitation rights are fathers. Fathers who have spent a great deal of time with their children cannot let go of them any easier than mothers can.

CHILD CUSTODY

If all fathers were as caring, time-involved and nurturant as Mr. Kramer, I would be totally enthusiastic about the notion of full or shared custody for fathers. After all, it does seem unfair that about 90 percent of the children of divorce are in their mothers' custody, and judges seem to continue to favor women in these cases. However, this is not necessarily *prima facie* proof of discrimination against men. As Nancy. D. Polikoff points out in her penetrating critique:

> If a father wants custody of his children and fights for them, the picture is very different from that which both popular belief and fathers' rights movement ideology would suggest. [In 1968, 20 percent of fathers requested sole or joint custody; by 1977, that percentage was down to 7.8—and 63 percent of the fathers who wanted physical custody got it.] . . . The power to decide child custody often lies with the father, not the mother. . . . By not wanting custody, men, and not judges, are responsible for the 90 percent figure.

Polikoff goes on to question why the fathers' rights movement focuses on getting the child during divorce rather than improving co-parenting during marriage, or helping father-child relationships become closer, or fighting for social and workplace change that would make it easier to *be* an involved father. This, it seems to me, is the difference between old-style fathers who are hooked on ownership and power, and new fathers whose focus is care and love.

Unfortunately, most men's efforts have centered on defeating the ex-wife regardless of the truth about which parent did or can do most of the care-giving, and regardless of the mother-child bond or the best interests of the child. Here are some of the problems that make me, at times, perceive father's rights as father's coercion:

• If both parents have been employed, it is often the father's claim that both have been equally involved in child-rearing. (As we've noted, in the typical family this is far from the case.)

• If the mother has been a full-time housewife but goes to work to support herself after the separation, the father says that she will have less time and interest in the child than he does—although he has always been working full-time. Writes Polikoff, "There is an undercurrent of punitiveness throughout custody decisions involving employed women, who, after all, comprise the majority of divorced and separated mothers."

• Rigid ideas about sex role identification (boys need fathers, girls need mothers, both need a man to establish the meaning of authority) allow fathers to argue on their behalf as *men,* not necessarily as *parents.*

• The popular belief that mother-headed households are inferior and create problem children often leads judges to favor the father without reference to his parenting ability.

• When financial ability is the criterion for custody, fathers almost always win. The idea is to keep women untrained, inexperienced and underpaid in the marketplace and then claim that they don't have the job security or income to support their children. Sometimes a man makes a custody claim against his ex-wife because she is a welfare mother when the reason she is on welfare is because he cut off his court-ordered child support.

• Because of the cultural preference for two-parent families, judges often give custody to the father, who is more often remarried, since a man—whatever his age—is more likely to find a new mate than is a woman if she is middle-aged. Many judges think all women are equally adept at childrearing by virtue of being female. Therefore, the father's new wife, or even his hired housekeeper, seem family enough (and better than the now poor single mother).

• Judges tend to "overrate small paternal contributions to parenting because they are still so noticeable," writes Polikoff. "In other words, the emphasis in evaluating mothers is on what they do not do, because they are expected to do everything. By this standard, men will always look good for doing more than nothing, and women will always look bad for doing less than everything."

TIME STUDIES

Yet, in terms of time alone, the typical American father has a long way to go to achieve equal parenthood. One famous study found that the average father interacts with his baby for less than 38 seconds a day.[11] In 38 seconds, you cannot change a diaper or sing three verses of "The Farmer in the Dell." The *most* time any father in this sample devoted to his infant in one day was 10 minutes, 26 seconds—barely enough time for a bottle and a burp. Other fathers studied have averaged 26 minutes a day interacting with a child under age five, and 16 minutes with children between the ages of six and seventeen. Still others have logged up to 15 minutes a day feeding their babies, compared to 1½ hours daily for mothers; almost half these fathers said they had *never* changed the baby's diapers, and three out of four had no regular caregiving responsibilities whatsoever.

Although some researchers make the point that "when the amount of time available to spend with children is considered, the father's involvement with his children is equal to that of the mother's"[12] they fail to examine the willingness to *make* time available or to differentiate the *content* of the time each parent spends with children. When playtime is measured, fathers may well equal or even surpass mothers; but when caring time is measured, fathers are again largely absent. Moreover, it is not enough to excuse men on the basis of their having less "available" time without questioning whether they have made themselves as available as possible or whether they have used masculine role imperatives to justify being *un*available.

Although no one is quite sure how to measure father-involvement with older children who require no feeding and diapering, we have only to look at children's survey responses to learn that what exists is not enough.

• In one study, half the preschool children questioned preferred the TV to their father.

• In another study, one child in ten (aged seven to eleven) said the person they fear most is their father;

• Half the children wished their fathers would spend more time with them; and

• Among children of divorce, only one-third said they see their fathers regularly.

When children were asked how TV fathers are different from real fathers, the TV fathers came out better in two areas: They don't yell as much as real fathers, said the kids, and they spend more time with their children than real fathers. A second-grader commented: "They're always there when the kids need them." "They care for children," added a fifth grader, "talk to children, show them they love them. Hug them."[13]

Most experts reassure harassed working mothers that what counts isn't the quantity but the quality of the time they spend with their children. For today's father, the challenge is to increase both quality *and* quantity. At this moment in history, caregiving fathering is still the exception; a choice— something a man can decide to do or not to do, and suffer no consequences if he doesn't. This may be changing, though, now that the experts are discovering fatherhood and legitimizing the "new" father.

Dr. Spock, for example. After twenty-seven years and book sales in the tens of millions, Benjamin Spock rewrote portions of his baby bible to make important nonsexist improvements, including this advice to fathers (which I highlighted in *Growing Up Free*):

Original: A man can be a warm father and a real man at the same time. . . . Of course I don't mean that the father has to give just as many bottles or change just as many diapers as the mother. But it's fine for him to do these things occasionally. He might make the formula on Sunday.	*Revision:* I think that a father with a full-time job—even where a mother is staying home—will do best by his children, his wife and himself if he takes on half or more of the management of the children (and also participates in the housework when he gets home from work and on weekends).

Dr. Spock also helped present and future fathers by retracting his advice about "sex-appropriate" toys. In his revised edition, he wrote:

> I think it is normal for little boys to want to play with dolls and for little girls to want to play with toy cars, and it's quite all right to let them have them. A boy's desire to play with dolls is parental rather than effeminate, and it should help him to be a good father.[14]

The fear of effeminacy causes parents to raise boys under severe sex role pressure to achieve something called "manhood"—which boys must earn and re-earn by establishing the many ways they are different from women. Primary in this proof-of-manhood-by-contrast is the relationship each sex is "supposed" to have with babies and children. And that relationship begins with doll play.

OF DOLLS AND MEN

The notion that doll play makes boys into "sissies" is a homophobic equation that clouds men's minds, obscuring the simple truth that when a boy plays with a doll, he is just modeling the parent–child relationship that he has known himself: He is pretending to be his own father. Presumably, in most cases, his own father is heterosexual. Thus, doll play is a boy's homage to the husband-father role, and one would expect it to be actively encouraged by those who believe heterosexual marriage and fatherhood are desirable for all males. But homophobia turns the culture against doll play for boys on the assumption that it turns boys into *mothers*. Somehow, heterosexist logic cannot imagine turning boys into fathers.

The crazy part is, by making doll play off-limits to boys and squelching their interest in "playing house" or caring for small children, *our culture creates an aversion to the very activities that make a man a good father.* In other words, boys are faced with two contradictory paradigms—the "real man" and the "good father"—and the latter is too often sacrificed for the former. The way to resolve this no-win situation is to reconcile the two masculine archetypes so that both embody the *same* human traits, not contradictory traits. Although a "real man" need not become a father, a man who *is* a father must be able to feel his manhood *confirmed* by active, caring fatherhood, rather than threatened by it.

The route to this state of mind is really quite simple. "Don't be the man you think you should be," I tell the men in my lecture audiences, "be the father you wish you'd had." And I think it is starting to happen—everywhere. In 1980, '81 and '82, I made the rounds of some thirty-five cities doing interviews on shows that take listeners' phone calls. To my surprise, the question that came up most often and aroused the most passion was how can men be better fathers?

• "My father never knew me," said an intense male voice over a Grand Rapids phone-in show. "I don't want to make the same mistakes with my own kids. I'm trying to learn how to father them while I still have time."

• "I'll never forget what happened when I was ten years old," recalled a seventy-year-old San Francisco man. "My mother had just died and my sister and I were standing beside the casket bawling. When my father saw my tears, he grabbed me and said, 'We're *men;* we're not going to cry. We're going to be strong.' I've swallowed my tears for sixty years and all I've got to show for it is a lifelong lump in my throat and mean memories of my father."

• An Indianapolis man said he had made a vow to learn how to take care of his kids after he heard about a local man who killed his entire family because his wife left him and he didn't know how to raise his four children.

• A New York City cab driver told me: "Being a father is more important to me than being a Baptist, being black, or being a man."

• A Washington, DC woman reported: "When our son said he'd be home from college on the day of my husband's office Christmas party, my husband asked him to come straight to the office. The boy bounded in, saw his father across the roomful of people, ran and threw his arms around my husband's neck and hugged and kissed him. At first I was embarrassed for my husband, but then I heard one man after another come up to him and say, 'I'd give the world if my son would do that with me.' "

It's a young phenomenon but the change is unmistakable. Fathering is becoming a new kind of verb—an active verb—that describes an enlarging role and new behaviors. Children are discovering their "other parent" and men are discovering their "other selves." Fathers are ripping off the stiff patriarchal collars of *their* fathers; men are writing about the old kind of father who couldn't tell his children his love or his fears, who "kept still and died in silence."[15] The American Psychoanalytic Association took up the subject of fatherhood at its 1982 conference, where scholars presented a paper on the rarely acknowledged traditional father, the father of the colonial period and the early years of this republic, who turns out to have had more in common with "the more nurturing" modern father than with the Victorian paterfamilias so sacred to "pro-family" conservatives.[16]

Everywhere, everyone, not just scholars, seems to be thinking and writing about the fathers they have or the fathers they are, and fatherhood is being redefined, reinvented, and redeemed. Men are taking more time away from the offices and factories where they have spent their lives being paid more *the more they stayed away from their families.* Old-style fathers, like Robert Townsend, the top Avis executive who wrote *Up the Organization,* have realized that the price paid for career supremacy was too dear: it cost him his family.

> I cheated them, worked like crazy—seven days a week, long hours. My children were an interruption. Today I don't know the oldest three at all. When I retired from business they were gone and it was too late. I'm sorry . . . because I've had more fun with the two youngest kids than I had in all those years of work.[17]

One economist claims that it is the "fear of uselessness" that keeps men out of the family circle and oriented toward the outside world. Because the disciplinarian-breadwinner had little to do around the house, he never got fully woven into the tapestry of family life. To compensate for that uselessness, for the emptiness of the old father role, men have concocted jobs, politics, sporting events, war, religion, and other "diversionary activities" that help them pretend to be important.[18]

The new father does not have to pretend. A man in Albuquerque, for example, loves being a father so much that he wanted to share his enthusiasm with a father-to-be. He gave his best pal a baby shower at which men friends gathered to toast the forthcoming baby with good will, good food, and a rap session about father feelings.[19] All over the country, men are materializing in childbirth courses, child-care centers, and early childhood education; they are staying home to care for their own children, braving the quizzical stares of cops and mothers as they push a baby carriage or watch their children in the playground; asking for joint custody; demanding paternity leave; and taking baby-care classes to prepare to be more skillful, better prepared fathers.

New research has given substance to the father role and its meaning to men and to children. At Yale, studies have shown that babies with stay-home fathers develop social and problem-solving skills at a precocious rate,[20] not because men are better at childrearing but because these babies are getting love and attention from *both* parents. (Unlike many working fathers, working mothers form these attachments to their infants even when they are not the full-time parent.) Other studies[21] reveal that men deeply share the highs and lows of childbearing: They get morning sickness, food cravings, and postpartum blues; fathers seem as adept as mothers at reading clues about what babies need; single fathers have been found to give "as much nurturance and warmth" as single mothers if they choose to, and giving it is as good for the father as it is for the child; and this newly acknowledged "fathering instinct" among human males has been corroborated in many other species.

Suddenly, magazines have discovered "Father Love," "A New Kind of Life with Father," and a "fathering boom."[22] Newspapers seem to be running more pictures of male sports stars and politicians holding or playing with their kids. The media made much of Senator Edward M. Kennedy's dropping out of the 1984 presidential race because of concern for his children. He claimed the pressures of a political campaign would be too hard on them so soon after the pain of their parents' divorce. "I believe that my first and overriding obligation now is to Patrick and Kara and Teddy," he said,[23] and though cynics may have raised a suspicious eyebrow, the fact is he made the announcement without apologies, with his children at his side, and with the confidence that his political future would survive it. In 1972, Edward Muskie ruined his career by showing "unmanly" emotion; ten years later, Teddy Kennedy could sacrifice power for love and still be a man.

At last, books and newsletters have been published by, for, and about the new father that do not address him as a glorified "mother's helper" but as a full participant in childrearing—whether his fathering fervor begins during the pregnancy, at birth, or at some midpoint in his children's lives, whether he is a co-parent or single parent.[24] Meanwhile, observing and evaluating these developments is the Fatherhood Project at the Bank Street College of Education, which will eventually issue a national report on men's actual involvement in parenthood, trends in child custody agreements, father education courses, and company policy on paternity leaves.[25]

New fathers, understandably, spawn new mothers, mothers willing to give up their preeminence in the nursery, mothers who never enjoyed being emotional surrogates for the too-busy Dad. Many women have begun to understand that nothing—no law or career breakthrough—will alter women's place more profoundly than men's increased fathercare. We are learning to relinquish whatever home-based power women exercise as monopolists of child development because that loss is more than offset by an increase in our personal freedom and the pleasures of shared parenthood. We too must give up power for love if we want more from our children's fathers than most of us got from our own.

As I write this, it is three weeks since my father died at the age of eighty-two. I have been stunned to discover that I remember every single thing he and I did together. There were so few. One visit to the zoo, one Sunday ice-skating, a horseback-riding adventure, a night at a street carnival, a few times at the circus, one—just one—family vacation, at the Top o' the World Lodge somewhere in the mountains, and my father's teaching me to drive. The rest is just a blur of his comings and goings—off to work, home for dinner, off to meetings, conventions, the synagogue. My father was parent to a dozen religious and charitable organizations; to me, he was judge and teacher, critic and goad. I remember bringing home an A-minus and being asked for an A. I remember trying to impress him, to charm him into wanting to be with me and my mother, trying to be smart for him, dressing to please him, but nothing I did could compete with his other world: the law, the war veterans, the bond drive, political campaigns, fundraising events, the Talmud, the Men's Club, his minions.

I know that some people have rich memories of fathers who were there when needed and I'm glad there is a growing literature about the very large ways fathers contribute to child development.[26] I've heard my women friends talk about watershed moments when their fathers helped them define who they were as women, what they would demand of life, and how much they might expect from men. One grown woman, facing the first Father's Day after the death of her father, composed a testimonial that describes the father many of us wish we'd had:

> As far as he was concerned, a child and parent should exchange love and respect every day, not save appreciation and recognition for special occasions. . . . I depended on him to be there, to catch me when I fell and put me back on my feet. I know that just being able to talk to my father, or to see him . . . was reassurance enough that, as Browning said, "All's right with the world."
>
> My father instilled confidence in me and my abilities, never doubting that I would succeed. His faith was so unswerving—and so unconditional. . . . Now I wonder if I'll ever stop aching over the loss of that tender, non-judgmental mirror that always reflected the me I so longed to be.[27]

The good news is long overdue. The truth-telling is cleansing. The reports of caregiving fathers are encouraging. But what makes me feel especially optimistic about the permanence of this phenomenon are three developments that could significantly legitimate the new father.

First, we are breaking the absurd linkage of Father with Breadwinner, understanding that one role is not dependent on the other and that neither role determines "masculinity." This is happening both because of the necessity for working mothers to share in the breadwinning, and because of the increased number of unemployed men in America. If that many men are out of work, all of them cannot be exhibiting a failure of "masculinity" or a lack of male role responsibility. Clearly, the fault is a larger failure, the economic and political failure of a system that has been allowed to blame the victim. Initially, the unemployed father feels guilty, inadequate, "unmanned." And then, judging by the men who speak out on TV talk shows and in press interviews, they begin to analyze what has happened and why they feel as they do.

TOM WAYNE: When your kid comes home and asks for a couple of dollars . . . what do you tell them when you ain't got it? . . . I mean when they're used to saying, "Dad, give me a couple of bucks," and you're used to pulling out your wallet and giving it to them. Now it's "sorry, son or daughter, I ain't got it."

PHIL DONAHUE: Do you feel like a failure?

TOM WAYNE: In a way, yes.

TERRY PERNA: Well, he said he feels like a failure; maybe he shouldn't. I don't know how you can get yourself from not feeling like a failure but it's not really his fault or anybody else's fault that they're not working.[28]

The cruel equation of Father with Breadwinner (money equals power, power equals manhood) results in nonworking fathers' feeling like non-men in their wives' and children's eyes, while Big Breadwinner fathers "earn" their manhood with a paycheck but sometimes lose their children in the process. Ironically, the misfortune of unemployment has had a positive side effect: It has introduced men to their children. Said a Detroit man about his layoff: "I've gotten to spend a whole lot more time with my kids. When I worked nights in the tire shop, I would never see them. Yeah. That's about the only good thing that's come out of it."[29]

And an unemployed executive with a graduate school degree confessed on the *Donahue* show:

. . . there are a lot of positives about this, too . . . and one of them is seeing my children walk for the first time and being there when they're in their bright and alert and awake hours rather than at the end of the day and the very beginning when they're just getting up or they're just ready to go to bed. That part has been an incredible joy to me and will be irreplaceable as long as I live.[30]

The second reason for my optimism is the dramatic change in the advertising images of men. Major advertisers are showing men diapering babies, giving middle-of-the-night bottles, helping kids brush their teeth, baking cookies—engaging in a three-dimensional fatherhood that far exceeds the old cardboard image of Dad carving the Thanksgiving turkey or driving the family car. If American business has begun to sell its products with the positive force of such fathering images, then that force must be formidable indeed.

Finally, I am optimistic because of the recent proliferation of child-care training courses for young *boys*. It started with an elective course for fifth-grade boys offered at a Manhattan private school, was given national visibility in a book called *Oh, Boy! Babies!*,[31] spread to other schools, and was further publicized by a made-for-TV movie based on the book. As with all social change, the old ideas about fathering cannot be permanently replaced until new ideas reach back and alter the *source* of our misconceptions. Childhood is that source; it is where our ideology of fatherhood takes root through experience with our own fathers, images of other fathers, and our own sex-role socialization. *Childhood is where fatherhood must be changed.* Thus, the baby-care class for boys, with its curriculum of care-giving skills development and its reinforcement of male nurturance, could forever eclipse the caricature of the formal or blundering father and replace it with a new father who wants to be involved, knows what to do and is proud he can do it.

Mike Clary is such a father. He spent two years as a full-time parent to his daughter Annie. He says that his kind of fatherhood taught him as much as moving to Walden Pond taught Thoreau:

> Annie makes me vulnerable—to longing, to daydreams, to fears, to pain. She has also made me capable of a love that seems boundless. That lack of constraint sometimes scares me. I feel responsible for that love, and wary of its energy, but I have grown comfortable with its weight.
>
> Annie has, finally, by making me a father, made me more of a man.[32]

This, then, is the new father. We've been waiting for him for a long, long time.

10

Familial Friendship: Love and Time Are All We Have

HAVE YOU EVER NOTICED how often people use family parallelisms to describe other experiences?

Actors say the cast of a long-running show is "as close as a family." An author writing about the importance of friendships calls her book *Friends as Family*.[1] Beloved servants are said to be treated "like part of the family." The Pittsburgh Pirates adopted the Sister Sledge record "We're a Family" as their theme song. Johnson & Johnson calls itself "A Family of Companies." IBM, among other corporations, has company picnics and gives employees birthday presents to create "a sense of family." Lebenthal & Company, a brokerage firm, promises clients "We treat you like family." The Swedes describe their homogeneous nation as "one big happy family." In his 1983 inaugural address, New York Governor Mario Cuomo said, "We must be the family of New York." And murderers or not, the Mafia is called a crime *family* because of its supreme loyalty.

Any impersonal group that tries to function in a close, caring way wants to conjure up the word "family" because in cultural mythology, if not always in fact, the family is the paradigm of mutual dedication. Yet many real families are not content to be "like a family"; instead, they model themselves after the very organizations that are eagerly imitating *them:*

THE CORPORATE MODEL

Dad is the chief executive officer. Mom, the operating officer, implements Dad's policy and manages the staff (children), who in turn have privileges and responsibilities based on their seniority. Since money is power, and Dad makes the most, he is the final word. In the corporate family, intimacy runs on the profit motive.

THE TEAM MODEL

Dad is head coach, Mom chef of the training table and head cheerleader. The children, suffering frequent performance anxiety, play by the rules and stay in shape with conformity calisthenics. That means when Dad wants everybody out for volleyball, he expects no laggards, no pause for poetry, no preference for physics. You can't reach the championships with a bunch of individuals running off in all directions, he insists. In the team family, competition is the name of the game and winning is everything.

THE MILITARY MODEL

Dad's the General. Mom always pulls KP and guard duty with a special assignment to the nurse corps when needed. The kids are the grunts. Rank justifies arbitrary behavior. Sympathy is for softies. Discipline is all. Unruly children are sent to the stockade; insubordinate wives risk dishonorable discharge. Punishment is swift and sadism is called character-building. For further details, see the movie *The Great Santini.*

THE BOARDING SCHOOL MODEL

Dad, the rector or headmaster, is in charge of training strong minds and bodies. Mom, the dorm counselor, oversees the realm of emotion, illness, good works, and bedwetting. The children are dutiful students. The parents, of course, have nothing left to learn; theirs is but to teach and test. When a family is run like a classroom, life is a continual report card and love a pass/fail course.

THE THEATRICAL MODEL

Dad, the producer, also plays the role of Father. Mom, the stage manager, doubles in the part of Mother. Children, the stagehands, also act the roles of Girls and Boys. No writer or director is necessary because the lines are scripted, the roles are sex stereotypes, the plot predictable. Improvisation is not allowed. When a family is a cast of characters, family life is an act.

Although I've posited two-parent units, these models may as readily be found in one-parent situations, collectives, step-families—wherever there are adults who need structures to prop up their self-esteem. My point is that, while other groups aspire to be families, families try to be something else because of the way family politics distort our world view.

Since companies, teams, armies, and such are, by their very nature, impersonal, male-dominated hierarchies, they hunger for what such groups find hardest to come by: care and warmth. When they catch a glimmer of either, they're quick to wrap it in the bunting of family in order to forge a connection between their sterile structure and the home— the apotheosis of human organizations.

The family, on the other hand, is thought of as women's and children's domain and, as we've seen, is largely left to fend for itself. Like any powerless group, the family seeks to approximate one of the more respectable, concrete social forms that have been dignified by money, status, and attention. Hungering for the semblance of power, family imitates its inferiors. However, while those pragmatic, impersonal struc-tures tend to bankrupt themselves and break under adversity, most families bend with their storms, bounce back with a modicum of help, and often outlast them all. As long as families persist in describing themselves in non-family terminology, let me propose an alternative model.

THE FRIENDSHIP MODEL

Mom, Dad, children, and other family members are best friends. Everyone gives care and takes care. Infants and small children demand more one-sided attention, but as in long-term friendship, the balance changes over time. Each person understands that the others may have different ways of giving support and expressing love at different times of their lives. Nevertheless, familial friendship rests on a rudimentary sort of equality, a kind of shared dignity. It does not allow one person to oppress another in order to feel strong. It offers both closeness and room to stretch. It crumbles under the weight of possessiveness, betrayal, exploitation, or abuse.

As is the case with dear friends, we choose to please our families or spend time with them because we love and enjoy them, not because we fear or tolerate them. They are our friends in need, but also in triumph. They are the people we lean on and the people who make leaning unnecessary.

When I ask friends if they can put their family relations to the test of friendship, many grow shamefaced. Viewed from that angle, they confess that their families get the worst of them and their friends the best: "I couldn't yell at my friends the way I yell at my husband. They'd never speak to me again." "If I humiliated my friends in public like I do my kids, I wouldn't *have* any friends." Might you ask a friend to serve you dinner every night or mend your clothes? I ask. "Of course not. That's not what friends are for." But is that what families are for? What did they do to deserve second-class treatment?

I think it was Robert Frost who said home is where, when you go there, they have to let you in. Our families see us at our most foolish or arrogant—and forgive us. They catch us being dumb, weak, envious, sick, sad, ugly, or drunk—and love us anyway. Divorce aside, they usually manage to overlook our mistakes, stick by us one way or another, and find something good to say about us at our funerals. Walk through any cemetery; you won't find epitaphs to a "Great Buddy," "Brilliant Comptroller" or "Fine Colleague." What ends up on our tombstones is "Beloved Wife, Mother, and Sister," "Beloved Husband, Father, and Grandfather," "Beloved Child." Our family credentials matter most at the end of life, but during it, most of us take our families for granted and show more consideration to a casual acquaintance.

Since friendship seems to bring out our best behavior, maybe it makes sense for us to try consciously to transform our families into our friends—not to invalidate family's special status, make parents into pals, or eliminate the boundaries between childhood and maturity (as so many fear[2]), but rather to hold family relations to the highest possible standard of human relations. Yet, as noted in Chapter Two and elsewhere in this book, structurally, emotionally, and developmentally, families offer far more than friendship, so in a way, it would be diminishing to expect them to emulate a less complex relationship. To reconcile these contradictions, what is needed is a conceptual framework that incorporates friendship's behavioral standards into family's enduring nest. That conceptual framework is what I am calling "familial friendship."

What is it? What happens between people to keep them as "close as a family"? One can give a thousand different answers—common interests, shared work, trust, adventures, exchanged confidences, a sense of humor, and so on—but underneath them all, in the purest, most profound sense, *love and time are all we have.* Familial friendship is embodied in the means by which *love is expressed* between and among us, and the way our *time is spent* together.

Naturally, we begin with love.

LOVE

For a long time, married love, like married sex, has had negative cultural connotations. "Getting hitched," the comedians used to say, "is the best cure for romance." When Nancy Mitford's *Love in a Cold Climate* was telecast, its advertising blurb was "They were brought up to marry—not fall in love." In contemporary magazine ads, the honeymoon is a turning point after which couples become no-nonsense consumers, shown furnishing their home, rearing their children and exhibiting almost no personal and sexual interest in one another. To Madison Avenue, courtship and weddings are romantic but marriage, clearly, is not.

A century ago, Oscar Wilde wrote, "The world has grown so suspicious of anything that looks like a happy married life;"[3]

in 1940, Denis de Rougemont proclaimed, "Now, passion and marriage are essentially irreconcilable,"[4] and in 1982, A. Alvarez, the British writer and critic, observed: "We have reached the point where a good marriage seems as unusual, almost as scandalous in some devious way, as divorce did a generation or two ago. People wonder if the partners are feeding each other's unhealthy dependency. The possibility that they might like each other's company and be friends and lovers seems impossible to contemplate."[5]

Among the social scientists, too, married love has had a bad press. In the 1930s, an influential sociologist named Willard Waller described marriage as "a private hell" and claimed that "romantic conventions conceal a fierce sexual struggle."[6] Romance in marriage was considered "immature" by experts, including Margaret Mead and Philip Slater. Love was supposed to be *replaced* by friendship, romance by respect and cooperation—people seemed unable to entertain the two ideals simultaneously. In the 1960s, hippies were "kicking the togetherness habit" altogether, and by the 1980s, in a complete reversal of the 1950s, romantic, happy marriages were entirely absent from prime time television, the barometer of mass social values.[7]

During the early years of the modern women's movement, the word was that romance was dead. If it hadn't already died with the flower children who courted irreverently if at all, it received a fatal blow from feminists who believed love was an opium of women as strongly as Marxists believed religion an opium of the people. "Romance, like the rabbit at the dog track," said Beverly Jones, "is the illusive, fake, and never attained reward which for the benefit and amusement of our masters keeps us running and thinking in safe circles."[8] Love, declared Ti-Grace Atkinson, is "woman's pitiful deluded attempt to attain the human" by making "an alliance with the powerful."[9] Germaine Greer thundered, "Love, love, love—all the wretched cant of it, masking egotism, lust, masochism, fantasy, under a mythology of sentimental postures, a welter of self-induced miseries and joys."[10]

"Is it the presence of romantic love that impedes women's power and authority in the public domain?" asked anthropologist Peggy R. Sanday after studying women's status in many cultures. "Is romantic love a mechanism for keeping women in their place and happy with their lot?"[11]

Many feminists answered yes: love between women and men sanitizes sexual politics; love hoodwinks women into giving men free sex and domestic service in return for a roof over their heads. Love blinds us to our status, saps our strength, steals women's time from work or art.

I accepted that analysis as far as it went, but it seemed strangely class-bound and unimaginative. It left no room for love unweighted by economic dependence, or love with a man who makes himself equally vulnerable. Moreover, no matter how "politically incorrect" it was at the time, I did not experience being in love as a trade-off for submission. It felt good: nourishing and empowering. In fact, I found love and feminism distinctly symbiotic.

Thankfully, throughout the 1970s, there were other voices of dissent.

After a tortured journey through man-hating, lesbianism, and celibacy, Ingrid Bengis admitted at the end of her book, *Combat in the Erogenous Zone,* "the thought of loving someone and being able to see them for four or five hours every day and spend the night sharing the daily accumulation of simple, silent warmth both sexual and nonsexual is one of the more inspiring aspects of life."[12] To the query "Is Romance Dead?" Barbara Harrison concluded, "I think the burial may have been premature."[13] Gerda Lerner, a founder of Women's Studies as a specific discipline in American colleges, confessed: "I also wanted to talk about marriage and love. I have had what people tell me is an unusual experience, a thirty-three-year-old happy marriage that ended with the death of my husband. This is not as unusual as people think, nor as unattainable as many feminists think."[14]

And there was even guidance from the past. For instance, Emma Goldman, the early-twentieth-century anarchist-feminist, warned that her attack on church, state, and private property was not a rejection of love. "Indeed, if partial emancipation is to become a true emancipation of women, it will have to do away with the ridiculous notion that to be loved, to be sweetheart and mother, is synonymous with being slave or subordinate."[15]

Many feminists reconsidered—not because of the way love is practiced, but because of its possibilities. I found those possibilities best expressed, oddly enough, in Shulamith Firestone's revolutionary tract, *The Dialectic of Sex:*

> . . . love is essentially a simple phenomenon—unless it has become complicated, corrupted or obstructed by an unequal balance of power.
>
> Love between two equals would be an enrichment, each enlarging himself through the other: instead of being one, locked in the cell of himself with only his own experience and view, he could participate in the existence of another—an extra window on the world. This accounts for the bliss that successful lovers experience: Lovers are temporarily freed from the burden of isolation that every individual bears.[16]

Successful lovers confirm that view. Their union enlarges rather than constricts. They see love not as the traditional ideal of two people becoming one, but of each *one* becoming two, living one's own life and a bonus life through the loved one.

Viola and Jim Berton, aged seventy-three and eighty-one, recently marked the fiftieth anniversary of what researchers call their "golden sunset" marriage—a union of well-matched, contented people who would do it all over again exactly the same way. The Bertons attribute their half-century love affair to their respect for each other and their self-celebration: "We continually try to do things that vary our life, that bring excitement to it," she says. "Just the simple idea of going out to breakfast can be different."

"Living with Mrs. Berton has been better and better every year," he says.

Apparently, this includes their sex life.

"Many people seem shocked to learn that older people are interested in sex," she says, "but we are. To be a good wife, I had to be a good sexual partner because he's interested."

"And how!" says he.

"If he sees a gleam in my eyes," she adds, twinkling, "it's not from my bifocals."[17]

SEX

> The idea that sex functions most naturally when it
> is "lived" instead of "performed" seems to escape
> many people. That sex can be "lived" in marriage
> seems to have escaped almost everyone.
>
> —*Masters and Johnson*[18]

My definition of sexual love is trust plus lust. Too often though, marriage kills the lust and infidelity kills the trust— so that in one way or another, sex destroys love. Strange, but true. The great libidinous waves that sweep two lovers into marriage are tamed by marital respectability, fatigue, lack of imagination, religious or moral strictures, misplaced modesty ("Now don't kiss me in front of the children"), all contributing to a cooling-down process that goes under the name of growing up. Then, for many, infidelity seems to provide the missing flame until it shows itself to be fire without heat— but fire enough to consume married trust.

In a sense, it's a miracle any of us has a healthy appetite for sexual love, especially within marriage. Caught as we are between the extremes of dehumanized pornography and desexualized religion, our options seem to be damnation on the one hand and degradation on the other.

Consider, just for an instance, the contradictions emanating from the Church of Rome.

October 11, 1980: Pope John Paul II stated that a man is guilty of "adultery in the heart" if he lusts for his wife.[19]

In other words, married sex that is exciting becomes illicit sex; true sexual desire—though every couple's ideal—is not religiously desirable.

October 25, 1980: His Eminence decreed that divorced Roman Catholics who remarry are not "separated from the Church" but must abstain from sex if they want to receive communion.[20]

Message: Remarriage will be tolerated but enjoying it is a sin.

December 15, 1981: The Pope condemned contraception as a "manipulation and degradation" of human sexuality but upheld the "rhythm" method of sexual abstinence.[21]

Translation: Married people who decide not to have children must pay for it by not having sexual pleasure; people who have sexual pleasure must pay for it by having children. If you have enough children, presumably you have had enough sexual love.

January 26, 1982 and July 4, 1982: Roman Catholic dioceses in Arizona and Illinois refused to allow two engaged couples to marry because in each case, the man was paralyzed and unable to consumate the union.[22]

Meaning you cannot have great sex in marriage but you cannot have marriage without *procreative* sex. "I was always taught that sex is secondary to love and understanding," objected one of the fiancés. A deputy of the Church insisted the couple could "have a friendship kind of love," but are incapable of marital love.

June 23, 1982: "Those who choose matrimony do well," said Pope John Paul II in a personal analysis of scripture. "But those who choose virginity or voluntary abstinence do better.[23]

Translation: No sex is best. It avoids two carnal nasties: babies and orgasms that do not result in pregnancy.

The Catholic Church doesn't mince words when dictating attitudes on sexual lust, but it is not alone; it is simply the most forthright repressor. Other, less overt influences leave a more subtle mark on sexual *trust* and the issue of infidelity. For example, studies of black women in the United States, England, and Trinidad found that class and culture influences attitudes toward fidelity and the importance of sex in a marriage. On the subject of the sexual rights of women, lower-class black women in Philadelphia might say, "Anything he can do, I can do," while the Trinidadians believe in "strong monogamous restrictions." As for a husband's infidelity middle-class women in all three societies, consider it catastrophic; "nothing would be more threatening to her marriage," while in the lower classes, the common wisdom accepts that "no man could be sexually satisfied with only one woman at a time."[24]

Men cheat and call it "meaningless," as though the more incidental the unfaithful act, the easier to forgive. Yet, the fact that a man would betray the fealty and honor of his wife for something he *himself* calls inconsequential has always seemed to me a disloyalty that desecrates the marriage all the more for having been undertaken so lightly. For most women, casual sex is not the answer because "Did you score?" is not the question. Yet not every woman is faithful. Depending on which sex poll you read, between 21 and 54 percent of American wives have had extramarital sex (husbands' cheating outnumbers wives' two-to-one).[25] The point is that women's affairs are seen as more "immoral" and threatening precisely because they are less casual than men's. Partly, this is due to the double standard—"wild oats" are supposed to dismiss a husband's fling but not a wife's—and partly it's because of what women were raised to believe about sex:

- Sex is bad without marriage.

- Sex is good only if you're in love.

It follows that most women did not have much sex before marriage. It also follows that most women married for love or called it love to sanitize, and "feminize," their sexual desire. But *after* marriage, the two axioms yield a new logic: "If I'm having an affair outside of marriage, I must *be* in love."

Thus, women's extramarital affairs tend to be experienced —or at least thought of—as *love* affairs (legitimating the sexual), and love affairs tend to break up a marriage.

The craziness of it all. Wouldn't it be a lot more sensible if both men and women were free to have lots of sex with or without love before they marry—and no affairs after. We would have to change, not one household at a time, but the moral priorities of the entire culture. Virginity would be seen as the patriarchal confidence game that it is: an ethic that keeps women sexually unawakened, ignorant, and undemanding, and that assures one man power over a woman's sexual appetites and control over the paternity of her children. In contrast, when and if men and women have equal power, multiple sexual experiences *before* marriage would be encouraged for the sake of both partners' maturation and physical enlightenment, and unfaithfulness *after* marriage would be more forcefully condemned. Society would judge marital infidelity wrong not because of sin or shame but because it betrays and defrauds the person one is supposed to love most in the world. Loving lust in marriage would make sex outside of marriage irrelevant. It also follows that lustful marriage would more likely exist between people who had chosen each other after having a basis of comparison by which to evaluate the varying intensities of love, of sex, and of sexual love. In this perfectable future, what I would hope for is a new morality that assures young people of the propriety of premarital sexual experimentation while also increasing the censure for marital unfaithfulness and the importance of marital trust.

HAPPILY EVER AFTER SOMETIMES HAPPENS

It *is* possible: love demonstrated openly, devotion without self-abnegation, joyful (not necessarily procreative) sexual love within marriage, that is what Viola and Jim Berton had as they reached their Golden Anniversary with the gleam still in their eyes. It would seem to be what awaits the couples that Dr. Helen Singer Kaplan is now studying, couples married from fifteen to twenty years who feel they are living the happily-ever-after dream.[26] What these enthusiastic long-lasting romances seem to have in common is "an enormous degree of communication and sensitivity," explains Dr. Kaplan,

almost as if his ear itches, she'll scratch it before he says anything. Each just knows how the other feels. And they're very excited about each other . . . very uncomfortable when they are apart and happy when they are together. They remain sexually attractive to each other, which is the most astounding thing. . . . They rarely quarrel, and if they do, it's only a brief flare-up because the distance is so painful they want to get the fight over with. Theirs is an inherent equality because they have an equal power to hurt each other. They are highly motivated to resolve their differences because closeness is so gratifying. It's not that they are unaware of each other's faults, but they don't dwell on them. There's total acceptance of each other. Total.

Dr. Kaplan is afraid that her study may create unrealistic goals among people whose bonds are not so idyllic. At the same time, she believes it important to publicize such marriages because through them we may learn that romantic monogamy may be "the natural tendency," the "norm" that has been perverted by the stresses and pathologies of modern life.

Whatever the objective truth, I'm not sure it matters. The fact that joyous, enduring love exists proves that it *can* exist, irrespective of modern pathologies and blasé cynicism. And if it does exist, if two people feel it and want to nurture it, it is also "politically correct." *From the perspective of family politics, the willingness to express love openly and to declare one's all-out need for another person is the gift of vulnerability—the polar opposite of dominance.*

Furthermore, that kind of vulnerability and demonstrativeness may be an amulet for good health. Studies show romantic love helps us separate from our family of origin and create a new intimacy group. Kissing is curative (a goodbye kiss in the morning seems to add five years to a man's life and reduces his likelihood of accidents and illness), hugs can reduce tension and depression, and warm affection from a wife seems to protect men against angina—a common heart ailment.* Couples who rate high on companionship (plus shared power and housework) are healthier and live longer.[27]

Oversimplified? Maybe. But the hugs and kisses, love notes, breakfast in bed, roses (including those *she* gives *him*), candlelight dinners (including those *he* gives *her*), satin sheets, private nicknames, intimate games, and continuing courtship rituals cannot be dismissed if they quicken the pulse between two people who have lived together for fifteen or fifty years.

THE HOUSEHOLD MOOD

Not only do overt acts of love and absolute fidelity demonstrate to one person the feelings of the other, but they establish the *emotional environment* of a family. When love rules that environment, chances are power hierarchies will not, and children will grow up seeing human relationships as sources of satisfaction, not exercises in dominance. This is also true in relationships *between* parents and children and among children, grandparents, and other relatives. I see the glow of such relationships not in romantic terms of course, but in the subordination of power to love. What I mean is this: In a traditional household, issues are resolved by the will of the most powerful member, but in a democratic family—as in a friendship—conflicting desires are reconciled by negotiation and the goal is to reduce the discontent of one party without adding to the discontent of another. A few examples illuminate the point:

> *Item:* The last time Edith Engel saw her two grandchildren was four years ago outside a courtroom. They were waiting to go before a judge who later rejected Mrs. Engel's plea for regular visits with the children of her runaway daughter. . . . The children's father, now remarried, opposes her request for visiting rights.[28]

---

* There are no studies measuring the effect on women of a goodbye kiss, hugs or warm affection from a husband.

Grandparents caught in the crossfire of a divorce may be denied access to their grandchildren for various reasons: One of the child's parents may claim that the grandparent is intrusive or sabotages the parent's child-rearing; hurting the grandparent may be a way to hurt the former spouse; or the grandparent may just be an unwitting reminder of the despised ex-spouse. Whatever the reason, breaking contact between children and their nanas and papas is an act of parent power, not love for children. This unfriendliest of gestures is a logical extension of the new twentieth-century hierarchy in which midlife adults now dominate both the very young and the very old. A "Grandparents Rights" Bill is currently pending in the U.S. Congress that would ensure grandparents the right to petition for visiting privileges with their grandchildren. What a pity that, once again, the love/power dichotomy has defeated human happiness and forced people to redress in court what family politics has destroyed.

Item: The kids [ages 15 and 11] are very aware of our financial situation. They know more about what's going on in my life and what I think and feel than they would if I were married. I'd probably shield them more. But I think as a result they can talk to me more freely about themselves. They know I don't claim to have all the answers.—*Single mother, New York*[29]

Because we are the responsible adults and our children are the inexperienced babes, we sometimes get trapped in the posture of the know-it-all or the I-can-handle-everything stoic. We're supposed to have the answers whether the child asks "Can I go out and play?" or "What should I do with my life?" Eventually, however, kids discover the miracle of parental fallibility. Once they understand that life is full of ambiguity and some problems are even too big for their parents, the know-it-all can become a foolish figure. Wise mothers and fathers avoid that trap. They balance authority with vulnerability. They wonder and ask as often as they direct and command. In other words, they are both parents and friends.

For the single parent, that balance is a daily struggle with critical consequences. Of necessity, children in one-parent families become more independent at an earlier age and assume more responsibility for housework and younger siblings. Often, they also contribute to household and financial decision-making, and provide emotional support to the parent.

"We're not equals," says one mother who routinely discusses her career with her fourteen-year-old son, "but I probably regard him more as an equal than I would if I lived with another adult."[30]

While the friendship–egalitarian approach runs the risk of making children somewhat insecure financially because they know so much, or of foreshortening the carefree years of childhood because they do so much, the benefits may outweigh the risks: Single parents' kids may benefit from having more rights and privileges, a more honest view of the world, and a greater demand on them for unselfish behavior.

> *Item:* Two fifteen-year-old girls who usually have a midnight curfew have been invited to the senior prom. The girls' dates and most of the group are seventeen and eighteen; they're good kids, some drink beer but none are rowdy. The plan is to go from the prom to an all-night house party to the beach at dawn, to a restaurant for breakfast and then home. Do the girls' parents let their daughters go?

One set of parents says no. They pride themselves on setting rules and living by them. A curfew is a curfew. A good girl shouldn't be out on the town at dawn. And how can they be sure whoever drives won't drink?

The other set of parents has made it a practice to decide disciplinary questions by putting themselves in their child's place rather than putting the child in her place. These parents believe that in general, empathy is a more significant character trait than obedience. They can see that the prom is a special occasion and deserves special consideration. They make inquiries and satisfy themselves that the young people will act with good judgment and the locations are safe. Moreover, they feel they know their own daughter and can trust her good sense. They end up saying yes.

The first set of parents insists on obedience to their authority regardless of the particular circumstances. The other parents ask themselves, would our daughter be deeply disappointed if she can't go and do we want to disappoint her if we don't have to? Would we be saying no because of her age? If so, can we prove a seventeen-year-old is any more "ready" for such an evening? If we say no because of the possibility of drinking, can we be certain no one ever drinks on those evenings when she comes home at twelve? Would we be saying no "on principle"? Can we make a case for our principles? Do we really believe it will harm her to miss a night's sleep? Did we ever stay up all night, or want to?

This sort of dialogue, plus discussion with the child, helps us reconcile yet another pair of contradictory impulses of parenthood: the wish to protect our children and the desire to train them for independent living. It is useful to identify our own true motives for coming down on one side or the other.

Asked at what age they would let their children ride a bike on the street, visit other children, go away to camp, travel alone on a plane, or babysit on weekends, the parents who granted daughters more independence at earlier ages were those with the most nontraditional sex role attitudes.[31] In another survey, most respondents said parents had no business interfering in their teenagers' choices about education, religion, or grooming, but they thought parents had a right to censor what a twelve-year-old boy reads, to make a fourteen-year-old girl wear a bra to school, and to insist a fifteen-year-old keep his door open during his girlfriend's visit.[32]

To be sure, setting limits protects our children and tells them we care about them. But sometimes we have to admit that our limits are arbitrary and what we call "protection" is an expression of parental hangups and the sheer flex of parental powers. Sometimes we have to care enough to give up control, and love them enough to let them go.

This may be especially hard to do when children become rebellious adolescents who seem to challenge absolutely everything their parents stand for. One minute they're dying their hair blue, the next minute they're dressed like bluebloods at a debutante ball. They have mood swings. They try to figure out who they are by using their friends as "raw material" and their friends' fads and styles as "inventory." What they need is stability at home while they do it. But many parents misinterpret their teenagers' behavior, says Dr. Vivian Seltzer, a developmental and clinical psychologist:

> Adolescence is a crucial developmental stage where friends, not parents, serve the primary educating role. Parents often mistake this growing process for rebellion, but they aren't seeing flight *from* parents as much as a powerful pull to the peer arena. In fact, it is home that provides a haven from the stress of the peer group rather than the other way around.[33]

There it is again, the idea of home as the place one goes for the ultimate friendship, the solid ground that offers relief from transitory friendships. If we did not insist on power over our children, we would not resent their friends' influence as challenge to that power. And if we did not take our teenagers' rebellion personally, they might find their self-image without disavowing us in the process.

TIME

Remember my contention at the start of this chapter: love and time are all we have. Time use *is* family history. What we do together counts. It adds up to years. It makes memories. "More than anything," reports a 1982 study, "Americans are looking for companionship in their leisure time and a person's spouse or romantic partner, children and close friends are the most important elements of that companionship."[34] Yet with all the talk of family togetherness and all the polls that show family to be supremely important, one out of four of us suffers from loneliness, and adolescents are the loneliest people of all.[35] More than three out of ten teenagers feel their fathers spend "too little time" with them, and 28 percent would like to spend more time talking with both parents.[36] In all, three out of four Americans consider it "very important" to do things as a family group.[37] But, sadly enough, what we do when we're together is spend our time in front of the TV set. In the 1982 study, 72 percent of families watched television every day (in contrast, about the same number of parents read to their children only once or twice a week)— and extended TV-watching has been found to deepen loneliness.[38] Another survey found:

> Television watching is the most frequently mentioned family activity, and 35 percent of the families are "total television households," meaning that their television sets are turned on all afternoon, at dinner time, and all evening. . . . A large number of families do little more than watch television together.[39]

I have my own theory about this and it has nothing to do with the attractions on the TV screen. I think most adults are ill at ease with children *unless* there is something to do. So many adults, accustomed to thinking in hierarchies, consider children charges, not persons; they do not know what to say to a child other than demanding information or issuing a command. Many do not know how to respond when kids talk to them. So, they become bored and impatient. They are afraid of letting down their guard and being too much of a pal. (The act of becoming a parent makes certain people lose touch with the child within themselves.) Or they are afraid the child will be bored with them and rather than risk rejection from an "inferior," they make no effort to connect. Thus, they watch TV side by side, mesmerized, unspeaking, unengaged. It is not the television itself that depersonalizes parent-child time, but our generation's use of television as *an escape from intimacy*.

For some families, vacations serve the same purpose. Experts say couples with "precursors for tension" will quarrel more on vacation,[40] and it seems safe to assume the same is true of families. Add to that the fact that three out of four American families take car trips (theme parks like Disney World are the most popular family destinations) and the second favorite activity is camping—and that families spend an average of five days together at a time[41]—and you have a lot of close-quarter intimacy to escape from and a lot of potential for tension.

Of course, things go wrong on vacations. We lose our way, miss connections, misplace baggage, get sunburn, insect bites, and cabin fever. Kids fight, parents fight, tempers fray, and, according to one survey at least, 11 percent of vacationers come home depressed.[42] But if families are friends at the core, and their activities during vacation times are not *intended* as an escape from intimacy, things can go right and something very precious can be gained. Besides the shared memories of what is seen and done in faraway places, there are the long stretches of uninterrupted time for each other, time to listen or relax in easy silence, and time for family members of different ages who usually have different interests to find things they like doing together, whether picking berries, playing word games, or riding the waves.

"We act better toward each other when we're on vacation," says one mother. "We're working toward a common goal. Having fun, having a good time, is when everybody is interested in what we're doing and content with one another."

To be sure, as John Updike reminds us, there is another side to this: ". . . families doing everything for each other out of imagined obligation and always getting in each other's way, what a tangle."[43] But I'm not talking about "obligation." Involuntary companionship is martyrdom, and who wants that? Notwithstanding my brief for spending and cherishing quality time together, I know not everyone is always going to want to do the same things at the same time—especially as children grow older. It is surely no tragedy to go our separate ways if Mom loves to ski and Dad hates the cold. Familial friendship feeds on more complex fare than the extremes of fairytale togetherness or TV oblivion.

When togetherness is voluntary and the time is spent creatively, what is produced can be a bonus above and beyond sweet memories. A University of Chicago study of very talented children measured the time and attention their parents gave them. Originally, the investigators hypothesized that the kids' remarkable abilities won the parents' inordinate time and attention, but the reverse proved true: The parents' attention seemed to create talented children. The most extraordinary swimmers, for example, got that way because their parents made sports and outdoor recreation a "regular part of family life." The great young pianists had parents who constantly played music, bought their kids records and musical toys, taught them to read notes, and sang together for fun.[44]

When families do things together, whether it is sports or music, going out or staying home, playing with toys, cooking, reading, talking, gardening, building, or fixing, it is the content of the parent-child interaction that matters. Clearly, certain situations are less conducive to interaction than others. For instance, a mother and a two-year-old navigating through the supermarket will average three or four squabbles per half hour,[45] while the same mother and child might share thirty minutes of pure pleasure during a half hour at home.

Now imagine that once a day, every day, you could be with your children for twenty minutes or a half hour just talking together. Imagine the whole family—parent, lover, friend, toddler, and teenager—in the same room at the same time without the distractions of play or work. Imagine them focused on one another, sharing experiences, solving problems, asking questions, watching reactions, teaching, learning, listening. In most households, those seemingly utopian encounters already happen, or could, every evening—and they're called dinnertimes.

I have chosen to end this book at the dinner table, not just because it is significant to our discussion of time use but because I consider dinnertime the quintessential metaphor for family life. We *are* our dinnertimes. Each family reveals itself by how it gathers around the table, where everyone sits, what is said, who serves, who speaks, how people listen, whether they linger, and how they each feel when it is over.

Although childrearing guides from John Locke (in 1689) to Benjamin Spock have been quite specific about when, what, and how much to feed children, I have yet to find advice on the meaning of mealtimes as a family experience. Yet day after day, year after year, those interludes add up—sometimes to as much as six thousand hours before the kids leave home. How do we spend those hours? Eating in front of the TV?

Wolfing food down in silence? Drifting through the kitchen one at a time, eating on whim? Feeding the kids first so the adults can have a more "civilized" meal, or bitterly enduring sibling struggles and gloppy high chairs?

Despite good reasons for each mealtime style—job schedules, kids' ages, level of parental energy, or whatever—I am convinced that many families would want to rethink their habits if they understood the great opportunity for intimacy and influence that mealtimes represent. By themselves, they cannot cure fundamental family estrangment, but in both emotional and intellectual areas, the positive potential of mealtimes is limitless.

To begin with, they are unbeatable for political education. Kathy Wilson, chair of the National Women's Political Caucus, says she acquired her ideology while eating: "My family was Republican and we discussed a lot of politics around the dinner table."[46]

Undoubtedly, there are also those who acquired their racism or misogyny or narrow-mindedness from digesting their parents' biases along with the stew and salad. But by the same token, many people can trace their appetite for social change or their understanding of the adult world to conversations around the oilcloth-covered kitchen tables of their youth.

In my childhood family, kids who got bored at large family dinners were free to leave the table. But if we were interested and quiet, if we didn't distract the grownups by fidgeting or knocking over glassware, we could stay in our chairs and listen or ask questions and get answers. After years of listening and asking, after hours of watching the adults pick at their cake crumbs while pressing their points, we knew enough, or thought we did, to chime in. If we said something inconsequential or simpleminded, their talk rolled over us like a tank. But if we had something to offer, they swept us into their discourse and at that moment each of us became a thinker— a *person*, not a child.

Eavesdropping on Reality. At the family dinner table, I heard the headlines from Hitler's Germany long before I could read them. I knew I should be grateful for my lamb chop because there were Jewish children like me starving in the

Warsaw ghetto. At five years old, I heard about the bombings, the concentration-camps, and the departure of my uncles to fight the Nazis. I'm not sure if my parents talked openly about Major Events because they thought I didn't understand, or because they wanted me to understand. I choose to believe the latter.

As far as I know, the only time the adults in my family spoke Yiddish—the language they used for keeping secrets from their American-born children—was when they talked about sex and divorce. In my childhood family, most supper seminars about serious subjects, apart from sex and war, were dominated by the fathers. It was the men who "went to business," so the men brought back the news of the world. The women reported bargains at the butcher shop, neighborhood news, gossip from the beauty parlor and what scandalous thing had happened to ruin which girl's reputation.

Consciously, I considered my father's news about his law clients and cases *real* conversation and my mother's stories background filler, like a radio heard through the wall of the next apartment. But unconsciously, I heard more. Along with the food she cooked, my mother fed me her female protein—sensitivity, diplomacy, kindness, budget trickery, flattery, poetry, and fibs—the stuff that gave her strength and dignity and disguised her powerlessness. I was not a receptive student back then.

On the other hand, a colleague of mine always found women's table talk as compelling as the political or theological discussions led by the men of her family. She noticed early on that women had more trenchant observations of people. At mealtimes on summer Sundays in her grandmother's house, if she sat quietly in the corner and shelled the peas or peeled the potatoes, they would forget to send her away when her racy Aunt Mae talked about sex or when her mother laughed about the foolish private behavior of the prominent white family she worked for. That's how she learned that "Big People didn't run their lives any better than ordinary folks."

Incidental Apprenticeships. If we have been nourished by a wide array of political and emotional motifs, a few of us also have gained rewarding professional legacies from our family dinner tables. One woman told me how her father, an oil millionaire, taught his children sophisticated principles of finance along with proper use of a knife and fork. He delighted in describing his company's business dilemmas and challenging the kids to find solutions. Today, that woman is the able vice president of the company she played games with at suppertime.

Miles from the nearest oil well, a far more commonplace middle-class family makes the same sort of intellectual capital out of mealtimes. The mother, a lexicographer, sets up spelling bees with her husband and sons between soup and dessert. Obviously, if intellectual entertainments arouse hostile rivalry or anxiety about winning the parents' approval, they are not worth the bonus in brainpower. But if they're undertaken in a spirit of fun, they can enrich children's education.

Nowadays, work-related discussions are as likely to be facilitated by the women of the family as the men. Any parent who describes hassles with a personnel director, volunteer agency, boss, unemployment office, or bank officer gives children an extracurricular course in self-sufficiency. The family time spent in such talk does more than relate to kids what we *do* all day. It educates them about the life force; tells them how to stoke the human spirit, survive corporate politics, beat the system, compromise, fight back, or forgive. Since twentieth-century children rarely have the opportunity to watch their parents on the job, these casual end-of-the day anecdotes become a modern version of the old apprenticeship system that introduced young people to the world of work.

The dinner hour also communicates the choreography of family life. Children notice who sits at the "head" of the table, which parent serves or gets served and which one, if any, seems to be the center of attention. Single parents, too, may send sex-role signals; for example, one father who has custody of his kids told me how he humiliated himself in front of them by drinking so much beer, he fell into a stupor during dinner. Later, he realized the guzzling had been a way to confirm his masculinity in front of a hard-drinking buddy he'd brought home for dinner—a man who thought that raising kids and cooking was not a man's job.

So much for exposing children to our world. To get more intimately familiar with *their* world, most parents resort to the classic dinner-table query: "What did you do today?" And they probably get a temperate, multisyllabic response no more than once a month. The only way to improve on that average is to behave with our children as we would behave with friends who came to dinner. Thus, we should not ask what the child did today unless we have the time and patience to listen to the answer. If we tune out just because they are meticulously recounting every play in their seven-inning softball game, we may not be made privy to other kinds of details when we want them. By the same token, if we've gotten out of touch, we cannot expect to "catch up" on our kids' lives with a barrage of questions. *Interrogation is not intimacy.* Children are especially expert at parrying unwanted questions with evasive grunts and wisecracks; they refuse to be cross-examined—and they're right. There is no shortcut to family intimacy; it is an organic result of putting in time and paying attention. It requires retention of family history and remembering from one day to the next what the child has told us, rather than starting from scratch with "What did you do today?" It comes from studying our children at mealtimes and taking seismic readings of their physical and emotional wellbeing according to the way they look, sound, sit, speak, pick at their food, or avoid our eyes.

What happens while food is being prepared, consumed, and cleared away teaches families many things about themselves, whether we choose to call mealtimes "educational" or not. Most people can conjure up their own childhood dinner table at the sight of a familiar salt shaker or the smell of a certain food. Therefore, who can doubt that mealtimes build memories more intense, evocative, and deeply imprinting than almost any we carry with us through our lives?

I am not naive enough to suggest that gathering the clan around the dinner table will spawn meaningful discussions every night or will automatically elicit cheerful moods, cooperative conversationalists, or a hunger for parental wisdom. Food fights will always be as close as the nearest squashed cupcake, and sullen faces, tantrums, and the expletive "Yucky!"

or "Gross!" will often greet a parent's well-meant discourse.

But if there is no regular daily effort to make intimate human contact between adult and child and among the children themselves, I question whether the entity called "family" can have any meaning. That meaning grows in families, as in friendships, when we routinely subsume our power in our love, and take the time to keep in touch with one another's lives.

Chapter Notes

Chapter 1: Whose Family Is It Anyway?

1. *Conservative Digest,* May/June 1980, pp. 2–3.

2. T. Lattaye, *The Battle for the Family,* Old Tappan, NJ: Revell, 1982; R. Kramer, *In Defense of the Family,* New York: Basic, 1983; B. Berger and P. L. Berger, *The War over the Family,* New York: Doubleday, 1983.

3. *The New York Times,** January 13, 1982; December 10, 1981; September 7 and August 17, 1980. See also Democratic Congressional Campaign Committee Report, April 30, 1980; "The Evangelical Right," American Jewish Congress Report, February 1981; Gallup Poll, *Public Opinion,* April/May 1981, pp. 20–41.

3a. D. Maguire, *The New Subversives,* New York: Continuum, 1982, p. 2. See also F. Conway and J. Siegelman, *Holy Terror: The Fundamentalist War on America's Freedoms in Religion, Politics and Our Private Lives,* Garden City, NY: Doubleday, 1982.

4. *Associated Press,* May 7, 1983; D. Yankelovitch, *Psychology Today,* April 1981, p. 60.

5. L. Cole-Alexander, director of the U.S. Labor Department Women's Bureau, quoted in *NYT,* February 6, 1982. See also G. Masnick and M. J. Bane, *The Nation's Families,* Cambridge, MA: Joint Center for Urban Studies of M.I.T. and Harvard, 1980.

6. J. Gasper, *The Right Woman,* May 1980.

7. *The Phyllis Schlafly Report,* May 1980. For more of Schlafly's family views, see her *PSR* of December 1982.

8. This is the definition promulgated by the Pro-Family Conference, 9700 Reseda Blvd., Northridge, CA 91324.

9. Supreme Court of the United States *Syllabus,* H.L. v. Matheson, Governor of Utah, *et al.,* decided March 23, 1981.

10. *The Eagle Forum,* October 1980, p. 1.

11. *World Press Review,* May 1982, p. 14.

---

* Henceforth *The New York Times* is abbreviated *NYT.*

---

12. *NYT,* February 14, 1982.

13. Sophocles, *Antigone,* Michael Townsend, trans., New York: Harper & Row, 1962, pp. 16–17.

14. Paul Weyrich, Committee for the Survival of a Free Congress, quoted in "Brayings of the New Right," a pamphlet published by Planned Parenthood of New York City, 380 Second Ave, New York, NY 10010. See also interview with Weyrich, *Conservative Digest,* May/June 1980, pp. 2–3.

15. *NYT,* September 9, 1982.

16. *New Directions for Women,* [a national newspaper] September/October 1982.

17. James Robison, television evangelist, quoted in "The Pro-Family Network's Dangerous Crusade," a Special Report of People for the American Way, 1015 18th St, NW, Washington, DC 20036

18. *Ms.* January 1981, p. 28.

19. C. Hymowitz and M. Weissman, *A History of Women in America,* New York: Bantam, 1978, pp. 83, 226, 329–31; E. C. DuBois, ed., *Elizabeth Cady Stanton—Susan B. Anthony: Correspondence, Writings, Speeches,* New York: Schocken, 1981, pp. 34, 132, 252; D. M. Scott and B. Wishy, eds., *America's Families: A Documentary History,* New York: Harper & Row, 1982, p. 514; E. Janeway, *The Powers of the Weak,* New York: Knopf, 1980, pp. 292–95; S. de Beauvoir, *The Second Sex,* New York: Bantam, 1961, pp. 99–102, 114, 116–18; S. M. Rothman *Woman's Proper Place: A History of Changing Ideals and Practices 1870 to the Present,* New York: Basic, 1978.

20. C. N. Degler, *At Odds: Women and the Family in America from the Revolution to the Present,* New York: Oxford, 1980, p. vi.

21. Quoted in "The Pro Family Network's Dangerous Crusade" (see note 17).

22. Quoted by Gloria Steinem in *Ms.,* November 1980, p. 21.

23. Request a copy of the Family Protection Act from your Senator or Representative. See also "The Pro-Family Movement and the New Right" in R. A. Viguerie, *The New Right: We're Ready to Lead,* Falls Church, VA: Viguerie, 1980.

24. *NYT,* May 24, 1981.

25. *National Center on Child Abuse,* Washington, DC

26. S. Abrahms, *Children in the Crossfire: The Tragedy of Parental Kidnapping,* New York: Atheneum, 1983; B. Lawrence and O. Taylor-Young, *The Child Snatchers,* Boston: Charles River, 1982; "Divorce American Style," *Newsweek,* January 10, 1983.

27. Gallup Poll, June 6, 1980.

28. A. Dworkin, *Right Wing Women*, New York: Perigee, 1983, chap. 1, "The Promise of the Ultra-Right."

29. J. Marcus, ed., *The Young Rebecca: Writings of Rebecca West: 1911–1917*, New York: Viking, 1982, p. 219.

30. S.M. Lipset, *Political Man: The Social Bases of Politics*, Garden City, NY: Doubleday, 1963; M. Horkheimer, "Authoritarianism and the Family Today," and E. Fromm, "The Oedipus Complex and the Oedipus Myth," both in R. N. Ansher, ed., *The Family: Its Function and Destiny*, New York: Harper & Bros., 1949, pp. 359–74, and 334–58; C. Lasch, *Haven in a Heartless World: The Family Besieged*, New York: Basic, 1977, pp. 87–93; P. Green, "Apple Pie Authoritarians," *The Nation*, July 3, 1982.

31. L. H. Fuchs, *Family Matters*, New York: Warner, 1971, p. 35.

32. *Ibid.*, p. 107

33. A. de Tocqueville, *Democracy in America*, vol. II, New York: Vintage, 1956, pp. 203–4.

34. Quoted in D. Maguire, *The New Subversives* (see note 3), p. 47

Chapter 2: The Enduring Nest

1. K. Pollitt, *The Nation*, April 5, 1980, p. 393.

2. C. P. Gilman, "The Home, Its Work and Influence," in D. M. Scott and B. Wishy, eds., *America's Families: A Documentary History*, New York: Harper & Row, 1982, pp. 459–64.

3. The following list represents a small sample of the wide range of books that examine the family as a social institution, each from its own perspective: J. B. Elshtain, ed., *The Family in Political Thought*, Amherst, MA: University of Massachusetts, 1982; J. Donzelot, *The Policing of Families*, New York: Pantheon, 1980; L. K. Howe, ed., *The Future of the Family*, New York: Simon and Schuster, 1972; C. N. Degler, *At Odds: Women and the Family in America from the Revolution to the Present*, New York: Oxford, 1980; K. Keniston and the Carnegie Council on Children, *All Our Children: The American Family Under Pressure*, New York: Harcourt Brace Jovanovich, 1977; I. Diamond, ed., *Families, Politics, and Public Policy*, New York: Longman, 1983; C. Lasch, *Haven in a Heartless World*, New York: Basic, 1977; M. Gordon, *The Nuclear Family in Crisis: The Search for an Alternative*, New York: Harper & Row, 1972; S. A. Levitan and R. S. Belous, *What's Happening to the American Family?* Baltimore: Johns Hopkins, 1981; M. Roman and P. E. Raley, *The Indelible Family*, New York: Rawson Wade, 1980; A. Toffler, *The Third Wave*, New York: William Morrow, 1980.

In addition, these provocative essays are worth reading: C. Greer, "Once Again the Family Question," *NYT* October 14, 1979; A. J. Cherlin, "The 50s Family and Today's," *NYT*, November 18, 1981; J. B. Orr, "The Changing Family: A Social Ethical Perspective," in V. Tufte and B. Myerhoff, eds., *Changing Images of the Family*, New Haven, CT: Yale, 1979, p. 377–

88; S. Keller, "Does the Family Have a Future?" in A. S. Skolnick and J. H. Skolnick, eds., *Family in Transition,* Boston: Little Brown, 1977; R. Baker, "What Is A Family For?," *NYT,* April 23, 1983.

4. R. N. Anshen, ed., *The Family: Its Function and Destiny,* New York: Harper & Bros., 1949 (especially the chapters by R. Benedict, T. Parsons, R. Linton, and R. N. Anshen); E. W. Burgess *et al., The Family: From Institution to Companionship,* 3rd ed., New York: American Book, 1963; W. N. Stephens, *The Family in Cross-Cultural Perspective,* New York: Holt, Rinehart & Winston, 1963; A. S. Skolnick and J. H. Skolnick, *Family in Transition,* (see note 3); P. Slater, "Changing the Family," in *Footholds: Understanding the Shifting Sexual and Family Tensions in Our Culture,* Boston: Beacon, 1977. M. J. Bane, *Here to Stay: American Families in the Twentieth Century,* New York: Basic, 1978; C. Lasch, *Haven in a Heartless World* (see note 3). For a critical look at the biases in the family literature, see R. Rapp, et al, "Examining Family History," *Feminist Studies,* Spring 1979, pp. 174–200.

5. J. Flax, "The Family in Contemporary Feminist Thought: A Critical Review," in J. B. Elshtain, ed., *The Family in Political Thought,* (see note 3) pp. 223–53.

6. B. Friedan, *The Feminine Mystique,* New York: W. W. Norton, 1963.

7. K. Millett, *Sexual Politics,* Garden City, NY: Doubleday, 1970.

8. S. Firestone, *The Dialectic of Sex,* New York: Morrow, 1970.

9. J. Mitchell, *Woman's Estate,* New York: Pantheon, 1971.

10. See Chapter 7.

11. G. Rubin, "The Traffic in Women: Notes on the 'Political Economy' of Sex," in R. R. Reiter, ed., *Toward An Anthropology of Women,* New York: Monthly Review Press, 1975.

12. D. Dinnerstein, *The Mermaid and The Minotaur,* New York: Harper and Row, 1976.

13. N. Chodorow, *The Reproduction of Mothering,* Berkeley, CA: The University of California, 1978.

14. W. D. Wandersee, *Women's Work and Family Values,* Cambridge, MA: Harvard, 1981, p. 121.

15. J. Flax (see note 5) p. 229; A. Simić, "White Ethnic and Chicano Families," in V. Tufte and B. Myerhoff, eds. (see note 3) pp. 251–69

16. C. B. Stack, "Sex Roles and Survival Strategies in an Urban Black Community," in M. Z. Rosaldo and L. Lamphere, eds., *Woman, Culture and Society,* Stanford, CA: Stanford, p. 114ff, 128; M. Dougherty, *Becoming a Woman in Rural Black Culture,* New York: Holt, Rinehart & Winston, 1978; L. F. Roders–Rose, *The Black Woman.* Beverly Hills, CA: Sage, 1980; B. B. Solomon and H. A. Mendes, "Black Families: A Social Welfare Perspective," in V. Tufte and B. Myerhoff, eds. (see note 3), p. 271.

17. *The Wall Street Journal,* December 23, 1982, p. 1; C. Berman, *Stepfamilies: A Growing Reality,* New York: Public Affairs Committee, 1982; A. J. Cherlin, *Marriage, Divorce, Remarriage,* Cambridge, MA: Harvard, 1981.

18. *NYT,* July 28 and August 4, 1981.

19. R. W. Smuts, *Women and Work in America,* New York: Schocken, 1971, pp. 14, 25, 140; G. Masnick and M. J. Bane, *The Nation's Families,* Cambridge, MA: Joint Center for Urban Studies of M.I.T. and Harvard, 1980.

20. Gallup Poll, March 1983; C. Lasch (see note 3), pp. 48, 124–33.

21. C. Degler (see note 3), pp. 453–54; K. C. Mikus, "Psychological Correlates of Early Family Formation," in D. G. McGuigan, ed., *Women's Lives: New Theory, Research and Policy,* Ann Arbor, MI: University of Michigan, 1980, pp. 119–21; L. S. Radloff, "Depression and the Empty Nest," *Sex Roles,* December 1980, pp. 775–81.

22. "Households, Families, Marital Status and Living Arrangements," *Current Population Reports,* Washington, D.C.: Bureau of the Census, March 1982.

23. *NYT,* July 2 and August 1, 1982.

24. National Center for Health Statistics, Washington, DC, 1982; *NYT,* May 18 and December 23, 1982; A. Thornton and D. Freedman, "Changing Attitudes Toward Marriage and Single Life," *Family Planning Perspectives,* Vol. 14, No. 6, November/December 1982.

25. K. Keniston, *The Uncommitted,* New York: Delta, 1965, p. 278.

26. Gallup Poll, June 1980.

27. *Ibid.*

28. D. Yankelovich, *Psychology Today,* April 1981.

29. Gallup Poll, reported in *NYT,* January 26, 1982. See also Institute of Life Insurance survey of April 1974; National Association of Secondary School Principals Survey, reported in a news release, September 6, 1974; and *Psychology Today,* July 1981, p. 61.

30. J. Veroff *et al., The Inner American: A Self-Portrait from 1957 to 1976,* New York: Basic, 1981.

31. Results of the study "Middletown III," reported in *NYT,* February 7, 1982.

32. H. B. Stowe, *Little Foxes,* chap. 1, quoted in E. Partnow, *The Quotable Woman,* Los Angeles: Corwin 1977, p. 36.

33. L. C. Pogrebin, *Ms.* April 1982, p. 66.

34. *NYT,* June 7, 1982.

35. *Ibid.*

36. C. Degler (see note 3), p. 452. See also B. Laslett, "The Significance of Family Membership," in V. Tufte and B. Myerhoff, eds. (see note 3), pp. 234, 249–50.

37. D. Dinnerstein, *Ms.*, August 1978, p. 45.

38. D. Dinnerstein (see note 12), p. 275.

39. D. Dinnerstein (see note 37), p. 92.

40. Quoted in *Ms.*, September 1981, p. 95.

41. *NYT,* July 5, 1982.

42. D. Dinnerstein (see note 37), p. 46.

43. C. R. Stimpson, *Ms.*, July/August 1982, p. 126.

44. J. Donzelot (see note 3), p. 91.

45. *Ibid.*, p. 52.

46. J. Humphries, "The Working Class Family: A Marxist Perspective," in J. B. Elshtain, ed. (see note 3), p. 219.

47. M. Horkheimer, "Authoritarianism and the Family Today," in R. Anshen, ed. (see note 4), p. 374.

48. C. Lasch (see note 3), p. 143.

49. J. B. Landes, "Hegel's Conception of the Family," in J. B. Elshtain, ed. (see note 3), pp. 131, 143.

50. General Mills *American Family Report*, 1976–77.

Chapter 3: Pedophobia:
Ambivalence and Hostility Toward Children

1. All facts and quotes relating to the Polovchak case have been drawn from the *NYT*, December 31, 1981; January 6, February 16, April 10, 17, 28, and October 7, 1982; *National Review*, March 18, 1983, p. 314; and *The Brief*, a history of the Polovchak case, Jan/Feb 1982, Illinois ACLU, 5 South Wabash, Chicago, IL 60603.

2. B. S. Miller and M. Price, eds., *The Gifted Child, the Family and the Community*, New York: Walker, 1981, pp. 9, 16.

3. Report to the President, White House Conference on Children, 1970.

4. *The Conservative Digest*, May/June 1980, p. 3.

5. For this insight, I thank Gloria Steinem. For the traditionalists' "pro-family" position, see B. Y. Pines, *Back to Basics: The Traditionalist Movement That Is Sweeping Grassroots America*, New York: Morrow, 1982, chap. 5, "Rallying Around the Family"; and R. Kramer, *In Defense of the Family*, New York: Basic, 1983; B. Berger and P. L. Berger, *The War over the Family*, New York: Doubleday, 1983.

6. N. Postman, *The Disappearance of Childhood.* New York: Delacorte, 1982, p. 152, 150, 140. See also M. Winn, *Children Without Childhood.* New York: Pantheon, 1983.

7. The information in this section was gleaned from the following sources: P. Aries, *Centuries of Childhood: A Social History of Family Life,* New

York: Knopf, 1962; E. Shorter, *The Making of the Modern Family,* New York: Basic, 1975, chap. 5; E. C. DuBois, ed. *Elizabeth Cady Stanton— Susan B. Anthony: Correspondence, Writings, Speeches,* New York: Schocken, 1981, p. 49; B. K. Greenleaf, *Children Through the Ages: A History of Childhood,* New York: McGraw-Hill, 1978; M. Cable, *The Little Darlings: A History of Child Rearing in America,* New York: Scribners, 1974; M. W. Piers, *Infanticide: Past and Present,* New York: Norton, 1978; D. M. Scott and B. Wishy, eds., *America's Families: A Documentary History,* New York: Harper & Row, 1982, pp. 570–75; M. Wollstonecraft, *Vindication of the Rights of Women* (1792), Middlesex, Eng.: Penguin, 1975, chap. 11.

8. For a critique of this legislation, see P. Edelman, "Child Labor Revisited," *The Nation,* August 21–28, 1982, pp. 136–38.

9. For insight into these developments, I am indebted to Verne Moberg, who translated two related articles by K. Stjarne that appeared in the Swedish newspaper *Dagens Nyheter,* September 26 and 30, 1982.

10. *NYT,* April 13, 1982, April 17, 1983. See also A. M. Yezer, "Housing Problems of Families," paper presented at the National Research Forum on Family Issues, Washington, DC, April 10, 1980. (Yezer is at George Washington University.)

11. R. J. Gelles, "Demythologizing Child Abuse," in A. S. Skolnick and J. H. Skolnick, eds., *Family in Transition.* Boston: Little Brown, 1977, pp. 385–94; L. Armstrong, *The Home Front,* New York: McGraw-Hill, 1983; *NYT,* January 4, 1983, pp. C1 and C2; January 24, 1982; December 27, 1981; July 21, 1981; and L. T. Sanford and M. E. Donovan, *Family Circle,* February 24, 1981.

12. *NYT,* June 12 and October 8, 1982. For more information on the problem of missing children, contact: *Find Me, Inc.* P.O. Box 1612, LaGrange, GA 30241; *National Coalition for Children's Justice,* 1214 Evergreen Rd., Yardley, PA 19067; *Family and Friends of Missing Persons,* P.O. Box 21444, Seattle, WA 98111; *Child Find, Inc.* Box 277, New Paltz, NY 12561 (or call toll free: 800-431-5005); *Search,* 560 Sylvan Ave., Englewood Cliffs, NJ 07632 (201-567-4040). For more information on other named problems, see *NYT,* January 9, 1983, September 23, October 17, and October 27, 1982. K. McCoy, *Coping with Teenage Depression,* New York: New American Library, 1982.

13. Quoted in Special Report, People for the American Way, 1015 18th St., NW, Suite 300, Washington, DC 20036; *NYT,* December 7, 1981.

14. P. York and D. York, *Toughlove,* Garden City, NY: Doubleday, 1982.

15. *Ms.,* April 1982, p. 24.

16. *NYT,* November 12, 1980.

17. C. Kleiman, *Chicago Tribune,* March 1981.

18. *NYT,* June 11, 1982.

19. *Time,* January 17, 1983, p. 47; *The Progressive,* May 1981, p. 27.

20. *Associated Press,* March 9, 1983; *NYT,* October 21, December 21, and April 24, 1982.

21. *NYT,* June 12, 1982. (See also note 12).

22. "A Nation at Risk," National Commission on Excellence in Education, Washington, D.C., April 1983.

23. *NYT,* May 2, March 23, 1983 and August 2, 1982.

24. *The New Yorker,* June 27, 1983, pp. 25–7. Also see, *NYT,* July 20, August 22, September 5 and 20, October 31, 1982, March 16, April 7, April 29, 1983. The best source for statistics on children's health and well-being is the Children's Defense Fund, 122 C St. NW, Washington, DC 20001.

25. *NYT,* July 6, 1982; *The New York Times Magazine,* January 2, 1983.

26. *NYT,* July 4, August 1, and November 1, 1982. See also R. Greenstein with J. Bickerman, "The Effect of the Administration's Budget, Tax and Military Policies on Low Income Americans," Center on Budget and Policy Priorities, 236 Massachusetts Ave., NE, Washington, DC 20002, January 1983.

27. This information is derived from Anthony Lewis' column in *NYT,* October 28, 1982, and from a report presented by Bob Greenstein at a seminar convened by the Children's Defense Fund for members of the press, December 3, 1981.

28. *NYT,* May 16, 1982. See also N. Bowers, "Young and Marginal: An Overview of Youth Employment," *Monthly Labor Review,* October 1979; L. C. Thurow, *Zero Sum Society,* New York: Basic, 1980, pp. 61–65, 187–88.

29. *NYT,* March 16, 1983.

30. Quoted in *NYT,* December 3, 1980.

31. "Better Health for Our Children: A National Strategy," Select Panel for the Promotion of Child Health, 1832 M St., NW, Room 711, Washington, DC 20036.

32. Source: Marion Wright Edelman, Children's Defense Fund (see note 24).

33. Infant Formula Action Coalition, 1701 University Ave, SE, Minneapolis, MN 55414; *NYT* (editorial) December 25, 1982.

34. National Mothers Survey, Ross Laboratories, 1980.

35. *NYT,* March 4, March 12, and March 13, 1982.

36. *NYT,* April 25, 1982.

37. *NYT,* (editorial), August 21, 1982.

38. *NYT,* January 21, May 9, June 9, October 8, 23 and December 22, 1982.

39. *NYT,* May 4, 1983.

40. Quoted in "Brayings of the New Right," Planned Parenthood of New York City, 380 Second Avenue, New York, NY 10010. See also J. Robison, *Attack on the Family,* Wheaton, IL: Tyndale, 1980.

41. Americans Against Abortion, P.O. Box 977, Tulsa, OK 74102.

42. *The Washington Star,* April 15, 1979.

43. *NYT,* July 23, 1981; *National NOW Times,* August 1982, p. 7.

44. *NYT,* April 28, 1982.

45. The Center for Early Adolescence, Carr Mill Mall, Carrboro, NC 27510 (April 1982).

46. Alan Guttmacher Institute, New York City; *NYT,* February 10 and February 26, 1982.

47. Alan Guttmacher Institute, New York City; Dr. Vladimir deLissovsoy and Gary Schilmoeller, Pennsylvania State University, 1979.

48. *NYT,* November 3, 1981; June 23, and October 12, 1982. See also Johns Hopkins University research reported in the *National NOW Times,* September 1982, p. 9.

49. Quoted in "Brayings of the New Right" (see note 40).

Chapter 4: Home Economics:
National Policy vs. the Family Interest

1. G. P. Kelly, *International Journal of Women's Studies,* July/August 1978, pp. 323–34.

2. F. Engels, *The Origins of the Family, Private Property and The State,* Eleanor Leacock, ed., New York: International, 1972; H. Taylor, "The Enfranchisement of Women" (1851) in J. S. Mill and Harriet Taylor, *Essays on Sex Equality,* Alice Rossi, ed., Chicago: University of Chicago, 1970; J. S. Mill, *The Subjection of Women* (1869), Cambridge, MA, and London, Eng.: M.I.T., 1976 edition; Z. R. Eisenstein, ed., *Capitalist Patriarchy and the Case for Socialist Feminism,* New York and London: Monthly Review Press, 1979 (pp. 5–55 contain Eisenstein's contribution to the discussion of power relations); J. Stacey, "When Patriarchy Kowtows: The Significance of the Chinese Family Revolution for Feminist Theory," in Z. R. Eisenstein, ed., *Capitalist Patriarchy* (see above), pp. 299–348 (provides illumination by cultural comparison); J. B. Elshtain, "Toward a Theory of the Family and Politics," and J. Flax, "The Family in Contemporary Feminist Thought: A Critical Review," both in J. B. Elshtain, ed., *The Family in Political Thought,* Amherst, MA: University of Massachusetts, 1982; and J. Flax, "Contempory American Families: Decline or Transformation?" in I. Diamond, ed. *Families, Politics, and Public Policy,* New York: Longman, 1983. (Although academic in style and tone, the Diamond and the Elshtain antholo-

gies are essential reading for anyone seriously interested in family politics). For a historical perspective, see J. Demos, "The American Family in Past time," *The American Scholar*, vol 43 (1974), pp. 422–46; J. B. Elshtain, "Hard Times for the American Family," *The Progressive*, May 1981, pp. 16–19.

3. K. Keniston, *The Uncommitted*, New York: Delta, 1965, p. 275.

4. P. Ariès, "The Family and the City in the Old World and the New," in V. Tufte and B. Myerhoff, eds., *Changing Images of the Family*, New Haven and London: Yale, 1979, pp. 29–42.

5. A. Skolnick, "Public Images, Private Realities: The American Family in Popular Culture and Social Science," in Tufte and Myerhoff (see note 4), p. 306–7.

6. For my own commentary on housework and female wage labor, and their relationship to patriarchy and capitalism, see chaps. 6 and 7. For more extensive analysis, see Z. Eisenstein, "The State, the Patriarchal Family and Working Mothers," and M. M. Ferree, "Housework: Rethinking the Costs and Benefits," both in I. Diamond ed., *Families, Politics and Public Policy* (see note 2); S. Rowbotham, *Women, Resistance and Revolution*, New York: Pantheon, 1972, chaps. 4 and 5; and E. Willis, "The Family: Love It or Leave It," in *Beginning to See the Light*, New York: Knopf, 1981.

7. J. Mitchell, "The Ideology of the Family," in *Women's Estate*, New York: Random House, 1971, p. 155.

8. Source: Speaker of the House of Representatives, Thomas P. O'Neill, Jr. quoted in *NYT*, July 13, 1982.

9. Gallup Poll, June 1980.

10. *Associated Press*, December 15, 1982.

11. For a fuller discussion of these issues, see *NYT*, February 24 and April 21, 1983; "Special Issue on Women and The American City," *Signs*, April 1980; M. C. Simms, "Women and Housing: The Impact of Government Housing Policy," in I. Diamond, ed. (see note 2); J. Goldstein, "Planning for Women in the New Towns: New Concepts and Dated Roles," in G. Kurian and R. Ghosh, eds., *Women in the Family and the Economy*, Westport, CT: Greenwood, 1981, pp. 73–80.

12. "Households, Families, Marital Status and Living Arrangements," *Current Population Reports*, Washington, DC: Bureau of the Census, March 1982.

13. *NYT*, June 3, 1981, April 17, 1983.

14. Quoted in *NYT*, April 17, 1982.

15. U.S. Department of Labor, Bureau of Labor Statistics Report 665, 1982; *Women and Work*, U.S. Department of Labor, April 1982.

16. *The Wall Street Journal,* October 21 and December 8, 1982; *NYT,* October 10, 14, 28, and November 3, 1982; February 2, 1983; *Psychology Today,* February 1981, p. 81; *Ms.,* January 1983, p. 20. P. M. Rayman, "The Private Tragedy Behind the Unemployment Statistics," *Brandeis Quarterly,* July 1982, p. 2.

17. Quoted in T. Wicker, *NYT,* July 13, 1982.

18. I am indebted to Sidney Kess, attorney, C.P.A., and lecturer, for his contributions to my thinking on tax policies, and to the visionary Tax Reform Resolutions passed at the Baltimore regional meeting of the White House Conference on Families, June 1980. For fact-checking assistance, I thank Arthur Bloom of the firm of Paneth, Haber and Zimmerman in New York.

19. "Child Support and Alimony: 1978" *Current Population Reports,* Washington, DC: Bureau of the Census, September 1981 (series p. 23, No. 112).

20. *NYT,* June 14, 1982.

21. Bureau of the Census Report, quoted in *NYT,* December 15, 1982; *NYT,* April 29, 1983.

22. Source: Bureau of Labor Statistics, December 1981.

23. "A Growing Crisis: Disadvantaged Women and Their Children," Washington, DC: *United States Commission on Civil Rights,* April 1983.

24. G. Gilder, *Wealth and Poverty* (1982) and *Sexual Suicide* (1975), both New York: Bantam.

25. C. Jencks, *Psychology Today,* November 1982, p. 73.

26. *NYT,* May 22 and March 3, 1982.

27. For more detailed analysis, see R. Greenstein with J. Bickerman, "The Effect of the Administration's Budget, Tax and Military Policies on Low Income Americans," Center on Budget and Policy Priorities, 236 Massachusetts Ave., NE, Washington, DC 20002; *NYT,* October 14, May 30, May 22, and May 4, 1982; *American Family,* February/March 1982.

28. Source: Marion Wright Edelman, Children's Defense Fund, 122 C St. NW, Washington, DC 20001; and Joan Ganz Cooney, *The New York Post,* November 21, 1981.

29. For a more thorough overview of the major problems in the foster care system, see B. Medsger, *The Progressive,* May 1981, pp. 21–25; R. Hubbell, *Foster Care and Families,* Philadelphia: Temple University, 1981; K. Hayes and A. Lazzarino, *Broken Promise,* New York: Fawcett-Crest, 1981; *NYT,* January 22, 1981, March 27, 1983; J. Goldstein, A. Freud and A. J. Solnit, *Beyond the Best Interests of the Child,* New York: Free Press, 1979.

30. D. Maguire, *The New Subversives,* New York: Continuum, 1982, p. 17.

31. *NYT,* January 15, 1982; March 28, 1983 (both Op-Ed page).

32. Quoted by Carl T. Rowan, in *The Washington Star*, March 19, 1980. See also *NYT*, May 24, 1982.

33. *NYT*, November 12, 1981.

34. *NYT*, July 21, 1981. (Justice Department statistics indicate a $10,000 annual cost per adult offender: *NYT*, April 25, 1983.)

35. Speech delivered December 3, 1981, at the Children's Defense Fund conference at Wye Plantation.

36. Quoted by A. Crittendon in *NYT*, July 9, 1982.

37. *NYT*, July 21, 1981.

38. L. C. Thurow, *The Zero Sum Society*, New York: Basic, 1980, p. 10.

39. Quoted by D. Yankelovich in *New Rules*, New York: Random House, 1981, p. 102.

40. L. C. Thurow (see note 38), p. 16.

41. *Ibid.*, p. 183.

42. Quoted by A. Crittendon (see note 36).

43. L. C. Thurow, (see note 38), p. 184.

44. *Ibid.*, p. 169.

45. A. Stein, *NYT*, March 28, 1983. See also J. Kurtz and J. A. Peckman, *NYT*, July 12, 1982.

46. L. C. Thurow (see note 38), p. 206.

47. The Family Support Project of the Bush Center in Child Development and Social Policy at Yale University, New Haven, CT, is producing a national directory. Until it is available, contact Heather Weiss, project director.

Chapter 5: Power Struggles on the Home Front

1. P. Slater, *Footholds*, Boston: Beacon, 1977, p. 15; A. Pietropinto and J. Simenauer, *Husbands and Wives*, New York: Times Books, 1979; B. Jones, "The Dynamics of Marriage and Motherhood," in R. Morgan, ed., *Sisterhood Is Powerful*, New York: Random House, 1970, p. 47.

2. J. Bernard, "The Paradox of the Happy Marriage," in V. Gornick and B. K. Moran, eds., *Woman in Sexist Society*, New York: Basic, 1971, pp. 85–96. Also see study cited in *Psychology Today*, December 1982, p. 83.

3. F. Lear, *NYT*, April 24, 1982.

4. Quoted in L. Rubin, *Worlds of Pain*, New York: Harper & Row, 1976, p. 118.

5. B. Ehrenreich, *Ms.*, May 1981, p. 46.

6. *NYT*, July 6, 1981.

7. Quoted in B. Ehrenreich (see note 5).

8. Helen Rowland, quoted in E. Partnow, *The Quotable Woman*, Los Angeles; 1977, p. 439.

9. *NYT,* November 9, 1981.

10. Quoted in *Time,* July 3, 1978, p. 20.

11. *God's Answer to Women's Lib,* published by Heirs of the Kingdom, P.O. Box 432, Tulsa, OK 74101.

12. *Psychology Today,* January 1981, p. 82.

13. L. Rubin (see note 4), p. 96.

14. L. Wheeler, ed., *Loving Warriors: Selected Letters of Lucy Stone and Henry Blackwell, 1853–1893,* New York: Dial, 1981, pp. 62, 21, 91; see also pp. 124–125.

15. L. Rubin (see note 4), p. 81.

16. C. Rivers, G. Baruch, and R. Barnett, *Lifeprints: New Patterns of Love and Work for Today's Woman,* New York: McGraw-Hill, 1983.

17. The Merit Report, November 29, 1982.

18. Roper–Virginia Slims Poll, 1980; *The New York Times Magazine,* March 22, 1981, p. 49.

19. The literature on power and family decision-making is voluminous; for example: G. H. Conklin, "Cultural Determinants of Power for Women in the Family: A Neglected Aspect of Family Research," in G. Kurian and R. Ghosh, eds., *Women in the Family and the Economy,* Westport, CT: Greenwood, 1981, pp. 9–27 (for a cross-cultural comparison, see pp. 217–30 in the same volume); for a lucid description of the differences among power, authority, and influence, see L. Lamphere, "Women in Domestic Groups," in M. Z. Rosaldo and L. Lamphere, eds., *Women in Culture and Society,* Stanford CA: Stanford University, 1974, pp. 98, 101, and 21 *n:* for the sound of struggle, see L. Rubin (see note 4), pp. 110–13.

20. *NYT* August 3, 1981.

21. M. A. Straus *et al., Behind Closed Doors,* Garden City, Doubleday, 1980.

22. University of Florida study reported in *National NOW Times,* September 1982, p. 9; A. Jones, *Women Who Kill,* New York; Holt, Rinehart & Winston, 1980; R. J. Gelles, "The Myth of Battered Husbands," *Ms.,* October 1979.

23. S. de Beauvoir, *The Second Sex,* New York: Bantam, 1961, p. 309.

24. *NYT,* August 3, 1981.

25. M. Straus *et al.* (see note 24), p. 31. American Bar Association Study of Domestic Violence, 1982; R. J. Gelles, *Violent Home,* Beverly Hills, CA: Sage, 1974; D. Martin, *Battered Wives,* San Francisco: Glide, 1976.

26. M. Straus *et al.* (see note 24), p. 3.; Southern Califoria Coalition on Battered Women, Santa Monica, CA, 1981; R. Langley and R. C. Levy, *Wife Beating,* New York: Dutton-Sunrise, 1977.

27. This was the consensus of speakers from the arenas of law, law enforcement and social science who addressed a 1981 meeting on the subject at the New York City Bar Association. Straus was a panelist and the session was chaired by Maria Marcus of Fordham University Law School. See also *Minneapolis Police Dept. Study of Police Tactics in Domestic Assault Cases,* Washington, DC: Police Foundation, April, 1983; L. Armstrong, *The Home Front: Notes from the Family War Zone,* New York: McGraw-Hill, 1983; L. G. Lerman, *Women's Rights Law Reporter,* Summer 1980, p. 271; G. N. McCarthy, *Getting Free,* Seattle, WA: Seal, 1982.

28. R. L. Shotland and M. K. Straw, *Journal of Personality and Social Psychology,* November 1976, pp. 990–99.

29. *National NOW Times,* October 1981 and June/July 1982.

30. *FBI Crime Report,* 1980.

31. *Equal Times,* July/August 1980.

32. M. L. Marcus "Conjugal Violence: The Law of Force and the Force of Law," *California Law Review,* December 1981, 1657–733. Marcus' brilliant article should be read by lay people as well as lawyers. For current data on patterns of family violence, contact Barbara E. Smith, Institute for Social Analysis, Reston, VA.

33. For more information and updated statistics, contact National Center on Women and Family Law, Room 402, 799 Broadway, New York, NY 10003; National Clearinghouse on Marital Rape, 2325 Oak St. Berkeley, CA 94708. See also *NYT,* June 1, 1981; L. Woods, "Litigation on Behalf of Battered Women," *Women's Rights Law Reporter,* Fall 1981, p. 41.

34. Quoted in *NYT,* November 29, 1982.

35. T. Beneke, *Men on Rape: What They Have to Say About Sex and Violence,* New York: St. Martin's, 1982; D. E. H. Russell, *Rape in Marriage,* New York: Macmillan, 1982; *Aegis: Magazine on Ending Violence Against Women,* Summer 1982 (from Feminist Alliance Against Rape, Box 21033, Washington, DC 20009).

36. R. Gelles, "Violence and Pregnancy," *The Family Coordinator,* January 1975, pp. 81–86; A. Dworkin, *Right Wing Women,* New York: Perigee, 1983, p. 143.

37. M. Straus (see note 27).

38. *NYT,* September 20, 1982.

39. *NYT,* September 11, 1980.

40. *Ms.,* November 1981; *NYT,* October 11, 1982 and February 2, 1983.

41. E. Fromm, "The Oedipus Complex and the Oedipus Myth," in R. N. Anshen, ed., *The Family: Its Function and Destiny,* New York: Harper & Bros, p. 338; see also L. Sheleff, *Generations Apart: Adult Hostility to Youth,* New York: McGraw-Hill, 1981, parts I and II.

42. *NYT,* July 22, 1981.

43. M. Straus *et al.* (see note 21), p. 102.

44. *Ibid.*, pp. 18–19.

45. R. J. Gelles, "Demythologizing Child Abuse," *The Family Coordinator,* April 1976, pp. 135–141. (See also Proverbs 1:8 and 13:24.)

46. M. Straus *et al.* (see note 24), p. 13.

47. *NYT,* September 27 and October 16, 1982.

48. J. Donzelot, *The Policing of Families,* New York: Pantheon, 1979, pp. 82–91.

49. M. Straus *et al.* (see note 21), p. 190, 193.

50. Judy Reed, Orange County, California—personal communication.

51. S. Weisskopf, "Maternal Sexuality and Asexual Motherhood," *Signs,* vol. 5 (1980), pp. 766–67; see also S. Lainson, *Ms.,* February 1983, p. 66.

52. *NYT,* January 10, 1983; *The Wall Street Journal,* December 23, 1982.

53. *Ms.,* November 1982, p. 114.

Chapter 6: Too Many Trade-Offs: When Work and Family Clash

1. *World of Work Report,* December 1979, p. 96; *NYT,* December 31, 1982; *Human Behavior,* April 1979, p. 35; E. Dienstag, *Whither Thou Goest,* New York: Dutton, 1976.

2. For various measures of these attitudes, see *Families at Work,* General Mills American Family Report, 1980–81, pp. 11, 43; Louis Harris speech, New York City, May 6, 1981; D. Yankelovitch, *Psychology Today,* April 1981, p. 76; B. G. Harrison *et at.,* "Locus of Control and Self-Esteem as Correlates of Role Orientation in Traditional and Nontraditional Women," *Sex Roles,* December 1981, p. 1185–86; Gallup Poll, 1980; R. Sidel, *Urban Survival: The World of Working Class Women,* Boston, Beacon 1978; Menninger Foundation study reported by C. A. Carmichael in *Chicago Tribune,* September 30, 1980.

3. For clarification of these statistics, see 1980 census data reported in *NYT* May 29, 1983, August 14, 1982; R. Bannon, "Dual-Earner Families: An Annotated Bibliography," *Monthly Labor Review,* February 1981, pp. 53–59; pp. 46–52; *Twenty Facts on Women Workers,* U.S. Department of Labor, 1980; *News Release,* Women's Bureau, U.S. Department of Labor, September 3, 1982; *Employment in Perspective,* Bureau of Labor Statistics Report 657, U.S. Department of Labor, Fourth Quarter 1981.

4. Gallup Poll, reported in *NYT,* August 15, 1982.

5. Source: Working Women United Institute, 593 Park Avenue, New York, NY 10021. See also, P. Kassell, "Going Underground Has Its Pitfalls," *New Directions for Women,* May/June 1982, p. 5.

6. *Twenty Facts on Women Workers* (see note 3).

7. Sources: *Economic Responsibilities of Working Women,* U.S. Department of Labor, September 1979; F. Horvath, "Working Wives Reduce Inequality in Distribution of Family Earnings," *Monthly Labor Review,* July 1980, pp. 51–53; *NYT,* January 20, 1982, and July 20, 1981; *The Wall Street Journal,* December 8, 1982.

8. R. G. Penner, *NYT,* April 25, 1982.

9. L. Haas, "Determinants of Role-Sharing Behavior," *Sex Roles,* July 1982, p. 756. For a more elaborate investigation of the origins and effects of sex segregation, see H. Hartmann, "Capitalism, Patriarchy, and Job Segregation By Sex," in Z. R. Eisenstein, ed., *Capitalist Patriarchy and the Case for Socialist Feminism,* New York and London: Monthly Review Press, 1979, pp. 206–46.

10. N. Erickson, *Women's Rights Law Reporter,* Fall 1981, p. 11.

11. *Geduldig* v. *Aiello; Gilbert* v. *G.E.; Satty* v. *Nashville Gas Co.*—all Supreme Court cases regarding maternity policies.

12. For an explanation of maternity entitlements, see *EEOC Guidelines on Discrimination Because of Sex and Questions and Answers Concerning the Pregnancy Discrimination Act,* Equal Employment Opportunity Commission, Washington, DC; M. Wheatley and M. S. Hirsh, *Managing Your Maternity Leave,* Boston: Houghton Mifflin, 1983; S. Kamerman, A. Kahn, and P. Kingston, *Maternity Policies and Working Women,* New York: Columbia University, 1983. The U.S. Supreme Court has ruled that the Act also covers benefits for wives of male employees: see *NYT,* June 21, 1983.

13. *Career and Family Bulletin,* May 1980 (published by Catalyst, 14 E. 60 St., New York, NY 10022).

14. For more information on occupational health, see W. Chavkin, ed., *Double Exposure: Women's Health Hazards on the Job and at Home,* New York: Monthly Review, 1983; V. R. Hunt, "Reproduction and Work," *Signs,* Winter 1975; J. M. Stellman, *Women's Work, Women's Health,* New York: Pantheon, 1977.

15. *The Wall Street Journal,* August 19, 1980, p. 31.

16. M. Vandervelde, *NYT,* March 11, 1979. See also the research of D. G. Winter at Wesleyan University, A. J. Stewart at Boston University, and D. McClelland at Harvard, reported in *Human Behavior,* November 1977.

17. Source: Menninger Center for Applied Behavioral Sciences, "Work and the Family: An American Dilemma," September 1980.

18. D. Maguire, *The New Subversives.* New York: Continuum, 1982, p. 130.

19. Relevent research reported in *NYT,* June 16, 1981 and *Radcliffe News,* April 1981, p. 9.

20. A. V. Horwitz, "Sex Role Expectations, Power and Psychological Distress," *Sex Roles*, June 1982, pp. 607–23.

21. To sample the provocative literature on power in marriage, see S. Yogev, "Happiness in Dual Career Couples: Changing Research, Changing Values, *Sex Roles*, June 1982, p. 597; S. J. Bahr, "Effects on Power and Division of Labor in the Family," in L. W. Hoffman and I. V. Nye, eds., *Working Mothers*, San Francisco: Jossey-Bass, 1974, pp. 167–185; L. Rubin, *Worlds of Pain*, New York: Basic, 1976, pp. 174–177; J. H. Scanzoni, *Sexual Bargaining: Power Politics in the American Marriage*, Englewood Cliffs, NJ: Prentice-Hall, 1972, pp. 67–70; B. W. Brown, "Wife Employment and the Emergence of Egalitarian Marital Role Prescriptions: 1900–74," and I. C. M. Cunningham and R. T. Green, "Working Wives in the United States and Venezuela: A Cross-National Study of Decision Making," both in G. Kurian and R. Ghosh, eds., *Women in the Family and the Economy*, Westport, CT: Greenwood, 1981, pp. 231–43 and 217–30.

22. C. Degler, *At Odds*, New York and London: Oxford, 1980, p. 436.

23. For example, see P. J. Andrisani, "Job Satisfaction Among Working Women," *Signs*, 1978, no. 3, p. 606; D. M. Haccoun and S. Stacy, "Perceptions of Male and Female Success in Relation to Spouse Encouragement and Sex Association of Occupation," *Sex Roles*, December 1980, pp. 819–31; R. Rapoport and R. N. Rapoport, "Further Considerations on the Dual Career Family," *Human Relations*, 1971, no. 24, 519–33; S. Yogev (see note 37). For a historical perspective on this phenomenon, see W. D. Wandersee, *Women, Work and Family Values: 1920–1940*, Cambridge, MA: Harvard, 1981. For specific focus on black women, see A. O. Harrison and J. H. Minor, "Interrole Conflict, Coping Strategies and Satisfaction Among Black Working Wives," in D. G. McGuigan, ed., *Women's Lives: New Research, Theory, Policy*, Ann Arbor, MI: University of Michigan, 1980, pp. 101–10.

24. D. Yankelovitch, *Psychology Today*, April 1981, p. 72.

25. S. de Beauvoir, *The Second Sex*, New York: Bantam, 1961, p. 653.

26. J. Hollender and L. Shafer, "Male Acceptance of Female Careers," *Sex Roles*, December 1981, pp. 1199–1203.

27. A. Hacker, *The New York Review of Books*, March 18, 1982, p. 39.

28. C. Bird, *The Two-Paycheck Marriage*, New York: Rawson-Wade, 1979.

29. R. B. Bryson, *et al.*, "The Professional Pair: Husband and Wife Psychologists," *American Psychologist*, 1976, no. 31, pp. 10–16; M. A. Foster, *et al.*, "Feminist Orientation and Job Seeking Behavior Among Dual Career Couples," *Sex Roles*, February 1980, pp. 59–65; B. S. Wallston *et al.*, "I Will Follow Him: Myth, Reality or Forced Choice—Job Seeking Experiences of Dual-Career Couples," *Psychology of Women Quarterly*, 1978, no. 3, pp. 9–21; M. Berger and M. Foster, "Finding Two Jobs," in R. Rapoport and R. N. Rapoport, eds., *Working Couples*, New York: Harper & Row,

1979, pp. 23–25; R. Rapoport and R. N. Rapoport, *Dual Career Families Re-examined*, New York: Harper & Row, 1976.

30. The Merit Report 1981, 120 Park Avenue, New York, NY 10017; C. Rubenstein, *Psychology Today*, Nov. 1982, pp. 36–41; A. Cherlin, *Marriage, Divorce, Remarriage*, Cambridge, MA: Harvard, 1982; *The Wall Street Journal*, December 8, 1982, p. 1.

31. J. G. Richardson and E. R. Mahoney, "The Perceived Social Status of Husbands and Wives in Dual Work Families as a Function of Achieved and Derived Occupational Status," *Sex Roles*, December 1981, pp. 1189–98; C. Safilios-Rothschild, "Dual Linkages Between the Occupational and Family Systems," in A. S. Skolnick and J. H. Skolnick, eds., *Family in Transition*, 2nd ed., Boston: Little Brown, 1977, pp. 555–64.

32. C. Degler (see note 22), chaps. 15 and 16; P. B. Scott, "Black Women and the World Experience," in D. G. McGuigan, ed. (see note 23), p. 169; L. Rubin (see note 21), p. 168; W. Slocum and F. I. Nye, "Provider and Housekeeper Roles," in F. I. Nye, ed., *Role Structure and Analysis of the Family*, Beverly Hills, CA: Sage, 1976, p. 82.

33. For example, see P. M. Keith and R. B. Schafer, "Role Strain and Depression in Two-Job Families," *Family Relations*, October 1980, pp. 483–88; A. Pines and D. Kafry, "Tedium in the Life and Work of Professional Women as Compared to Men," *Sex Roles*, October 1981, pp. 963–77; P. J. Andrisano (note 23), p. 602.

34. Source: Marta Mooney, Fordham University Graduate School of Business, quoted in C. Kleiman, *Chicago Tribune*, March 29, 1982.

35. *Families at Work* (see note 2) p. 19.

36. F. P. Stafford, "Women's Use of Time Converging With Men's," *Monthly Labor Review*, December 1980, p. 57, 58. Also see, C. Russell Hill and F. P. Stafford, "Parental Care of Children: Time Diary Estimates of Quality, Pedictability and Variety," *Journal of Human Resources*, Spring 1980, pp. 219–39.

37. *Corporations and Two-Career Families: Directions for the Future*, New York: Catalyst, 1981 (see note 13).

38. J. H. Pleck, G. L. Staines and L. Lang, "Conflicts Between Work and Family Life," *Monthly Labor Review*, March 1980, pp. 29–32; G. L. Staines and P. O'Connor, "Conflicts Among Work, Leisure and Family Roles," *Monthly Labor Review*, August 1980, pp. 35–9; P. La Rossa and M. M. LaRossa, *Transition to Parenthood*, Beverly Hills, CA: Sage, 1981.

39. Quoted in L. C. Pogrebin, *The New York Times Book Review*, June 17, 1973.

40. C. Degler (see note 22), p. 434.

41. Health study reported in *NYT*, April 15, 1980.

42. J. A. Levine, *Who Will Raise the Children?* Philadephia and New York: Lippincott, 1976.

43. J. N. Hedges and E. S. Sekscenski, "Workers on Late Shifts in a Changing Economy," *Monthly Labor Review,* September 1979, pp. 14–22; H. B. Presser and V. S. Cain, "Couples Working Different Shifts," *Science,* February 1983.

44. S. Kamerman, *Parenting in an Unresponsive Society,* New York: Free Press, 1980, pp. 139–66; C. Joffe, "Child Care: Destroying the Family or Strengthening It?" in L. K. Howe, ed., *The Future of the Family,* New York: Simon & Schuster, 1972, p. 261; S. Kamerman and A. J. Kahn, *National Study of Child Care Systems,* (1983), order from Kamerman, Columbia University School of Social Work, 622 W. 113 St., N.Y. NY 10025.

45. M. J. Bane *et al.,* "Child Care Arrangements of Working Parents," *Monthly Labor Review,* October 1979, p. 52. See also A. S. Grossman, "Working Mothers and Their Children," *Monthly Labor Review,* May 1981, p. 52; T. W. Schultz, ed., *Economics of the Family,* Chicago, IL: University of Chicago, 1974, pp. 3, 19, 546. *The Child Care Handbook: Needs, Programs and Possibilities,* Children's Defense Fund, Washington, DC, 1982, pp. 2–35; *Women & Work,* January 1983 (Director's Journal), U.S. Department of Labor, Office of Information, Washington, DC 20210.

46. *Child Care and Equal Opportunity for Women,* U.S. Commission on Civil Rights, Washington, DC, 1981, pp. 50–51; *Monthly Labor Review,* February 1981, p. 54; *Employed Parents and Their Children,* Children's Defense Fund, Washington, DC, pp. 7–8; S. B. Kamerman and A. J. Kahn, eds., *Family Policy: Government and Families in Fourteen Countries,* New York: Columbia, 1978.

47. *The Child Care Handbook* (see note 45).

48 A. Clarke-Stewart, *Daycare,* Cambridge, MA: Harvard, 1982.

49. *NYT,* August 7, 1982; *America's Children and Their Families: Key Facts,* Children's Defense Fund, Washington, DC, 1979, p.10.

50. *Ms.* February 1983, p. 85; *NYT,* June 17, 1982.

51. LeRoy Robinson, *NYT,* August 23, 1982.

52. M. J. Bane (see note 45) p. 52.

53. For a small sample of these findings, see D. Rosenthal and J. Hansen, "The Impact of Maternal Employment on Children's Perceptions of Parents and Personal Development," *Sex Roles,* June 1981, pp. 593–98; D. Sobel, *NYT,* December 13, 1981; B. Romano of Loyola University, Chicago, research reported in *Psychology Today,* November 1981; J. Kagan, *The Growth of the Child,* New York: Norton, 1978, p. 96; C. Drum, University of Iowa Humanities/Science News Service, October 14, 1981; L. C. Pogrebin, *Ladies' Home Journal,* October 1979, p. 68; K. A. Moore and S. L. Hofferth, "Women and Their Children," in R. E. Smith, ed., *The Subtle Revolution,* Washington, DC: Urban Institute, 1979, pp. 143–52; J. Reis and R. Burton, "An Exploration of Mothers' Socialization Practices as Related to Type of Maternal Employment," unpublished (available from J.

Reis, Northwestern University, Center for Health Services and Policy Research, Evanston, IL 60201).

54. C. I. Waxman, *Single Parent Families: A Challenge to the Jewish Community,* Institute of Human Relations, New York City, February 1980, pp. 6–7 and "Men in Early Childhood Education," Film or videotape from Davidson Films, 850 O'Neill Ave, Belmont, CA 94002.

55. My recommended booklist would include B. Siegel-Gorelick, *The Working Parents' Guide to Child Care,* Boston: Little Brown, 1983; R. K. Baden, A. Genser, J. A. Levine, and M. Seligson, *School-Age Child Care: An Action Manual,* Boston: Auburn House, 1982; *The Child Care Handbook: Needs, Programs and Possibilities* (see note 45); S. Auerbach, *Confronting the Child Care Crisis,* Boston: Beacon, 1979; S. Auerbach, *Choosing Childcare: A Guide for Parents,* New York: Dutton, 1981; E. Galinsky and W. H. Hooks, *The New Extended Family: Day Care That Works,* Boston: Houghton Mifflin, 1977; R. C. Endsley, *Quality Day Care: A Handbook of Choices for Parents and Caregivers,* Englewood Cliffs, NJ: Prentice-Hall, 1981; G. Mitchell, *The Day Care Book: A Guide for Working Parents to Help Them Find the Best Possible Day Care for Their Children,* Briarcliff Manor, NY: Stein & Day, 1979; B. M. Glickman, *Who Cares for the Baby? Choices in Child Care,* New York: Schocken, 1978. For answers to specific questions, contact the new national information resource, Child Care Action Now, 1602 17 St. NW, Washington, DC 20009.

56. Study by L. Long (Loyola College) and T. Long (Catholic University), noted in Women's Equity Action League *Washington Report,* April/May 1981, p. 3.

57. For example: *Recommended Corporate Policies for Working Mothers/ Parents,* Women Employed Institute, 5 South Wabash, Chicago, IL 60603 ($2.50); *A Corporate Reader: Work and Family Life in the 1980s,* Children's Defense Fund, 122 C St. NW, Washington, DC 20001 (1983). *Frontiers of Corporate Competition: Linkages Between Work and Family,* Aspen Institute Seminar, August 1981, Foundation for Child Development, Washington, DC; A. R. Cohen and H. Gadon, *Alternative Work Schedules: Integrating Individual and Organizational Needs,* Reading, MA: Addison-Wesley, 1978; N. S. Barrett, "Women in the Job Market: Unemployment and Work Schedules," in R. E. Smith, ed. (see note 53), pp. 63–98; S. Kamerman (see note 44), chap. 7; C. Bird (see note 28), Part IV.

58. R. A. Winett and M. S. Neale, "Results of an Experimental Study on Flexitime and Family Life," *Monthly Labor Review,* November 1980, p. 29; H. H. Bohen and A. Viveros-Long, eds., *Balancing Jobs and Family Life,* Philadelphia: Temple University, 1981.

59. E. B. Jones and J. E. Long, *Women and Part-Time Work,* U.S. Department of Labor, Employment and Training Administration, 1978.

60. *Permanent Part-time Employment: The Manager's Perspective,* National Technical Information Service, Springfield, VA 22151 ($6.50).

61. Source: Bureau of Labor Statistics, U.S. Department of Labor.

62. *New Ways to Work*, National Clearinghouse on Job Sharing, 149 Ninth Street, San Francisco, CA 94103; Workshare, 311 East 50 Street, New York, NY 10022; S. Grady, *Working Woman*, March 1981, p. 79.

63. *Catalyst Career & Family Bulletin*, Fall 1981, pp. 2–5. (see note 13).

64. *Ibid.*, May 1981, p. 8.

65. A. V. Horwitz (see note 20).

66. A. Campbell, "Changes in Psychological Well-Being During the 1970s of Homemakers and Employed Wives," in D. G. McGuigan, ed. (see note 23).

67. *Women's Wear Daily*, March 28, 1979, p. 4.

68. *Corporate Relocation Practices: A Report on a Nationwide Survey* (1983) published by Catalyst (see note 13).

69. J. S. Lublin, *The Wall Street Journal*, November 18, 1977, p. 1.

70. For up-to-date information, see *Career and Family: Maternity and Parental Leaves of Absence* (1983) published by Catalyst, (see note 13).

71. B. Banon, *Ms.*, April 1978, pp. 83–86; *Employers and Child Care: Establishing Services Through the Workplace*, The Women's Bureau, U.S. Department of Labor, Washington, DC 20210. Marian Wright Edelman of The Children's Defense Fund, Washington, DC and Sheila Kamerman of Columbia University seem most knowledgeable on fast-breaking developments in this area. Employers should consult *Child Care Assistance: Issues for Employer Consideration*, Hewitt Associates, 600 Third Avenue, New York, NY 10016 (1982).

72. A. P. Beutel II Day Care Center, cited in *The Child Care Handbook* (see note 45). Also Nyloncraft, Inc., in Indianapolis, reported in *National NOW Times*, September 1982, p. 9.

73. *NYT*, June 23, 1983.

74. R. P. Quinn and G. Staines, *The 1977 Quality of Employment Survey*, Institute for Social Research, University of Michigan, 1979.

75. *Ms.*, December 1982, p. 45.

Chapter 7: Just Housework

1. General Mills *American Family Report* 1976–77, p. 132.

2. M. Straus *et al.*, *Behind Closed Doors*, New York: Anchor, 1980, pp. 156–58.

3. General Mills *American Family Report* 1976–77, p. 96.

4. R. Andre, *Homemakers: The Forgotten Workers*, Chicago: University of Chicago, 1981; S. Strasser, *Never Done: A History of American Housework*,

New York: Pantheon, 1982; P. Kome, *Whose Work Is Housework?* Toronto: McClelland & Stewart, 1982.

5. R. Theobald, "Redefining Work and Family," in *Families and Work,* project report of the American Association of University Women, Washington, DC (1982), p. 72.

6. H. I. Hartmann, "The Family as the Locus of Gender, Class and Political Struggle: The Example of Housework," *Signs,* 1981, no. 3, p. 377.

7. The major studies are K. Walker and M. Woods, *Time Use: A Measure of Household Production of Family Goods and Services,* Center for the Family, American Home Economics Association, 1976; J. Robinson, *How Americans Use Time: A Social Psychological Analysis,* New York: Praeger, 1977; S. F. Berk, ed., *Women and Household Labor,* Beverly Hills, CA: Sage, 1980; M. Meissner *et al.,* "No Exit for Wives: Sexual Division of Labor and the Cumulation of Household Demands," *Canadian Review of Sociology and Anthropology,* 1975, no. 12, pp. 424–39.

8. See the studies referenced in note 7, as well as K. E. Walker, "Time Spent in Household Work by Homemakers," *Family Economics Review,* 1969, pp. 5–6; K. E. Walker, "Time Spent by Husbands in Household Work," *Family Economics Review,* 1970, pp. 8–11; H. Hartmann (see note 6), pp. 377 *n,* 378 *n.*

9. See notes 7 and 8, as well as C. Safilios-Rothschild, "The Influence of the Wife's Degree of Work Commitment Upon Some Aspects of Family Organizations and Dynamics," *Journal of Marriage and the Family,* 1970, no. 32, pp. 681–91; M. M. Poloma and T. N. Garland, "The Married Professional Woman: A Study in Tolerance of Domestication," *Journal of Marriage and the Family,* 1971, no. 33, pp. 531–40.

10. Benton and Bowles Research Services, 909 Third Avenue, New York, NY 10022 (1980). See also S. McCall, University of Texas study reported in *Ms.,* October 1979, p. 30.

11. H. Hartmann (see note 6), p. 383.

12. S. K. Kamerman, *Parenting in an Unresponsive Society,* New York: Free Press, 1980, pp. 64–71.

13. J. H. Pleck, "Husbands' Paid Work and Family Roles: Current Research Issues," prepared for H. Z. Lopata and J. H. Pleck, eds., *Research on the Interweave of Social Roles, vol. 3. Families and Jobs,* Greenwich, CT: JAI 1983; J. H. Pleck, "Changing Patterns of Work and Family Roles," paper presented at American Psychological Association Conference, Los Angeles, August 1981; J. H. Pleck, "Men's Family Work: Three Perspectives and Some New Data," *The Family Coordinator,* October 1979, pp. 481–88; J. H. Pleck and M. Rustad, "Husband's and Wife's Time in Family and Paid Work in the 1975–76 Study of Time Use," draft version, March 1980. See also, F. P. Stafford, "Women's Use of Time Converging With Men's," *Monthly Labor Review,* December 1980, p. 57.

14. The General Mills *American Family Report*, 1976–77, p. 90; W. Shepard, "Mothers and Fathers, Sons and Daughters," *Sex Roles*, June 1980, pp. 424–26; J. Klemesrud, *NYT*, June 27, 1981; I. F. Nye, "Emerging and Declining Family Roles," *Journal of Marriage and the Family*, 1974, no. 36, pp. 238–45; L. L. Holmstrom, *The Two-Career Family*, Cambridge, MA: Schenkman, 1972, pp. 66–72.

15. H. Hartmann (see note 6), p. 385; H. P. McAdoo, "Black Families," in *Families and Work* (see note 8), p. 31.

16. Cunningham and Walsh survey reported in *The New York Post*, July 31, 1980.

17. *Ibid.*, and *NYT*, June 8, 1982, advertisement for Intermarketing (*TV Guide*).

18. E. C. Stanton, *Eighty Years and More*, London: T. Fisher Unwin, 1898.

19. S. de Beauvoir, *The Second Sex*, New York: Knopf, 1968, p. 451.

20. Quoted by G. Steinem in *Ms.*, August 1972, p. 38.

21. S. Plath, *Ariel*, New York: Harper & Row, 1965, p. 30.

22. J. Colony, *The New York Times Magazine*, December 6, 1981.

23. A. Oakley, "The Sociology of Housework," in A. S. Skolnick and J. H. Skolnick, eds., *Family in Transition*, Boston: Little Brown, 1977, pp. 186–88.

24. R. Seidenberg and K. De Crow, *Women Who Marry Houses: Panic and Protest in Agoraphobia*, New York: McGraw-Hill, 1983. For more on the "housewife's disease," see J. Davidson, *The Fall of a Doll's House*, New York: Holt, Rinehart & Winston, 1980, pp. 189–90; *Homeworkers' Health/ Business Reporter*, P.O. Box 4333, San Diego, CA 92104.

25. S. Kaufman, *The Diary of a Mad Housewife*, New York: Random House, 1967. See also L. Rubin, *Worlds of Pain*, New York: Basic, 1976, p. 103.

26. J. Syfers, "I Want a Wife," *Ms.*, Spring 1972, p. 56.

27. M. Piercy, "What's That Smell in the Kitchen?" in *Circles on the Water*, New York: Knopf, 1982.

28. B. Ehrenreich, *Ms.*, October 1979, p. 80.

29. L. Ross *et al.*, "Television Viewing and Adult Sex Role Attitudes," *Sex Roles*, June 1982, pp. 589–92.

30. P. D. Mamay and R. L. Simpson, "Three Female Roles in Television Commercials," *Sex Roles*, December 1981, pp. 1223–32.

31. *Ibid.*, p. 1230.

32. L. Rubin (see note 25), p. 100.

33. B. Friedan, *The Feminine Mystique*, New York: Norton, 1963, chap. 1.

34. R. L. Coser, *Signs*, Spring 1981, p. 490.

35. L. Rubin (see note 25), p. 105.

36. General Mills *American Family Report,* 1980–81, pp. 74–75.

37. P. Mainardi, "The Politics of Housework," in D. M. Scott and B. Wishy, eds., *America's Families: A Documentary History,* New York: Harper & Row, 1982, pp. 515–20.

38. H. Hartmann (see note 6), p. 372.

39. T. Veblen, *The Theory of the Leisure Class,* New York: Macmillan, 1899.

40. A. R. Markusen, "City Spatial Structure, Women's Household Work and National Urban Policy," *Signs,* Spring 1980, pp. S32–S44.

41. J. Tognoli, "Differences in Women's and Men's Responses to Domestic Space," *Sex Roles,* December 1980, pp. 833–42.

42. General Mills *American Family Report,* 1976–77, p. 128.

43. H. Hartmann (see note 6), pp. 367–68.

44. R. W. Smuts *Women and Work in America,* New York: Schocken, 1971, p. 28; *Ms.,* October 1979, p. 50; J. A. McGaw, "Women and the History of American Technology," *Signs,* Summer 1982, pp. 813–21; M. M. Dunsing, "Changes in Economic Aspects of Family Life," *Illinois Teacher,* March/April 1981, p. 172; H. Hartmann (see note 6), p. 385.

45. A. Buchwald, *The New York Post,* November 20, 1982.

46. A. S. Grossman, "Women in Domestic Work: Yesterday and Today," *Monthly Labor Review,* August 1980, p. 17.

47. E. M. Stern, *American Mercury,* January 1949.

48. Speech delivered September 22, 1982, at the Women's Forum meeting, 21 Club, New York City.

49. H. Hartmann (see note 6), p. 389, *n*54; *NYT,* September 19, 1982.

50. J. Bernard, *The Future of Motherhood,* New York: Dial, 1974, p. 336.

51. S. L. Manning, "New Perspectives on Production in the Home: The Historical View," paper presented at the Family Economics—Home Management Section Workshop, Lindewood College, St. Charles, MO, June 1979.

52. Although this is contradicted by the more recent studies cited in note 7, it has gained currency and is cited in M. Spencer, *Contemporary Economics,* 2nd ed., New York: Worth, 1974, p. 127.

53. Analysis by Michael Minton reported in *National NOW Times,* June 1981.

54. *National NOW Times,* January/February 1982.

55. *NYT,* December 16, 1982.

56. J. S. Mill, *The Subjection of Women* (1869) Cambridge, MA and London, Eng.: M.I.T., 1976 reprint.

57. "Child Support and Alimony: 1978," *Current Population Reports*, Washington, DC: Bureau of the Census, 1981.

58. C. P. Gilman, *Women and Economics* (1898), Carl Degler, ed., New York: Harper 1966 reprint. See also, W. Edmond and S. Fleming, eds., *All Work and No Pay: Women and Housework and the Wages Due*, London: Falling Wall Press, 1975; A. Myrdal and V. Klein, *Women's Two Roles: Home and Work*, London: Routledge and Kegan Paul, 1956; T. Fee, "Domestic Labor: An Analysis of Housework and Its Relation to the Production Process," *Review of Radical Political Economics*, Spring 1976, pp. 1–8.

59. J. K. Galbraith, *Economics and the Public Purpose*, Boston: Houghton Mifflin, 1973.

60. W. H. Brody, "Economic Value of a Housewife," Research and Statistics Note, U.S. Department of Health, Education and Welfare, Social Security Administration Office of Research and Statistics, August 28, 1975. See also N. Glazer-Malbin, "Housework," *Signs*, Summer 1976, pp. 905–22; M. Murphy, "The Measurement and Valuation of Nonmarket Economic Activities," paper presented at the Family Economics—Home Management Section Workshop, Lindewood College, St. Charles, MO, June 1979. Graduate economists may be interested in R. Gronan, "The Effect of Children on the Housewife's Value of Time," in T. W. Schultz, ed., *Economics of the Family: Marriage, Children and Human Capital*, Chicago: University of Chicago, 1974, pp. 457–88.

61. General Mills *American Family Report, 1980–81*, p. 37.

62. Dr. Conrad Berenson, economist, City University of New York, personal interview, September 5, 1982; also, N. R. Hauserman and C. Fethke, "Valuation of a Homemaker's Services," *The Trial Lawyer's Guide*, Fall 1978; D. Johnsen, *The Economic Value of Housework*, senior essay, Yale University, January 10, 1983.

63. R. Corbett, C. C. Fethke, and N. R. Hauserman, "A Practical Program to Achieve Economic Justice for Homemakers," *Journal of Home Economics*, Summer 1980; N. R. Hauserman, "The American Homemaker: Policy Proposals," in D. G. McGuigan, ed., *Women's Lives: New Theory, Research and Policy*, Ann Arbor, MI: University of Michigan, 1980, pp. 397–403; A. Witte, *Ms.*, October 1979, p. 85.

64. K. Newland, "Families, Work and Government Policy" in *Families and Work* (see note 5), p. 49.

Chapter 8: The Politics of Pregnancy and Motherhood

1. Reported in "On Campus #31," *Project on the Status and Education of Women*, Association of American Colleges, Summer 1981, p. 6.

2. R. Rapp *et al.*, "Examining Family History," *Feminist Studies*, Spring 1979, p. 182.

3. Testimony by Representative Pat Schroder, quoted in *National NOW Times,* April 1982, p. 5. See also *NYT,* October 26, 1981, and December 5, 1982.

4. See *New York University Review of Law and Social Change,* vol. IX, (1979–80), pp. 231–269.

5. *Ms.,* July/August 1982, pp. 154–58; *NYT,* January 17, 1983.

6. *NYT,* July 18, 1982. See also a report from the international perspective in *NYT,* October 28, 1982.

7. *NYT,* October 26, 1982; *Chicago Tribune,* October 28, 1982.

8. *Vogue,* June 1982; *Time,* February 22, 1982; *Savvy,* June 1982.

9. B. Stephen, *New York Daily News,* June 24, 1982. See also M. K. Blakely, *NYT,* June 17, 1982.

10. Public Agenda Foundation Survey, "Today's American Woman," December 1980, p. 29.

11. S. Cahil, ed., *Motherhood: A Reader for Men and Women,* New York: Avon, 1982; A. Oakley, *Becoming a Mother,* New York: Schocken, 1980; P. Chesler, *With Child,* New York: Crowell, 1979; S. Spinner, ed., *Motherlove: Stories by Women about Motherhood,* New York: Dell, 1978; A. B. McBride, *The Growth and Development of Mothers,* New York: Harper & Row, 1973; E. Whelan, *A Baby? . . . Maybe: A Guide to Making the Most Fateful Decision of Your Life,* New York: Bobbs-Merrill, 1975; J. Price, *You're Not Too Old to Have a Baby,* New York: Penguin, 1978; M. Bombardieri, *The Baby Decision,* New York: Rawson-Wade, 1981; A. Rich, *Of Woman Born,* New York: Norton, 1976; J. Bernard, *The Future of Motherhood,* New York: Dial, 1974; J. Bernard, *Women, Wives and Mothers,* Chicago: Aldine, 1975, pp. 97–160; E. Badinter, *Mother Love: Myth and Reality— Motherhood in Modern History,* New York: Macmillan, 1981; N. Chodorow, *The Reproduction of Mothering,* Berkeley, CA: University of California, 1978; D. Dinnerstein, *The Mermaid and the Minotaur,* New York: Harper & Row, 1976; A. Martin-Leff in *New Directions for Women,* September/ October, 1981, p. 7; *Off Our Backs,* February 1980, p. 23; Ti-Grace Atkinson in *Off Our Backs,* December 1979. S. L. Atlas, *Single Parenting,* Englewood Cliffs, NJ: Prentice-Hall, 1981; K. Hope and N. Young, *MOMMA: The Sourcebook for Single Mothers,* New York: New American Library, 1976; E. Einstein, *The Stepfamily,* New York: Macmillan, 1982; G. E. Hanscombe and J. Forster, *Rocking the Cradle: Lesbian Mothers—A Challenge in Family Living,* Boston: Alyson Publications, 1982; J. Horner Plumez, *Successful Adoption,* New York: Harmony, 1982; C. Ware, *Sharing Parenthood after Divorce,* New York: Viking, 1982; I. Ricci, *Mom's House, Dad's House,* New York: Macmillan, 1980.

12. *Time,* February 22, 1982, p. 58; *NYT,* February 16, 18, 21, 25, 1982.

13. *NYT,* March 21, 1982.

14. *The New York Times Magazine,* October 17 and November 21, 1982; *NYT,* January 19, 1983.

15. *Phyllis Schlafly Report,* December 1982, p. 1.

16. L. Smith, *The Mother Book,* Garden City, NY: Doubleday, 1978, p. 129.

17. *NYT* (Op Ed page), August 8, 1980; K. Millett, *Sexual Politics,* New York: Doubleday, 1970, pp. 172–73.

18. G. Steinem, *Ms.,* October 1980, p. 88.

19. *NYT,* April 18, 1982.

20. *The Washington Post,* October 24, October 29, and November 12, 1980; *Chicago Sun-Times,* October 23, 1980; *Chicago Tribune,* April 20, 1981. For more information on these and other such custody cases, contact WEAL Fund, 805 15th Street, NW, Suite 822, Washington, DC 20005; Child Custody Project, National Center on Women and Family Law, 799 Broadway, Room 402, New York, NY 10003; or the Committee for Mother and Child Rights, Box 481, Chappaqua, NY 10514.

21. For more information about the LuAnn Stevenson case and other lesbian mother custody suits, write National Gay Task Force, 80 Fifth Avenue, New York, NY 10011. See also *Ms.* September 1976, p. 72; and C. G. Gibson and M. J. Risher, *By Her Own Admission: A Lesbian Mother's Fight to Keep Her Son,* Garden City, NY: Doubleday, 1977.

22. *New Directions for Women,* November/December 1982, p. 6.

23. *NYT,* December 11, 1982.

24. *NYT,* November 18 and 22, 1982; March 15, 1983.

25. Source: Harriet Pilpel, counsel to Planned Parenthood, New York City.

26. *NYT,* March 17 and May 18, 1981.

27. H. Gregory, ed., *The Religious Case for Abortion,* Asheville, NC: Madison and Polk, 1983.

28. *NYT,* May 21, 1981; Dr. Clifford Grobstein quoted, May 4, 1981; Letters to the Editor, May 31, 1981; Dr. John C. Fletcher quoted, August 14, 1981.

29. U.S. Supreme Court decision in *Roe* v. *Wade,* January 22, 1973.

30. *The Sacramento* (CA) *Bee,* July 5, 1980; March 13, 1981; Senator Hyde's H.R. 900 and Senator Helms' S.J. Res. 19 would prohibit abortion with no exception for rape, incest, or saving the life of the mother. Senator Grassley's S.J. Res. 18 provides no exception for rape and incest. According to *NYT,* June 14, 1981, that is President Reagan's position, too.

31. *NYT* (editorial) March 30, 1983.

32. *Ms.,* June 1981, p. 100.

33. *The Conservative Digest,* 1980; *NYT,* January 30, 1983.

34. Harriet Pilpel (see note 25). Additional sources for facts about abortion: Alan Guttmacher Institute, Washington, DC; Planned Parenthood, New

York City; Religious Coalition for Abortion Rights, New York City; Reproductive Rights National Network, New York City; Abortion Rights Mobilization, New York City; and National Abortion Rights Action League, Washington, DC.

35. For copies of pending legislation or news of current developments, write to your senator or congressperson. A detailed consideration of the constitutional issues involved may be found in S. Estreicher, "Congressional Power and Constitutional Rights: Reflections on Proposed Human Rights Legislation," *Virginia Law Review,* February 1982.

36. E. Ross, quoted in R. Rapp *et al.* (see note 2), p. 187.

37. U.S. Supreme Court decision, *Planned Parenthood of Missouri* v. *Danforth.* See also "Abortion as Fatherhood Lost," *Family Coordinator,* October 1979, p. 569.

38. *NYT,* May 21, 1981.

39. A. Dworkin, *Right Wing Women,* New York: Perigee, 1983, chap. 3.

40. *NYT,* January 17, 1982.

41. Richard H. Feen, post-doctoral thesis, Harvard Divinity School, quoted in *NYT,* May 31, 1981.

42. Mary Daly, *Commonweal,* March 12, 1971.

43. *Ibid.*

44. *NYT,* June 14, 1981; *Ms.,* February 1981; *The National NOW Times,* June/July 1982.

45. A. Dworkin (see note 39), p. 232 *n.*

46. *NYT,* February 23, 1982.

47. *NYT* (Letter to the Editors), August 16, 1982.

Chapter 9: The New Father

1. For example, D. Ehrensaft, "When Women and Men Mother," *Socialist Review,* January/February 1980, p. 37; L. B. Rubin, *Intimate Strangers,* New York: Harper & Row, 1983, p. 200.

2. Quoted in E. Partnow, *The Quotable Woman,* Los Angeles, CA: Corwin, 1977.

3. D. Moynihan, "A Family Policy for the Nation," in L. Rainwater and W. Yancey, eds., *The Moynihan Report and the Politics of Controversy,* Cambridge, MA: M.I.T., 1967. See also L. M. Synder, "The Deserting Nonsupporting Father," *Family Coordinator,* October 1979, pp. 594–98.

4. W. S. Matthews, "Sex-Role Perception, Portrayal and Preference in the Fantasy Play of Young Children," *Sex Roles,* October 1981, p. 986.

5. R. Warren, *Primary Support Systems and the Blue Collar Working Woman,* paper presented at the Conference on New Research on Women, Ann Arbor, MI, 1975.

6. C. Gilligan, *Psychology Today,* June 1980, p. 68: See also L. Eichenbaum and S. Orbach, *What Do Women Want? Exploding the Myth of Dependency,* New York: Coward, McCann & Geoghegan, 1983.

7. *Ms.,* April 1983, pp. 77–80; *Chicago Tribune,* March 7, 1982; I. Ricci, *Mom's House, Dad's House,* New York: Macmillan, 1980.

8. *Child Support and Alimony Bureau of the Census,* September 1981, Report no. 112, p. 23, and telephone update February 8, 1983.

9. *NYT,* February 11, 1982.

10. N. D. Polikoff, "Gender and Child Custody Determinations: Exploding the Myths," in I. Diamond, ed. *Families, Politics, and Public Policy,* New York: Longman, 1983, Chapter 10. For statistics in brackets, see Carol Berman, *NYT,* May 19, 1983 (Letters to the Editor).

11. Unless otherwise noted, the data in this section are excerpted from L. C. Pogrebin, *Growing Up Free,* New York: McGraw-Hill, 1980, pp. 141–42 where the original sources are referenced, or have been obtained from Joseph Pleck, who is studying fathers' family time for the Wellesley Center for Research.

12. A. Booth and J. N. Edwards, "Fathers: The Invisible Parent," *Sex Roles,* June 1980, p. 445.

13. H. L. Klapper, "Children's Perceptions of the Realism of Televised Fiction," unpublished thesis, New York University, 1978.

14. Quotations may be found in B. Spock, *Baby and Child Care,* New York: Meredith, 1968, pp. 30–31; B. Spock, *Baby and Child Care* (rev. ed.), New York: Pocket Books, 1976, p. 47 and p. 42.

15. A. Brandt, *Psychology Today,* April 1982; M. Richler, *Esquire,* August 1982; Z. Rubin, *Psychology Today,* June 1982.

16. *NYT,* May 17, 1982.

17. Personal communication.

18. J. Eggert, "On the Uselessness of Men," *Anvil #38,* December/January 1982, University of Wisconsin.

19. N. O'Malia, *Ms.,* February 1982.

20. *Psychology Today,* January 1983, p. 71.

21. Sources: G. L. Grief. "Dads Raising Kids," *Single Parent,* December 1982; *NYT,* December 20, September 6, May 1, April 10 and March 6, 1982, April 6, 1981; *Newsweek,* November 30, 1981, p. 94; K. M. Rosenthal and H. F. Keshet, *Fathers Without Partners.* Totowa, NJ: Rowman and Littlefield, 1980.

22. *Esquire,* November 1982, p. 81; *Newsweek* (note 21); *Ms.,* February 1982; *New Age,* June 1981.

23. *NYT,* December 2, 1982, p. 1.

24. L. Yablonsky, *Fathers and Sons.* New York: Simon and Schuster, 1982; S. N. Katz and M. L. Inker, *Fathers, Husbands and Lovers: Legal Rights and Responsibilities.* New York: American Bar Association Press, 1979; L.

Salk, *My Father, My Son*. New York: G. P. Putnam's, 1982; M. Galper, *Joint Custody and Co-Parenting*. Philadelphia, Pa: The Running Press, 1982; G. A. and M. Silver, *Weekend Fathers*. New York: Stratford Press, 1981; S. A. Sullivan, *The Father's Almanac*. Garden City, New York: Doubleday, 1980; J. R. Covington, *Confessions of a Single Father*. New York: Pilgrim Press, 1982; Alliance for Perinatal Research and Services, *The Father Book*, Washington, DC: Acropolis, 1981; C. Shedd, *A Dad Is for Spending Time With*, Mission, KS: Sheed Andrews and McNeel, 1978; M. Roman and W. Haddad, *The Disposable Parent: The Case for Joint Custody*, New York: Holt, Rinehart & Winston, 1978; E. A. Daley, *Father Feelings*, New York: Morrow, 1978; D. Steinberg, *Father Journal*, Santa Cruz, CA: Times Change Press, 1977; R. H. Gatley and D. Koulack, *The Single Father's Handbook*, Garden City, NY: Doubleday, 1979; *Co-Parent Magazine*, P.O. Box 92262, Milwaukee, WI 53202 ($2 per copy); *Single Dad's Lifestyle*, P.O. Box 4842, Scottsdale, AZ 85258 ($12 per year); J. Heinowitz, *Pregnant Fathers*, Englewood Cliffs, NJ: Prentice-Hall, 1982; R. Meister, *Fathers*, New York: Richard Marek, 1981; A. Colman, *Earth Father Sky Father: The Changing Concept of Fathering*, Englewood Cliffs, NJ: Prentice-Hall, 1981.

25. The Fatherhood Project, Bank Street College of Education, 610 West 112 Street, New York, NY 10025.

26. S. Price-Bonham *et al.*, "The Father Role: An Update" (twenty-four-page bibliography), *Infant Mental Health Journal*, Winter 1981; A. Booth and J. N. Edwards, "Fathers: The Invisible Parent" (see note 12); Special Issue: "Men's Roles in the Family," *Family Coordinator*, October 1979; S. Cath *et al.*, eds., *Father and Child: Developmental and Clinical Perspectives*, Boston: Little, Brown, 1982; R. D. Parke and D. B. Sawin, "The Father's Role in Infancy: A Re-evaluation," *Family Coordinator*, no. 25, 1976, pp. 489–512; W. S. Appleton, *Fathers and Daughters: A Father's Powerful Influence on a Woman's Life*, Garden City, NY: Doubleday, 1981.

27. M. Rosenberg, in *NYT* (Op-Ed page). June 20, 1981.

28. *Phil Donahue Show* transcript #08192, p. 3 (available from Multimedia Program Productions, P.O. Box 2111, Cincinnati, OH 45201), 1982.

29. *NYT*, November 23, 1981.

30. *Phil Donahue Show* transcript #12282 (see note 28), p. 6.

31. A. C. Herzig and J. L. Mali, *Oh, Boy! Babies!*, Boston: Little Brown, 1980.

32. M. Clary, *Daddy's Home*, New York: Seaview, 1982, p. 222.

Chapter 10: Familial Friendship

1. K. Lindsey, *Friends as Family*, Boston: Beacon, 1981.

2. Recent examples: M. Winn, *Children Without Childhood*, New York: Pantheon, 1983; R. Kramer, *In Defense of the Family*, New York: Basic,

1983; N. Postman, *The Disappearance of Childhood*, New York: Delacorte, 1982; J. Westin, *The Coming Parent Revolution*, Chicago: Rand McNally, 1981.

3. Quoted in *Women Pro and Con*, Mount Vernon, NY: Peter Pauper, 1958.

4. D. de Rougemont, *Love in the Western World*, New York: Harcourt Brace 1940 ed., Pantheon, 1956 ed., p. 288.

5. Quoted in *NYT*, March 1, 1982.

6. Quoted in C. Lasch, *Haven in a Heartless World*, New York: Basic, 1977, pp. 51–53, 59.

7. J. Greenfield, *TV Guide*, April 17, 1982; J. Dailey, *TV Guide*, June 19, 1982.

8. B. Jones, "The Dynamics of Marriage and Motherhood," in R. Morgan, ed., *Sisterhood Is Powerful*, New York: Random House, 1970, p. 59.

9. T.-G. Atkinson, "Radical Feminism and Love," *October 17 Movement*, (position paper) New York City, April 12, 1969.

10. G. Greer, *The Female Eunuch*, New York: McGraw-Hill, 1971, p. 165.

11. P. R. Sanday, "Female Status in the Public Domain," in M. Z. Rosaldo and L. Lamphere, eds., *Women in Culture and Society*, Stanford, CA: Stanford University, 1974, pp. 199–200.

12. I. Bengis, *Combat in the Erogenous Zone*, New York: Knopf, 1972, pp. 252–53.

13. *Ms.*, July 1974.

14. *Ms.*, September 1981.

15. Quoted by N. Barko in *Ms.*, March 1982.

16. S. Firestone, *The Dialectic of Sex*, New York: Morrow, 1970, pp. 145, 146.

17. *NYT*, November 9, 1981.

18. *McCall's*, June 1980, p. 26.

19. *NYT*, October 12, 1980.

20. *NYT*, October 26, 1980, p. 1.

21. *NYT*, December 16, 1981.

22. *NYT*, January 27 and July 5, 1982.

23. *United Press International*, June 24, 1982.

24. R. R. Bell, "Comparative Attitudes about Marital Sex among Negro Women in the U.S., Great Britain and Trinidad," in G. Kurian and R. Ghosh, eds., *Women in the Family and the Economy*, Westport, CT: Greenwood, 1981, pp. 197–207.

25. *McCall's*, June 1980, p. 22; *Time*, January 31, 1983, p. 80; A. Pietropinto and J. Simenauer, *Husbands and Wives*, New York: Times Books, 1979, pp. xxvi and 279.

26. Personal interview, August 7, 1982; *Savvy,* July 1982, pp. 45–47.

27. Sources: W. J. Goode, "The Theoretical Importance of Love," in R. L. Coser, ed., *The Family: Its Structure and Function,* New York: St. Martin's, 1974, pp. 143–56; kissing study reported in personal communication by C. Kleiman, *Chicago Tribune,* 1980; hugs theory offered by Dr. Virginia Satir, quoted in *Bottom Line,* June 15, 1981; angina study reported in *Psychology Today,* December 1982, p. 81; companionship study described in L. Pratt, *Journal of Marriage and the Family,* February 1972.

28. *NYT,* December 17, 1982; for a provocative discussion of skip-a-generation friendship, see A. Kornhaber and K. L. Woodward, *Grandparents/Grandchildren: The Vital Connection,* Garden City, NY: Doubleday, 1981.

29. *NYT,* May 6, 1982.

30. *Ibid.*

31. R. C. Barnett, "Parental Sex-Role Attitudes and Child-Rearing Values," *Sex Roles,* August 1981.

32. *Psychology Today,* October 1982, p. 18.

33. Quoted in *NYT,* December 7, 1981.

34. "Where Does the Time Go? The United Media Enterprises Report on Leisure in America." Reported in *NYT,* December 15, 1982.

35. C. Rubenstein and P. Shaver, *In Search of Intimacy,* New York: Delacorte, 1982.

36. General Mills *American Family Report* 1980–81, pp. 63–66.

37. *The Connecticut Mutual Life Report on American Values in the 80's: Research & Forecasts,* 1981.

38. "Where Does The Time Go?" (see note 34); C. Rubenstein and P. Shaver (see note 35).

39. E. A. Medrich *et al., The Serious Business of Growing Up: A Study of Children's Lives Outside School,* Berkeley, CA: University of California, 1982.

40. Quoted in *NYT,* July 12, 1982.

41. Study reported in *Ladies Home Journal,* August 1980, pp. 108–110.

42. *Ibid.,* pp. 108.

43. J. Updike, *Rabbit Is Rich,* New York: Fawcett, 1981, p. 302.

44. Study reported in *NYT,* March 30, 1982.

45. G. Holden, University of North Carolina, reported in *Psychology Today,* November 1981.

46. Quoted in *NYT,* July 14, 1981.

Index